CONFLICT, DOMINATION AND VIOLENCE

Studies in Latin American and Spanish History

Series Editors:
Scott Eastman, Creighton University, USA
Vicente Sanz Rozalén, Universitat Jaume I, Spain

Editorial Board:
Carlos Illades, Universidad Autónoma Metropolitana, Mexico
Mercedes Yusta, Université Paris 8, France
Xosé Manoel Núñez-Seixas, Ludwig-Maximilians München Universität, Germany
Dominique Soucy, Université de Franche-Comté, France
Gabe Paquette, Johns Hopkins University, USA
Karen Racine, University of Guelph, Canada
David Sartorius, University of Maryland, USA
Claudia Guarisco, El Colegio Mexiquense, Mexico
Natalia Sobrevilla Perea, University of Kent, United Kingdom

This series bridges the divide between studies of Latin America and peninsular Spain by employing transnational and comparative approaches that shed light on the complex societies, cultures, and economies of the modern age. Focusing on the cross-pollination that was the legacy of colonialism on both sides of the Atlantic, these monographs and collections explore a variety of issues such as race, class, gender, and politics in the Spanish-speaking world.

Volume 1
Metaphors of Spain: Representations of Spanish National Identity in the Twentieth Century
Edited by Javier Moreno Luzón and Xosé M. Núñez Seixas

Volume 2
Conflict, Domination and Violence: Episodes in Mexican Social History
Carlos Illades

Conflict, Domination and Violence

Episodes in Mexican Social History

Carlos Illades

Translated from Spanish by Philip Daniels

berghahn
NEW YORK · OXFORD
www.berghahnbooks.com

Published in 2017 by
Berghahn Books
www.berghahnbooks.com

English-language edition © 2017, 2020 Carlos Illades
First paperback edition published in 2020

Originally published in Spanish by Editorial Gedisa in 2015 as
Conflicto, dominación y violencia. Capítulos de historia social

Library of Congress Cataloging-in-Publication Data

A C.I.P. cataloging record is available from the Library of Congress

British Library Cataloguing in Publication Data

A catalogue record for this book is available from the British Library

ISBN 978-1-78533-530-3 hardback
ISBN 978-1-78920-529-9 paperback
ISBN 978-1-78533-531-0 ebook

Contents

The ragged people rapidly joined the youths and the ferryboys jumped to the shore, armed with long, thick oars ... and the youths' shouting and the horrible injustice being done ... aroused the instinctive hatred towards the police, and true popular anger showed itself. Again, the cops drew their long swords, then bands of men replaced the boys and stones began to hail down on the bastard police until they fled with bleeding heads and battered swords.

—Manuel Payno

For my sisters

Spanish Terms Used in This Book

autodefensas	community-based vigilante or self-defence groups, also known as *Policia Comunitaria* (Community Police), that arose in the Gulf and South Mexico regions between 2012 and 2013
cacicazgo	the area under a *cacique*'s control
cacique	a local political boss; traditionally, peasants allied themselves with regional *caciques*
ejido	communal agricultural land, where community members individually farm designated parcels
fuero/desafuero	political immunity from prosecution/termination of the same
gachupín	a Spanish settler in Latin America

List of Organizations

Asamblea Nacional Popular (ANP) – National People's Congress

Asamblea Popular de los Pueblos de Oaxaca (APPO) – Popular Assembly of the Peoples of Oaxaca

Asamblea Popular de los Pueblos de Oriente – Popular Assembly of the Towns of the East

Asociación Cívica Guerrerense (ACG) – Guerrero Civic Association

Asociación Cívica Nacional Revolucionaria (ACNR) – National Revolutionary Civic Association

Asociación de Copreros – Copra Farmers Association

Bloque Negro – Black Bloc

Brigada Campesina de Ajusticiamiento – Peasant Execution Brigade.

Brigada Popular de Ajusticiamiento 26 de Septiembre – 26 September Popular Justice Brigade

Caravana por el Desarrollo y la Paz – Caravan for Peace and Development

CCF/FAI-México – the Conspiracy of Cells of Fire/Informal Anarchist Federation Mexico

Células Autónomas de Revolución Inmediata Práxedis G. Guerrero – Práxedis G. Guerrero Autonomous Cells for Immediate Revolution

Coalición de Organizaciones Populares – Coalition of Popular Organizations

Comando Magonista de Liberación – Magonista Liberation Commando

Comando Popular Revolucionario La Patria es Primero (CPR-LPEP) – The Country Comes First – Popular Revolutionary Commando

Comandos Armados de Liberación – Armed Liberation Commandos

Comisión Consultiva de Indemnizaciones – Advisory Committee on Compensation Claims

Comisión Mixta Hispano Mexicana de Reclamaciones – Joint Hispano-Mexican Claims Commission

Comisión Nacional de Derechos Humanos (CNDH) – National Human Rights Commission

Comité Cívico Guerrerense (CCG) – Guerrero Civic Committee

Comité Clandestino Revolucionario Indígena-Comandancia General del EZLN – Clandestine Indigenous Revolutionary Committee-General Command of the EZLN

Consejo Ciudadano de Seguridad Pública – Citizen Council for Public Security

Consejo de Ejidos y Comunidades Opositoras a La Parota – Council of Ejidos and Communities Opposed to La Parota

Consejo de los Pueblos Nahuas del Alto Balsas (CNPNAB) – Alto Balsas Council of Nahua Towns

Consejo General de Huelga – General Strike Council

Consejo Guerrerense 500 Años de Resistencia – Guerrero Council 500 Years of Resistance

Consejo Nacional Indígena – National Indigenous Council

Coordinadora de las Sombras – Coordination of Shadows

Coordinadora Estatal de Trabajadores de la Educación de Guerrero (CETEG) – State Coordinator of Education Workers of Guerrero

Coordinadora Estudiantil Anarquista – Anarchist Student Coordination

Coordinadora Nacional de Trabajadores de la Educación (CNTE) – National Coordinator of Education Workers

Coordinadora Regional de Autoridades Comunitarias-Policía Comunitaria (CRAC-PC) – Regional Coordinator of Community Authorities – Community Police

Cruz Negra – Black Cross

Ejército Libertador del Sur – Liberation Army of the South

Ejército Popular Revolucionario (EPR) – Popular Revolutionary Army

Ejército Revolucionario del Pueblo Insurgente (EPRI) – Revolutionary Army of the Insurgent People

Ejército Zapatista de Liberación Nacional (EZLN) – Zapatista Army of National Liberation

Federación Anarquista Informal (FAI – Informal Anarchist Federation)

Federación de Estudiantes Campesinos y Socialistas de México (FECSM) – Mexican Federation of Socialist and Peasant Students

Frente de Liberación Animal – Animal Liberation Front

Frente de Liberación de la Tierra – Earth Liberation Front

Frente de Pueblos en Defensa de la Tierra (FPDF) – Community Front for the Defence of Land

Frente Oriente – Eastern Front

Frente Popular Revolucionario – Popular Revolutionary Front

Grupo Interdisciplinario de Expertos Independientes (GIEI) –
Interdisciplinary Group of Independent Experts

Individualidades Inclinadas hacia lo Salvaje – Individualities Inclined
to Savagery

Iniciativa Anarco-Insurreccionalista de Ofensiva y Solidaridad
Julio Chávez López-FAI – Julio Chavez Lopez-FAI Anarcho-
Insurrectionalist Initiatiative of Offence and Solidarity Julio
Chavez Lopez-FAI

Instituto Nacional Electoral – National Electoral Institute

Liga de Campesinos de Atoyac – Atoyac Peasants League

México Unido contra la Delincuencia – Mexico United Against Crime

Movimiento Libertario de Regeneración Económica Mexicana –
Libertarian Movement for Mexican Economic Regeneration

Movimiento por la Paz con Justicia y Dignidad (MPJD) – Movement
for Peace with Justice and Dignity

Núcleo Antagonista Anarquista de Ajusticiamiento 25 de Noviembre-
FAI – 25 November-FAI Antagonist Anarchist Execution Nucleus

Organización Campesina de la Sierra del Sur (OCSS) – Peasant
Organization of the Southern Sierra

Organización Ecologista de la Sierra – Environmentalist
Organization of the Sierra

Partido Comunista Mexicano (PCM) – Mexican Communist Party

Partido de los Pobres (PdlP) – Party of the Poor

Partido Obrero de Acapulco (POA) – Acapulco Workers' Party

Partido Obrero de Tecpan – Tecpan Workers' Party

Partido Revolucionario Obrero Clandestino Unión del Pueblo – Union
of the People – Clandestine Revolutionary Workers Party

Procuraduría General de Justicia (PGR) – Attorney General's Office

Secretaría de Comunicaciones y Transportes – Ministry of
Communications and Transport

Sindicato Mexicano de Electricistas (SME) – Mexican Electricians
Union

Sindicato Nacional de Trabajadores de la Educación (SNTE) –
National Union of Education Workers

Tendencia Democrática Revolucionaria-Ejército del Pueblo –
Revolutionary Democratic Tendency-People's Army

Tercer Congreso Nacional Indígena – Third National Indigenous
Congress

Unión Popular Emiliano Zapata (UPEZ) – Emiliano Zapata Popular
Union

Figures, Illustrations and Tables

Figures

Illustrations

Tables

Preface

This book deals with diverse social movements scattered throughout Mexico's history and geography, to which the tools of social history attempt to provide some coherence that is at least factual and at best explanatory. Preceded by a historiographical discussion, the book's main subjects are the origins of the labour movement, the 'Pueblos Unidos' rebellion in Querétaro and Guanajuato at the beginning of the Porfiriato, the attacks on Spanish-owned shops in Mexico City in the critical year of 1915, the cycles of social violence in the far south of the country in the twentieth century, current urban neo-anarchism, public protest during the democratic transition and the social mobilization stemming from the forced disappearance of 43 students from the Ayotzinapa teacher training college.

Conflict, domination and violence are not only the heuristic guide to the eight chapters, but are also a recording of the usual pulse of a diverse, unfair, unequal and class-conscious society. They also provide a compendium of a history of organization, resistance and collective action aimed at reversing this condition, to reduce its negative consequences or to wreak revenge on the propertied classes. Artisans, rural communities, revolutionary armies, university students or marginalized youngsters, as well as ordinary people, are the star players in this social fabric that they share with caciques, employers, government officials, businessmen, police, hitmen and soldiers.

The props for popular mobilization were the sociable interactions, both traditional and modern, interacting with liberal, socialist and anarchist ideologies. The Sierra Gorda uprising sought support in the towns to end the dispossession of their lands, making use of the revolutionary ideology of 1848 to bring order to their demands and map out the social democratic republic, while the working classes developed mutualism (founded on liberal principles), and subsequently trade unionism, to provide them with support in case of need and collective bargaining with employers on working conditions and wages; under the influence of anarchism, they established the Casa del Obrero in

1912. Associationism was clearly instrumental for the formation of a democratic civil society prior to the Mexican Revolution, even though certain elite groups that seethed with class prejudice regarded the 'dangerous classes' with suspicion and the crowd with dread.

With the Revolution, society became an arena of conflict where land disputes, democratic expectations, old resentments and new problems flourished. One example of this was the confrontation between the popular armies and foreign minorities. Violence against Spanish residents was driven largely by the fact that these immigrants worked in economic niches (groceries, farms, cantinas and textile factories) where they came into frequent conflict with the low-income population, in addition to their having links with the Porfirio Diaz regime. This conflict is moreover an element in the construction of national identity which is affirmed in opposition to the 'historic enemies' of Mexican identity, the Spanish colony and the United States.

While in many ways the country was modernized in the twentieth century, the legitimacy of the regime was based on its revolutionary origin and the welfare state 'a la Mexicana', whose foundations were laid during the presidency of Lázaro Cardenas, rather than on a democratic mandate. The caciques in rural areas and the 'charro' leaders within the workers' movement were the intermediaries between the popular classes and the executive (at the local, state and federal levels), to which the other branches of government obsequiously subordinated themselves. When those intermediaries were overwhelmed by subordinates, co-optation and force were used over and over again. Guerrero, the most violent state according to recent official statistics, is today the victim of organized crime and the secular victim of social and political violence. As such, Guerrero is the radical synthesis (rather than the exception) of economic backwardness, social inequality and cacique domination, a fact that is sadly illustrated by the forced disappearance of 43 students from the Ayotzinapa teacher training college in Iguala. Popular mobilization has also been constant, as has state repression, resulting in the formation of guerrilla and community *auto-defensa* groups, the latter being the rearguard of a rural society that is confronting violence fostered by organized crime and by the state, the initiator of this unwinnable internal war.

To date in the twenty-first century, public protest has been recurrent and widespread, not so much because public freedoms have increased since the democratic transition (i.e. the PRI's loss of the presidency), but because of the dysfunctional relationship between the governed and the governors. From the 2001 Neo-Zapatista Tour, demanding a law recognizing the rights of indigenous peoples, to the demonstrations demanding the presentation alive of the 43 Ayotzinapa students (from 2014 to date), state responses have been pitiful or nonexistent, which has bred democratic disenchantment, coupled with war, insecurity, the poverty of half of the population and social inequality that is growing rather than diminishing.

After the disappointing Partido Acción Nacional (PAN – National Action Party) administrations, the second of which caused violence in Mexico to increase to levels not seen since the Revolution, the return of the Partido Revolucionario Institucional (PRI – Institutional Revolutionary Party) to the presidency triggered violent demonstrations by neo-anarchists who for years had carried out small acts of sabotage against the symbols of capitalist power (mainly transnational companies and bank branches), occasionally sending explosive devices to government officials, religious leaders, executives of large consortia and scientists involved in biotechnology. The return to power of the PRI, the party that had dominated the country for 70 years, and the government of Mexico City being in the hands of the PRD (Party of the Democratic Revolution) a 'social democratic' left-wing party fuelled the conviction in these neo-anarchist groups that change would be impossible so long as these parties were the only political options available.

The sources used in this study are varied, including documents from court and diplomatic records, Mexican and foreign newspapers, declassified Department of State reports, webpages of various entities, in addition to pamphlets, press releases and manifestos of radical organizations. The first results of these searches led to communications in Mexico, Spain, the United States, Brazil, France and Finland, which have been reworked for this edition. To José Rosales Suasti, I am grateful for the generous supporting documentation that supports Chapter 3, while Professor Marcelo Badaró, of the Universidad Federal Fluminense in Rio de Janeiro, and my assistant Guillén Torres, provided me with several of the sources used in Chapter 7. I am indebted to my longstanding friend Vicent Sanz, who encouraged me to publish the English edition of this volume in the series he co-edits with Professor Scott Eastman. I want to thank Chris Chappell, Senior Editor at Berghahn Books, for making it possible in such a pleasant way. I should also like to thank Philip Daniels for his conscientious translation of the manuscript. Matias Gonzalez Field prepared the index. Romuald de Richemont kindly allowed me to use the powerful photographs from his series 'Mexico: 43 Still Missing Students' that illustrate the intensity of public protest. Despite the contributions of so many, all errors of fact or interpretation that the reader may find in the text are the sole responsibility of the author.

Chapultepec, November 2016

Chapter 1

The Historiography
of Social Movements

Halfway through the twentieth century, Fernand Braudel raised a call for establishing a productive dialogue between history and the social sciences whereby history might freely employ indispensable concepts that it was incapable of developing by itself, and the social sciences might acquire the temporal depth they lacked. He went on to state that there would be no social science 'other than by the reconciliation in a simultaneous practice of our different crafts'. The convergence of history with the social sciences was baptized 'social history' and later, in the United States, as 'historical sociology' to underline sociologists' shift towards historiography.[1]

At the first international congress of historical sciences held after the Second World War in Paris, 1950, Eric Hobsbawm was involved in the section on social history, 'probably the first in any historical congress', as he recalls in his autobiography.[2] It gained momentum in 1952 with the creation of the British journal *Past and Present*, which brought together a group of Marxist historians (Hobsbawm himself, Christopher Hill, Rodney Hilton, George Rudé, and E.P. Thompson), joined by such prominent scholars as Lawrence Stone, John Elliot and Moses Finley. Meanwhile, in the United States, historical sociology took its first steps forward with Barrington Moore, the Harvard teacher of Charles Tilly.

It would be very hard to find a sociologist who has taken better advantage of history than Tilly. With the exception of his first book, on the counter-revolution in the Vendée (published in 1964), long duration, which Braudel conceptualized as the history of structures, is the time-frame for Tilly's analysis, whether it be of social struggles in France, state systems, European revolutions, democracy or social movements worldwide. By 1970, George Rudé had already drawn attention to Tilly's articles 'on the concerns of manual and "pre-industrial" labour in nineteenth-century France'. Five years later, the historians from the

German Democratic Republic who developed the concept of 'proto-industrialization' to explain the transition from feudalism to capitalism recognized the debt this concept owed to the pioneering work carried out by 'American historians Franklin F. Mendels and Charles and Richard Tilly' in the 1960s.[3]

With their 250-year history, social movements have been common ground for historians and sociologists for half a century. They are the subject of the last book Charles Tilly published during his lifetime. Tilly was assisted by Lesley J. Wood, whom he asked to work on the book 'perhaps knowing that he wouldn't be able to finish it before his death'.[4] The exposition made here seeks to locate it within the problematic field where both disciplines came together, to present the previous developments of social history – particularly the work of Hobsbawm, Rudé and Thompson – and thus to place Tilly's studies in perspective in order to weigh his historiographical contribution and to comment on certain texts on social movements drawn from historical sociology, which, like those of Sidney Tarrow, have interacted with his work.

Social History on Stage

In 1959, two books were published that would bring their authors prominence as notable exponents of social history, at that time identified with the movement known as 'history from below'. I refer here to Hobsbawm's *Primitive Rebels* and Rudé's *The French Revolution*. One is concerned with elucidating the 'archaic forms of social movements in the nineteenth and twentieth centuries' (banditry, millenarianism, etc.) and the other with discovering the motivations and the social composition of the revolutionary people.[5]

More than anyone else, Rudé strove to reveal the internal logic of eighteenth- and nineteenth-century popular protest in response to what the common people considered grievances, injustices or unilateral breaking of the covenant between social groups, or between them and the state. Taking a stand against the widely shared perception, originating in the nineteenth century and theorized by Gustave Le Bon's social psychology, to the effect that the crowd is irrational and guided by purely emotional impulses, and moreover questioning the supposition of methodological individualism according to which rational choice is an exclusively individual attribute, Rudé found patterns of behaviour that could explain collective action and the repertoire available for achieving collective goals. He dedicated his best-remembered book to the study of 'what sociologists have termed the "aggressive mob" or the "hostile outburst" – to such activities as strikes, riots, rebellions, insurrections, and revolutions'.[6]

The French rural revolts in the eighteenth century, motivated by what Ernest Labrousse characterized as a subsistence crisis, were in no sense intended to overthrow the government or to bring down the established order; they simply sought to avoid hunger. In addition to this pressing need, in English cities the crowd protested against the employment of Irish labour, for the freedom of dissidents or for the repeal of certain laws that they considered unjust. The French Revolution triggered the mobilization of artisans who demanded better wages, (but ended up losing the right to freedom of association under the 1791 Le Chapelier Law), the mobilization of the popular classes who sought to stop the prices of basic foodstuffs rising and to practise direct democracy, and the reactionary revolts 'by the Church and king' (the Vendée) which were quelled by the government of the National Convention. In Britain, the nineteenth century saw the effectiveness of direct action, with the calculated reinforcement of threatening letters directed to owners and authorities through Luddism, Captain Swing and Rebecca's Daughters, the latter being unwilling to pay taxes they saw as unfair:

> Rebecca (as her historian reminds us) was strictly Sabbatarian: she never worked on Sundays and even studiously avoided late night sessions on Saturdays and Monday early mornings. She was remarkably discriminating: only toll gates considered to be 'unjust' were dealt with, particularly those studding the side roads, which, through their proliferation, placed a heavy extra cost on the carting of lime.[7]

In addition to the immediate motivations of social actors (hunger, work disputes, rights trampled on, etc.) and the organizations that arose (*compagnonnages*, cells, etc.), it was the forms under which they rationalized their social condition that was fundamental for Rudé. In order to do this, he turned to the concept of ideology, which he considered comprises two overlapping levels: on the one hand, 'inherent' ideas arising from everyday experience (a basic notion of rights, of justice or of what is proper); and, on the other hand, 'derived' ideas that come from structured political speeches (liberal, conservative or socialist). Synthesis of these was the role of intellectuals, in the Gramscian sense of the term.[8]

In 1969, Hobsbawm and Rudé published the classic text on the great revolt of English labourers confronting rural mechanization. After analysing the structure of the rising of 1830, its central episodes and following step by step the fate of the insurrectionists deported to Australia, they found that, in spite of the violence, 'the attacks were

directed against property, not people's lives'. Based on 'the silent consensus of the poor', the dogged struggle of Captain Swing represented
the last resistance of the 'traditional society against its destroyers'. By
1870, modern trade unionism would take charge of the demands of
farm workers. Thus, the spontaneous and horizontal protest of subordinates, who were apolitical and often anonymous, and who finally
resorted to direct action in order to put pressure on the ruling classes,
were clearing the ground for the workers' movement: organized, with
visible leaderships and a structured ideology; disciplined, having explicit political demands; and using strikes as a bargaining tool.[9]

Outside the English-speaking world, the French historian Georges
Lefebvre in *The Great Fear of 1789* (1932) studied peasants' expectations, attitudes and behaviour towards the Revolution. Albert Soboul,
his most eminent disciple, says that Lefebvre changed the standpoint
from which the phenomenon of revolution had been studied precisely
by looking at it 'from below'. And, as far as he was concerned, he shifted
the interest in rural areas to the city and made a complex characterization of the popular movement of Year II, that of the sans-culottes,
which brought together artisans, the unemployed, small business owners and the little people who stood for the control of prices and practised direct democracy in 1793.[10]

We cannot end this brief review of the studies of preindustrial crowds
without mentioning *The World Turned Upside Down* (1972), a formidable book by Christopher Hill on the egalitarian and radical sects (the
Diggers, the Ranters and the Levellers, among others) who made the
British monarchy tremble during the English Revolution. This popular
alternative to the dominant aristocratic culture, which was preceded
by the Gunpowder Plot (1605) perpetrated by Guy Fawkes, whose
iconic mask hides the faces of postmodernist rebels and that antici-
pated the nineteenth-century Luddite movement, would undoubtedly
have stood the world on its head:

> There was, however, another revolution which never happened,
> though from time to time it threatened. This might have established
> communal property, a far wider democracy in political and legal in-
> stitutions, might have disestablished the state church and rejected
> the protestant ethic.[11]

An exploration of some of these historical 'dead ends' was the area of
study of the twentieth century's most important social historian: E.P.
Thompson.

Thompson's influential book on the formation of the English working class,[12] as well as his later studies on the crowd, took aim, among

other things, at the criteria historians used for classification – their distinctions between archaic and modern, preindustrial and industrial, pre-political and political social movements – because he believed that the working class originates from this crowd, as he held that working-class forms of consciousness were one of the substrates upon which the workers' traditions were founded.

In the 1960s, Thompson and Perry Anderson debated the contemporary crisis in English society and its underlying historical causes, leading them to inquire why there had been no revolution in England like the French Revolution and the consequences this had had for the later development of conservative political culture in the country. Broadly speaking, Anderson argued that the landed aristocracy gradually became an agrarian bourgeoisie (the source of the conservative gene that it never lost), while Thompson argued that the development of the *gentry* was relatively independent and contradictory, and that it was moreover erroneous to assume that there was an ideal type of bourgeois revolution (the French Revolution), in contrast with an accumulation of imperfect or degraded historical experiences. Where Anderson saw a submissive working class, Thompson highlighted the complexity of its culture and potential for conflict, as shown by Luddism.[13]

In the 1970s, in an effort to understand this, Thompson focused on the conflict between the upper and lower classes in the eighteenth century from which modern social classes emerged. The landed aristocracy, triumphant in the Revolution of 1688, consolidated its political and cultural supremacy over society as a whole, a supremacy that was intermittently challenged by subordinate groups. This confrontation went from disputes accompanying a rise in the cost of food, opposing the people's 'moral economy' with the economy of the free market, to the poaching that defied rural landowners' property rights. The repertoire of actions available to the subordinated population was limited to mocking the gentry, replicating rituals the gentry considered scandalous, or at least in poor taste, and small daily acts of rebellion. The eighteenth-century mob was rebellious and irreverent, 'but rebellious in defence of custom'.[14]

The polarization of these two social blocks occurred in parallel with the Industrial Revolution, which, with the 'accompanying demographic revolution were the backgrounds to the greatest transformation in history, in revolutionising "needs" and in destroying the authority of customary expectations'.[15] In this way, the experiences of mechanization, labour discipline and wage labour came together in this process of pre-existing cultural conflict at the heart of paternalistic society. In addition, the picture of the emergence of the working class is completed by both the organization that both brought Methodism to its congregation and the dissemination of Thomas Paine's ideas to craftsmen and small landowners, reinforcing the belief that the Englishman is 'born free' (merging spontaneous ideas with elaborate ideologies, as we saw in Rudé). Thus, 'From 1830 onwards a more clearly defined class consciousness, in the customary Marxist sense, was maturing',[16] allowing the working population to constitute itself as an autonomous subject and claim its political rights in the Chartist movement.

Thompson thought of class as a historical formation and not a mere agent in the economic and social structure, as was considered to be the case by certain contemporary sociologists 'obsessively concerned with methodology'. Thompson brought three interrelated categories into play: class, experience and awareness. Class involves common interests formed through everyday experience. These interests do not arise arbitrarily, since they are linked to the productive relationships in which individuals are joined together, that is, they have a basis in social materiality and are objectified through experience, which transforms individual human groups into social classes. From this perspective, class exists through its own experience. For this reason, Anthony Giddens recognized that Thompson, author of *The Making of the English Working Class,* placed strong emphasis 'upon the capability of the human agents to shape actively and to reshape the conditions of their existence', and Tarrow noted his suggestion 'to substitute for the materialist version of Marxism a focus on class *self*-creation'.[17]

From the linguistic side of things, the American William H. Sewell Jr. studied the corporate speech of French craftsmen and the emergence of associative speech during the July Revolution, through which working-class consciousness was made explicit (in approximately the same period studied by Thompson for the English case).[18] Meanwhile, the British historian Gareth Stedman Jones demonstrated the difficulty of considering language as a mere vector of consciousness and not as an epistemological problem in itself, as well as the failure of Marxist political theory, despite the recovery of Gramscian categories by Hobsbawm, Rudé and Thompson.

While in *Outcast London* (1971) Stedman Jones addressed social conflict in the Victorian era, in *Languages of Class* (1983) he revised his theses, especially after reconsidering Chartism, and refuted essentialist conceptions of social classes (Rudé, Hobsbawm and Thompson) in which the 'social being' is both its constituent element and the substance of its objective materiality, shifting the analysis towards political languages (as the Cambridge School also did in intellectual history) through which the social being is identified as such. To that extent, it is not possible to 'decode political language to reach a primal and material expression of interest since it is the discursive structure of political language which conceives and defines interest in the first place'.[19]

The Contribution of Historical Sociology

The work of Braudel, Hobsbawm, Rudé and Thompson provided significant reference points for Tilly, who did not hesitate to admit his intellectual debt to them, even though, at the same time, he distanced himself from the progressive vision of social movements (the step from lower to higher forms of struggle), ascribing to Hobsbawm and Rudé the methodological error of confusing the forms of collective action with the occasions when they occur. Even with the passage of time, Tilly saw no value in making a distinction between archaic and modern movements, nor would he share the implicit assumption that the advance of 'revolutionary consciousness and organization would eventually sweep away spontaneous and useless protest'.[20] Tilly, in fact, shifts his analysis away from the strong concepts of Marxism (economic structure, ideology, consciousness) and the constitution of social subjects (classes) to the basic components of every concerted collective action, the way in which these combine, the mobilization of resources, the structure of political opportunities and external constraints – that is, everything that shapes contentious politics.

Tilly and Wood dated the origin of the social movement to the second half of the eighteenth century, with the synthesis of three pre-existing elements, which thereafter combined in various ways, giving rise to a wide range of movements. These elements were collective claims on the authorities that were related to a programme, an identity or a position (a campaign); the use of various forms of political action (social movement repertoire), incorporating not only what people do but also what they are capable of doing; concerted public representations of worthiness, unity, numbers, and commitment by participants and their constituencies (abbreviated as WUNC displays).[21]

Building on Rudé, Tilly and Wood stressed that the London demonstrations that swept John Wilkes into Parliament in 1768 – the repercussions reaching as far as South Carolina, citizenship being the privilege of a very narrow segment of the population at the time – presented a considerable novelty because an election campaign became 'an occasion for display of popular solidarity and determination'. Even so, it was not until after the Napoleonic Wars that British politics institutionalized social movements. Tilly and Wood recorded the changes that the turn of the nineteenth century brought for social movements: the repertoire 'separated increasingly from older forms of signalling support or opposition such as forced illuminations, Rough Music, serenades, and the sacking of houses' and consequently there was a spread of 'public meetings, petition drives, public declarations, demonstrations, and shared symbols of membership'.[22]

Freedom of association, the right that had been hard-won by the working class after bloody battles, was an essential factor for uniting social movements, strengthening their identity elements, creating coalitions and networks (even international ones – for example, the International Workers' Association) as well as channelling collective demands to the public powers in an organized and effective way to achieve a certain degree of dialogue. Tilly and Wood did not overlook the emergence of the labour movement, and their chapter on the nineteenth century begins with the silk weavers (*canuts*) of Lyons who, on 25 February 1848, singing the 'Marseillaise', left the Croix-Rousse quarter where they had their workshops and marched to the town hall. It was a well-organized campaign reinforced by a varied repertoire with convincing demonstrations of worthiness, unity, numbers and commitment that strengthened the demand to declare the Republic.[23] The Chartists would try to do the same thing in England to obtain universal male suffrage, reducing or annulling the census requirements that favoured the propertied classes exclusively.

These examples lead us to the theme of popular politics – a trait of modern social movements according to Hobsbawm and Rudé – and to the link between social mobilization and the process of democratization that greatly interested Tilly and Wood. Tilly and Wood's conclusion, after analysing much of the available empirical evidence, was that, on the one hand, there is no necessary connection between social movements and democracy, and, on the other, the evidence suggests that social movements usually arrive after democratization. When this does not occur, as in authoritarian regimes, they weaken.[24]

The journey through the twentieth century skips the revolutions that Tilly wrote about shortly after the collapse of the Soviet Union,[25] stopping at the youth movements of the 1960s. These 'new social movements' started out as a questioning of post-industrial society and a world ruled by adults[26] – or, if we think of Mexico, of authoritarianism – incorporating claims as diverse as those of feminism, gay rights, environmental protection, the rights of indigenous peoples and the decriminalization of drugs. Meanwhile, in Eastern Europe, people were exhorted to exercise popular sovereignty. Never before had social movements spread over so much of the world and never, without downplaying local diversity, had they been so homogeneous, happily combining uniqueness with general patterns, which brings us back to the fundamental question Wood poses in the preface to the second edition of Tilly's book: 'Why do social movements look so similar around the world, and how and why have such movements become a major form of political action globally?'[27]

This question also brings us into the twenty-first century and the process of the internationalization of social movements. In the nineteenth century, migration flows had driven this tendency, both in the labour movement and other social movements (anarchism in South America and white supremacism in the United States being two prominent cases), but clearly it was a century later when the labour movement became more important, supported by the mass consumption of new technologies that 'tied social movement participants more firmly to other users of the same technologies as they separated participants from nonusers of those technologies'. However, despite appearances, the availability of state-of-the-art communication technology increased the divides between different corners of the globe instead of reducing them. The distance between the First World and the Third World is even greater nowadays, and 'most of the world's people still [lack] access to social movements as a way to voice popular claims'.[28]

Tilly and Wood consider the hypothesis that in the future, social movements will disappear or change into radically different political forms, though this would merely be a different way of expressing the same social demands. And this is precisely the thesis of Alain Touraine, who thinks that we are not only entering a post-social era, but that the nature of demands is also changing because 'the current crisis witnesses the disappearance of the actors of the industrial society'. The crisis in the global economy not only threw millions into precarious circumstances, unemployment and poverty, but also destroyed the capitalist society that we had previously known, since the social actors were virtually wiped out when the cleavage between them and the system was finalized, and subordinates are now no longer able to form a unified force capable of resisting unregulated capitalism. The economy became autonomous to the extent that there is no socially controlled power that governs it; thus, henceforth, the conflicts (and a possible reconfiguration of community life) will be between the financial economy, which gobbled up the actual economy, and moral subjects, sovereign individuals and holders of universal rights, united by ties of solidarity based 'on the recognition of the other, since we all have the same fundamental rights'. For Touraine, the disappearance of the social 'leaves the logic of *calculation* face to face with the logic of *conscience*'.[29]

While Touraine considers that in the 'post-social situation' the class struggle is no longer the main source of conflict and proponent of collective demands, Tarrow's viewpoint is that this never was the case, because he finds in the states and in capitalism 'the two major sources and targets of contentious politics'. This is seen in social responses against tax burdens, struggles for the extension of suffrage to subordinates and the creation of a professional police force to contain popular unrest, as occurred in England after the Peterloo Massacre in Manchester in 1819 or in the United States to guarantee the functioning of the free market, according to David Montgomery's pioneering studies.[30]

For Tarrow, social movements arise at the same time as the modern state and are sequences of political action based on compact, internal social networks, accompanied by 'collective action frames' that have the ability to challenge powerful opponents, whether they be other political coalitions, classes or the state itself. And this collective action becomes contentious when employed by groups that do not have regular access to institutions, being an expression of the popular politics that, Tarrow says, always overlaps with the formal politics practised by the elites. Once states were consolidated, certain forms of popular protest became institutionalized, forcing governments to accept certain 'forms of collective action whose legitimacy they had earlier resisted, while suppressing others'.[31]

Tarrow uses the concept of 'cycles of collective action' when these extend to society as a whole and can spread through different though often contiguous geographical areas. The first of the modern era corresponds to the revolutions of 1848, whose repercussions spread as far as Latin America by encouraging the development of the first socialism[32] – and the most recent to the Arab Spring. In the twentieth century, the 1968 student movements or the Velvet Revolutions of 1989–91 stand out. The temptation to use the singular and consider them as fragments of a single process oversimplifies their diversity and confuses their underlying causes. Tarrow therefore cautions that they 'must be disaggregated into innovations they produce, campaigns and coalitions, and mechanisms of mobilization and demobilization'.[33]

'Anti-systemic movements' is the concept used by Giovanni Arrighi, Terence K. Hopkins and Immanuel Wallerstein to analyse cycles of collective action. Like Tarrow, they recognize the centrality of the state by stating that 'the actual structures of classes and ethnic groups have been dependent on the creation of the modern states'.[34] As theorists of the 'capitalist world-economy', they consider that anti-systemic movements began with the romantic revolutions of 1848, with ramifications that have continued up to the present day:

The social movements of the late nineteenth century were rooted in the intensification of the processes of capitalist centralization, and rationalization of economic activities. A large variety of social groups (servants and peasants, craftsmen and low-status professionals, small traders and shopkeepers), which had up to then coped more or less with the spread of market competition, suddenly found their established patterns of life and work threatened by widening and deepening proletarianization, and reacted to the threat through a wide variety of struggles.[35]

Taking the only global revolutions that have occurred to date as a framework, those of 1848 and 1968 (whose extensions were the Velvet and other Revolutions of 1989), systemic movements developed in three directions: firstly, as the vindication of rights, social improvements and political participation within the state (social democracy in the West); secondly, as the seizure of political power on the periphery (communism in the East and in Asia); and thirdly, as wars of national liberation in backward countries (anti-imperialism in the Third World). However, postwar capitalism transformed the structure of the workforce by developing segments of salaried professionals, employees in the service sector (with a large female contingent) and the semiskilled or unskilled workforce (into which migrant workers were incorporated). This would be the basis of the new social movements of the 1960s: the pacifistic/environmental/alternative movements, feminist movements and those of the ethnic minorities. Noteworthy consequences of 1968 were 'the changes in power relations between status-groups such as age-groups, genders, and "ethnicities"', which proved 'to be far more lasting than the movements which brought them to world attention'.[36]

Conclusion

While, around the middle of the nineteenth century, the author of *History of the French Social Movements from 1789 to the Present* (1850), the German Lorenz von Stein, thematized social movements and the French writer Jules Michelet did the same in his *The People* (1846), it was not until a hundred years later that these were incorporated into the agenda of professional historiography stimulated by the flourishing of British social history and French historiography. The former proposed to explain the emergence and development of the modern labour movement, while the latter dealt with the popular side of the French Revolution.

The articulation between the economy and society was one of the key problems addressed by social historians, given that developments in economic history suggested a quite optimistic vision of the Industrial Revolution by emphasizing the material progress it brought and obliterating the social damage it produced. Friedrich A. Hayek, for example, tried to extinguish 'the legend that the situation of the working classes worsened as a result of the implementation of "capitalism"'.[37] And he would find the answer in Hobsbawm's early studies of workers in Thompson's classic on the same subject, where Thompson detected that: 'In some of the lost causes of the people of the Industrial Revolution we may discover insights into social evils which we have yet to cure.'[38]

Although in Hobsbawm, one has already seen a shift in the labour movement towards the history of the working class, that is, the passage from 'old' to 'new' social history, it would be Thompson who would make this statement. With it, the working class ceases to be a linear result of the economic process (the Industrial Revolution), acquiring a central role in the process of its formation that, moreover, is inextricably linked to the consciousness of itself, so that the class exists when it identifies itself and acts as such.

It should be noted that the link between class consciousness and social mobilization interested Rudé greatly and was the subject of one of his books, in which he dealt with the articulation between the spontaneous ideas of social actors and the ideologies developed by intellectuals. But, like Hobsbawm and Thompson, social class continues to be Rudé's subject. Touraine reintroduced the factor of consciousness, though dissociated from social class; in other words, conceived in moral terms and at the same time as universality (it should be recalled that for Marx, the working class was the universal class that would unify all the oppressed behind it).

While old social history focuses on structural (mainly economic and technological) elements that make social movements possible, as well as the formation of classes, we observe in Thompson the recovery of culture in the anthropological sense as a dimension of social analysis and, in Montgomery, but also especially in Stedman Jones, a rethinking of politics, in addition to an interest in the languages of class that the latter shares with Sewell Jr.

In spite of the points of confluence with social history, the approach of historical sociology is different. Tilly and Tarrow, who opted for broad temporal perspectives, in the same way as Braudel in his time proposed for historical discipline, taking into consideration social classes and their motivations, but what mainly attracts his attention are the mechanisms that trigger collective action and make a particular thing happen at a particular time in a particular place. In this way, the structural analysis that makes explicit the conditions of possibility for events to happen – as Arrighi, Hopkins and Wallerstein suggest – revolves around the specific factors that activate what Tilly called 'contentious politics', highlighting how indispensable elements combine to create a particular social mobilization, particular available resources, the particular structure of political opportunities and external constraints (often those of the state). Social movements, Tilly and Wood conclude, contribute to democracy when they help 'to expand the circle of participants in public politics', equalize them 'in terms of importance', prevent 'categorical inequalities' from being translated into public policy and integrate into this 'previously segmented trust networks'.[39]

Notes

1. Braudel, *History and the Social Sciences*; Casanova, *La historia social y los historiadores*.
2. Hobsbawm, *Interesting Times*.
3. Rudé, *The Crowd in History*; Kriedte, Medick and Schlumbohm, *Industrialization before Industrialization*.
4. Tilly and Wood, *Social Movements, 1768–2008*.
5. Hobsbawm, *Primitive Rebels*; Rudé, *The Crowd in the French Revolution*.
6. Rudé, *The Crowd in History*.
7. Ibid.
8. Rudé, *Ideology and Class Consciousness* in Rudé.
9. Hobsbawm and Rudé, *Captain Swing*; Rudé, The *Ideology of Popular Protest*, in Rudé, *Ideology and Popular Protest*; Rudé, *The Crowd in History*. I cite the former. To place the Swing Riots in the context of the more widespread, two-century phenomenon of destruction of machines, see Hobsbawm, *Worlds of Labour*.
10. Soboul, *The French Revolution*, 1975, my emphasis; Soboul, *A Short History of the French Revolution*, 1977.
11. Hill, *The World Turned Upside Down*.
12. Some of E.P. Thompson's comments on Rudé's studies of the preindustrial crowd are in Thompson, *The Making of the English Working Class,* I. Rudé, for his part, regretted not having been able to refer to Thompson's work in greater detail. His *The Crowd in History* was well-nigh in press (published in 1964) when Thompson's book appeared in 1963. See Rudé, *The Crowd in History*. There is a constant dialogue with Thompson's work in Rudé's *Ideology and Class Consciousness* (published in London in 1980).
13. Anderson, *The Repressive Culture*; Thompson, *The Peculiarities of the English*.
14. Thompson, *Customs in Common*.

15. Ibid.
16. Ibid.; Thompson, *The Making of the English Working Class*, I.
17. Thompson, *The Making of the English Working Class*; Giddens, *Out of the Orrery*; Tarrow, *Power in Movement*, my emphasis.
18. Sewell, Jr., *Work and Revolution in France*.
19. Stedman Jones, *Languages of Class*.
20. Tarrow, *Power in Movement*; Tilly, *Contention and the Urban Poor in Eighteenth- and Nineteenth-Century Latin America*. I cite the latter.
21. Tilly and Wood, *Social Movements, 1768–2008*; Tarrow, *Power in Movement*.
22. Ibid.
23. Tilly and Wood, *Social Movements, 1768–2008*. Despite its evocative exposition, one misses Bezucha's classic study, *Modern European Social History*.
24. This thesis is more fully developed in Tilly, *Democracy*.
25. Tilly, *European Revolutions, 1492–1992* (Chapters 6, 7) addresses the revolutions in Eastern Europe.
26. Hobsbawm, *Age of Extremes*. 'By the late '60s, the culture gap separating young people from their parents was perhaps greater than at any point since the early 19th century.' Judt, *Ill Fares the Land*.
27. Tilly and Wood, *Social Movements, 1768–2008*.
28. Ibid. In 'the post-social situation', Alain Touraine points out, 'the most important conflicts no longer arise within a system of production, but oppose the globalized economy with the defence of rights that are strictly human, and not only social.' Touraine, *After the Crisis*.
29. Tilly and Wood, *Social Movements, 1768–2008*; Touraine, *After the Crisis*, my emphasis.
30. Montgomery, *Citizen Worker*; Tarrow, *Power in Movement*.
31. Tarrow, *Power in Movement*.
32. Illades and Schelchkov, *Mundos posibles*.
33. Tarrow, *Power in Movement*.
34. Arrighi, Hopkins and Wallerstein, *Antisystemic Movements*.
35. Ibid.
36. Ibid.
37. Hayek, *History and Politics*.
38. Ibid.; Hobsbawm, *Worlds of Labour*, Chapters 5, 6, 7; Thompson, *The Making of the English Working Class*, I.
39. Tilly and Wood, *Social Movements, 1768–2008*.

Chapter 2

The Organization and Collective Action of Craftsmen

In the early decades of Mexico as a nation, the corporate institutions that brought urban craftsmen together, the guilds and brotherhoods, broke up. The guilds had guaranteed a monopoly over work, the market and craft knowledge; the brotherhoods, linked to the Catholic Church, provided basic safety nets to provide aid to artisans facing hard times. In the early years of independence, both groups declined, in such a way that associationism expanded in the second half of the nineteenth century in response to this decline, the economic setbacks of the early decades of independence, forced recruitment into the army and the liberal order, which nonetheless contributed to the formation of civil society.

While they enjoyed a freedom that corporations did not have, mutual societies were not powerful structures that could participate forcefully in labour disputes. However, despite lacking any roots in the production process, they did make a decisive contribution to the socialization of free artisans, workers in the service trades and a segment of industrial workers. They were organizations that were primarily concerned with relief for workers in the event of illness or death. They recognized the equality of their members, were obedient to democratic principles and were careful to avoid internal conflict, for which reason they expressly forbade any political or religious discussion. When they managed to amalgamate and gain greater strength, being used for political purposes brought about their downfall. This failure was the common fate of workers' congresses in the 1870s and, later, of the *Casa del Obrero Mundial*.

Except for minor local government positions, the representatives of the working classes did not attain elected office during the nineteenth century. Inasmuch as they were collective actors, workers were relegated from the world of institutional politics, and the leadership groups provided the link between the two spheres. Their role, in the absence of defined rules, was by and large discretionary, and the weakness of the link was always evident. Given this limitation in terms of their origins, workers' political action moved into the symbolic field, with civic festivities providing the opportunity for collective representation.

Mutual Societies

In Mexico's most important cities, there were a large number of artisans who were qualified in traditional trades,[1] though finding work was difficult because of very low rates of job growth in the period of stagnation after independence, unfavourable competition from imported textiles, economic instability caused by wars and internal conflict, inertial population growth, inelasticity of demand and the low status of their trades.[2]

The *Sociedad Mexicana Protectora de Artes y Oficios* (Mexican Society for the Protection of Arts and Trades), founded in 1843 in Mexico City, and the *Compañía de Artesanos de Guadalajara* (Company of Artisans of Guadalajara), founded in 1850, were among the first artisan organizations in the country. The former, which still retained such guild remnants as guaranteeing the performance of work to customers or providing basic education to artisans, also had provisions for assistance in the case of a worker's illness or death, as well as in various other cases. Over time, labour associations became more mutualistic and, by the 1870s, some had evolved towards cooperativism.[3] After the Revolution, the state would take charge of social security, fostering the protection of workers through workers' insurance, implemented during the Alvaro Obregon presidency (1921) and, later on, via the enactment of the Federal Labour Law (1931).

In Mexico City, the first to organize themselves were hatters and tailors, who, along with shoemakers and carpenters, were among the most important trades in the nineteenth century in terms of size. In 1854, they described the purpose of their association to the Ministry for Development thus:

> Gathered together, and having authority's leave, we propose to form a company to which all individuals in the trade will have the right to belong, should they so desire. We have no other purpose than to help one another in those of life's circumstances when an unlucky craftsman, overwhelmed by the burden of a horrible disease, finds himself without resources, perhaps lacking the wherewithal to provide for

his own health or the nourishment of his family, for it should not be concealed from your excellency that upon this class falls misery and need.[4]

In spite of the difficulties, some trades did acquire a tradition of organization; there are even assemblies on record that formed in the second half of the nineteenth century and survived into the twentieth century (Table 2.1). Such was the case of the Mutual Society of the Trade of Tailors, the Great Family of Artisans, the Fraternal Society of the Trade of Seamstresses, the 'Union and Concord' Company of Waiters, the 'Xicoténcatl' Society of Foundrymen and Patternmakers, and the Bakers' 'Union and Friendship' Society. Others became unions during the revolutionary period, resulting in, for example, the Restaurant Employees' Union or the Graphic Arts Union.[5]

Membership in mutual societies was voluntary, which, in combination with the non-existent support within the productive structure, economic insecurity and the instability inherent in craftsmen's jobs, accentuated the weaknesses of the societies, leaving them at the mercy of certain leadership groups whose members, though democratically voted into office, changed little, as they had greater economic power, perhaps via owning workshops or through having links with the local government.[6]

Practising a trade, working in an industry, having a profession or a 'means of making an honest living', in addition to displaying good behaviour and high moral standards, were the basic requirements for belonging to a mutual society. Formally, decisions were based on the members' secret vote and, as noted above, religious or political issues were avoided in meetings. To assist members or their families, these associations included savings funds financed by contributions from each member. These were sporadically used to make loans to members, support striking workers, establish cooperative workshops and provide education. The number of affiliated workers could be important, but economic insecurity and voluntary affiliation made it impossible to consolidate a stable base of unionized workers.[7]

On 26 November 1871, the printers Juan de Mata Rivera and Francisco de Paula Gonzalez, with another ten artisans, founded the Society of Workers of the North Pole, which admitted workers of all classes. From this emerged the *Gran Círculo de Obreros de México* (Great Circle of Workers of Mexico), which sought to improve the economic and moral situation of working-class members, train them and broaden their civic knowledge, defend them from the excesses of both capitalists and master craftsmen, bring workers together nationally, and pro-

Table 2.1 Craftsmen's Organizations

Guilds 1788	Mutual Societies 1853–76	Associations 1918
Masons	Stonecutters and Masons	
The art of reading	Socialist Society of Mexican Typographers Mexican Typography Printers Regenerator of the Most Noble Art of Gutenberg Fraternal Society of Bookbinders	Association of Graphic Arts and Adjuncts of the Federal District Union of Graphic Arts Typesetters 'Diaz de Leon' Typographical Society Union of Bookbinders, Scribers and Similar Lino-typographical Union Union of Typographical Press Operators
Apothecaries	Pharmaceutical Fraternal Society	'Practical Pharmacy' Society
	Great Family of Artisans	Great Family of Artisans
Stonecutters	Stonecutters Mutual Society	Union of Mexican Stonecutters
Carpenters	Progressive Society of the Trade of Carpenters Fraternal Society of Carpenters	Union of Carpenters, Woodcarvers and Similar
Coach Builders	Workers of the Future of the Trade of Coach Builders	
	Fraternal Society of the Trade of Seamstresses	Fraternal Society of Seamstresses
Tanners	Fraternal Society of the Trade of Tanners	
	'Xicoténcatl' Society of Foundrymen and Patternmakers	'Xicoténcatl' Society of Foundrymen and Patternmakers
Musicians	Philharmonic of Mutual Aid	Philharmonic Union Philharmonic Co-fraternity
	'Union and Concord' of the Trade of Waiters	'Union and Concord' of the Trade of Waiters Union of Restaurant Workers Union of Restaurant Employees Cosmopolitan Centre of Waiters Mutual Society of Restaurant Waiters
	'Union and Friendship' Society of the Trade of Bakers	'Union and Friendship' Society of the Trade of Bakers

Hairdressers	Hairdressers and Phlebotomists	Fraternal Society of Hairdressers
Silversmiths	Silversmiths and Sheet-Beaters	
Tailors	Trade of Tailoring for Mutual Aid	Mutual Society of the Trade of Tailors
Hatters	Private Society of Mutual Aid Hatters' Fraternal society Union of Hatters Hatters' Mutual Society	
Reformer of the Trade of Hatters	Union of Rope-Makers and Hatters	
Silk Weavers	Fraternal Union of Weavers	Guild of Cotton Thread and Cloth Workers
Shoemakers	Hope of Shoemakers	Union of Shoemakers 'Santa Cruz' Guild of Shoemakers

Sources: 'Relación de los gremios, artes y oficios que hay en la nobilísima Ciudad de México (1788)' [Report of the Guilds, Arts and Trades Existing in the Most Noble City of México (1788)], Biblioteca Nacional, ms. 1388 (451), in Kicza, *Colonial Entrepreneurs*, 1983; Illades, *Hacia la república del trabajo* [*Towards a Republic of Work*], pp. 109–10; 'Asociaciones registradas en el Departamento de Trabajo hasta mayo del año de 1913' [Associations Registered with the Department of Work up to May 1913]; 'Directorio de asociaciones en la República' [Directory of Associations in the Republic], pp. 52–55.

tect industry and development of trades. The *Gran Círculo* established branches in factories bordering the capital, in others around the country and at mutual societies in Mexico City, for example, the branch established at the Águila factory in Contreras in 1872. Membership increased rapidly. By 1873, there were four branches; two years later, there were twenty-eight; and by 1878, the total came to thirty-four. It also had about forty mutual societies in Mexico City itself.

The *Gran Círculo* shared a newspaper with a number of Mexico City mutual associations. This was *El Socialista,* founded by Juan de Mata Rivera in July 1871, with a weekly column describing its activities and helping to coordinate its membership. The organization's original rules are unknown. At the outset, the *Gran Círculo* was probably a kind of mutual society, accepting individual and collective membership. Statutory reform on 25 May 1874 concentrated power in the leadership, subordinating members and branches to the central board's decisions. It proposed the formation of a general savings fund, distinguished the central circle (consisting of members living in Mexico City and branch members from outside the capital who, if they were unable to attend, were represented by Mexico City residents) from the branches scattered around the country, each of which was to have a minimum of twenty members, established that the board of directors would be formed by the executive (president, vice president, accountant, archivist, four secretaries and two pro-secretaries as alternates, plus a finance committee and one representative for every twenty members) and empowered the branches to appoint deputies to the centre circle, including the option of ceding the seat to members who lived in the capital.[8]

Largely thanks to the work of the *Gran Círculo*, on 5 March 1876, the Constituent Workers' Congress was inaugurated in the presence of thirty-five deputies accredited by the various associations, which grew to 173 in June, when the Congress had its largest attendance. On 16 September, it promulgated the 'Act of Constitution of the Great Confederation of Associations of Workers of the United Mexican States', providing a six-month period for the drafting of its internal constitution, which would only deal with the more general aspects. Subsequent steps, aimed at refining the regulatory text, would require the approval of the majority of organizations assembled at the Congress to acquire force of law, giving rise to the First Constitutional Assembly. Pending this, the Congress would continue in office, though this did not actually happen as it was suspended several months later.[9]

The Second Workers' Congress, attended by thirty-three representatives from twelve different associations, began work on 14 December 1879 in Mexico City. Its numbers gradually diminished until none but the representatives from the *Gran Círculo* remained. Nonetheless, the standing committee – whose members included Pedro Ordóñez and José María González y González, who had also participated in the 1876 Congress – remained in operation until 1894. After the schism that gave rise to the National Labour Congress, the Second Workers' Congress was reorganized in January 1895 and continued for a further eight years.

Workers and the Public Sector

It was at civic festivities that the public presence of organized workers was fully recognized. The civic ritual, with its republican character, was at once a sphere for representation and a source of legitimacy. At these celebrations, the authorities (once religious, now civil) assigned workers a place and gave them a public voice. Civic festivities helped to consolidate workers as collective subjects by providing a space for their companionship within the symbolic republican field.

In colonial times, artisans participated in religious festivals. Year after year, urban workers came together en masse at the Corpus Christi procession, which was the most popular in Mexico City. Workers marched, each flourishing the banner of their respective brotherhoods. Each trade, convened as a guild, had its patron saint, who they celebrated on his or her saint's day. After independence, without forsaking their participation in church celebrations, workers gravitated towards the civil arena. Mutual societies were jealous practitioners of funerary rites when one of their members died, and the *Gran Círculo* was invariably present at republican anniversaries: the tributes to Benito Juarez, the *Grito de Dolores* and the 5 May celebrations. They also commemorated heroes and great patriotic events by selecting a meaningful date for the inauguration of a workshop, starting a conference, opening a library, distributing diplomas or investing an executive board.[10]

In the restored republic, the anniversaries in which workers participated were secular. Emphasis was placed on the birth of the independent nation, the fate of the republic and the defence of sovereignty. Hidalgo, Juarez and Zaragoza were the most important figures in the workers' pantheon, though Juarez was pre-eminent. By exalting these heroes, they not only made them their own, but also reminded the state of their own contribution to the makeup of the country. Public holidays thus gave status within the body politic to citizens of the republic of work.[11]

The relationship between mutual societies and President Juarez could not have been better. Several of their members enrolled on the republican side during the French intervention and, when the republic emerged victorious, mutual societies increased nationwide. Juarez himself supported these groups directly. Upon his death, workers were stricken with grief. The *Gran Círculo* attended Juarez's funeral and the commemorations of the anniversary of his death. In 1872, they sent a large assembly to the San Fernando Cemetery, carrying the banner of 'Peace and Progress, in mourning and veiled in black'; 'All the arts and trades were represented there, as well as some societies'. Their banner was placed on one side of the platform 'as a sign of distinction of the *Gran Círculo de Obreros*'; on the other side was 'the flag of the president's honour guard', as one newspaper reporter pointed out. The tailor Victoriano Mereles spoke on behalf of the organization, stressing the crucial importance of the Reform Laws for workers, because it was thanks to these that 'the Mexican people pulled down the rampart raised by the clergy, destroying the progress of man who must undertake a historic mission on earth: the conquest of social rights'.[12]

On the following anniversary of Juarez's death, the *Gran Círculo* invited all its members in the capital, 'including any able to attend from nearby towns to take part in this popular demonstration', whereby 'on this day, the children of labour honour the memory of an illustrious man'. After meeting at the building of the *Gran Círculo*, the affiliated societies lined up their representatives, based on seniority. The commission of the *Gran Círculo* brought up the rear of the parade, which, accompanied by a military band, would march down the streets of Plateros, Profesa, San Francisco and Santa Isabel, then along the Avenida de los Hombres Ilustres to the San Fernando Cemetery. These parades always took place on Sunday, even if this was not the exact anniversary of Juarez's death. Neighbours were also asked to decorate their homes. Finally, speakers would ascend an expressly constructed platform and recite poems that had been written specially for the event. And this would continue, year in, year out.[13]

Confronted by the suspicion that they harboured secret political ambitions regarding the presidential election of 1876, the organizers were forced to clarify that this was merely a 'proper tribute to the man who had given Mexico its constitution and reform laws, and who had defended the country's rights from the foreign enemy with a firm hand'. On this occasion, the parade was complemented by a literary evening presided over by the son of Juarez himself, Benito Juárez Maza, who was given 'a special invitation from the board of the *Gran Círculo*'. Having committed themselves thus far, the leaders of the group took the opportunity to put him forward as a representative on the Workers' Congress that was taking place at the time. The idea was 'enthusiastically accepted', though nothing came of it. Once the speeches and poems had come to an end, 'the young Juarez thanked the *Gran Círculo* and the speakers for the demonstrations of sympathy directed to his father'. Later on, 'he was accompanied to the street by many individuals who had taken part in the ceremony, all carrying lights in their hands as a sign of great affection'. The article closes by congratulating 'the artisans of Mexico' on the commemoration, as 'honouring the memory of Juárez is honouring patriotism, it is strengthening democracy, strengthening law and order in our country'.[14]

Punishment and reward guided the state's relationship with the *Gran Círculo*, while subordination governed the behaviour of its leaders. In the end, intervention in party politics led to the organization's downfall. The first important conflict occurred when a significant contingent of representatives of the 1876 Workers' Congress decided to endorse Sebastián Lerdo de Tejada as candidate for president against José María Iglesias and Porfirio Díaz. Subsequently, another campaign that contributed to the fragmentation of the *Gran Círculo* was when Trinidad García de la Cadena's political aspirations found support among the membership, whereas General Porfirio Diaz supported Manuel Gonzalez.[15] The price was paid in 1882: the *Gran Círculo* lost its government subsidies as well as custody of the St Peter and St Paul building in central Mexico City.

If the labour movement that emerged during the restored republic was weak, the Porfirio Diaz regime managed to render it ineffective until just before major strikes broke out in 1906. A symptom of this change in the labour movement was the *Convención Radical*, an association founded in May 1886 by Colonel Enrique A. Knight, who also published a newspaper of the same name. Later that year, its founders were displaced by the group headed by Pedro Ordóñez, who emphasized its mutualist policy and marginalized Knight's civic project, which aimed to instruct the working classes in republican values and practices. The conflict came to an end when the Colonel's group was expelled on charges of attempting to put an unmistakably political stamp on the organization. Political participation would be guaranteed as the right of the individual, but in no case should the society 'as a corporation' be involved. The plan of action drafted in 1888 broke with this apolitical direction, summoning the working classes to participate in public affairs, form an alliance with the government, forgo strikes and promote industrial development policies. From this moment until around 1903, the *Convención Radical* was associated with the Second Workers' Congress, maintaining its commitment to the Constitution of 1857.[16]

Collective Action

The freedom that the Constitution of Cádiz gave workers to exercise their trades was not accompanied by the protection that had characterized production under guilds. The power of craft guilds in New Spain was based on monopolies of work (including the process of trade apprenticeships), the market and corporate representation within the state, and so the opening up of the market undermined the guild's privileged position. The first major response was the Parian riot in November 1828, when a crowd of about five thousand people ransacked and destroyed several luxury shops in the Parian building located in the heart of Mexico City. The problem persisted throughout the century and, in November 1861, a group of about two thousand craftsmen and some women, led by the tailor Juan Cano, comptroller of the *Gran Familia de Artesanos*, marched through the Alameda demanding protection for domestic industry and jobs. They managed to get the Chamber of Deputies to listen to them, but not to deal with their demands. The

liberal press turned against them, arguing both that they had no right
to break into the Congress and that the leaders had manipulated the
workers because free trade made goods cheaper, which increased their
purchasing power. In the event, it was a Catholic newspaper that supported the protectionist petition.[17]

In any event, the affected artisans' interest in their own sector did
become a matter of public debate and highlighted the obstacles to a
possible alliance between workers and the Liberal government, for
while it was true that the Liberal government was sympathetic to associationism, it was also defined by its doctrinal postulates that ascribed
the status of natural law to its economic dogmas. After the French
intervention, Juárez offered 'protection' to mutual societies.

In the 1870s, the tailors, hatters and typographers of several Mexico City establishments went on strike. The waistcoat makers of *Casa
Cousin* stopped work in August 1872 because the owner lowered the
price of finished garments by two reales. And in May 1875, the milliners
in the centre of the capital stopped work because their daily wages had
been reduced. After three months and following official arbitration,
workers grouped together in the *Sociedad Reformadora del Ramo de
Sombrerería* – Branch 24 of the *Gran Círculo* – managed to renegotiate
their work rates. The typographers of the *Imprenta del Supremo Gobierno* unsuccessfully attempted the same thing in August 1878.[18]

Although worker protest died down during the Porfiriato, it revived
towards the end of the dictatorship, with strikes at Cananea and Rio
Blanco, and increased again during the Revolution, when it became
easier for workers to associate and the armed struggle undermined the
working classes' standard of living. The Madero administration set up
the Labour Department to regulate the labour sector and arbitrate between the factors of production. One of the first conflicts it dealt with
was the textile workers' strike in Mexico City, Puebla, Veracruz and
Tlaxcala, in which those striking demanded increased wages and a ten-
hour working day. In January 1912, Madero received a commission of
the strikers and listened to their requests. Before the end of the month,
industrialists and workers agreed to shorter working hours and a wage
increase of 10 per cent, which ended the strike, but did not settle the
dispute, as employers found ways to swindle workers out of the promised wage increase.[19]

The *Casa del Obrero*, founded in September 1912 and renamed the
following year as the *Casa del Obrero Mundial* (COM), brought together
a small number of Mexico City mutual societies, comprising stonema-
sons, textile workers, tailors and coachmen. Having been silenced under
the Huerta dictatorship, the COM entered a pact with Constitutional-

ist forces in 1915 to restrain the *Convencionista* armies of Villa and Zapata, but also tried to seize the opportunity to expand its presence in the country. This ended the relationship with the Constitutionalists, leading to the dissolution of the 'Red Battalions' within six months.[20] While this happened, the capital city suffered shortages and galloping inflation, the COM supporting both strikes and worker unionization. In November 1915 alone, the following workers' groups were formed or reorganized:

> cigarette and cigar makers, carpenters and carvers, tailor operators, tailors' cutters, Foundrymen and Patternmakers, hatters, shoemakers, drivers of carriages for hire, seamstresses, hairdressers, dyers, Federation of Workers and Employees of the Tramways Company of Mexico, Federation of Workers in Yarn, Fabric and Similar, Federation of National Artillery Repair Workers.[21]

Various productive divisions suspended activities in 1915, notably masons, restaurant workers, drivers of carriages for hire, tailors, electricians and streetcar workers. In November, bakery and graphic arts workers went on strike. The bakery workers, said to number over three thousand, demanded 'a slight increase in their wages, an increase which is the more justified when the high cost of necessities and the exaggerated profits obtained by the owners of bakeries are taken into account'. Meanwhile, the Graphic Arts Union was demanding 'increased wages, *recognition* of its character as a union, abolition of fines and everything that workers should require who wish to emancipate themselves', the objective being accomplished by a strike lasting little over a week. Moreover, the spinning and weaving workers of San Antonio Abad 'who recently went on strike to require of their employers, among other things, increased wages, division of capital at some factories and recognition of their union, have just obtained an important part of their negotiations'.[22]

Other guilds resorted to negotiations to improve workers' wages. This was the case of carpenters, who presented a memorandum of demands to owners, among which a wage increase of 150 per cent stands out:

> To this end, a meeting was called between the industry's owners and workers, so that both parties could explain their reasons in defence of their interests. After a session that lasted several hours, the owners agreed fully to the rates that would determine wages from that date.

> In addition, they have achieved recognition of their union, an 8-hour working day and certain other benefits.[23]

Female workers also became unionized and were extremely combative in their protests. Accordingly, in November 1915, 'some 300 comrades assembled, including cigarette makers, seamstresses and corset-makers' at the COM 'to exchange ideas and find out how they could unionize'. In addition, cork-makers and bonnet-makers created a union, while affiliation to the Seamstresses' Union climbed to over 300.[24]

At the 'El Salvador' and 'La Perfeccionada' factories, bonnet-makers went on strike on numerous occasions because administrators refused to increase their wages, and as these were extremely low, 'they had declared a strike after exhausting all the means of persuasion they had at their disposal'. After several days on strike, workers at 'El Salvador' negotiated 'a salary increase of 100%', while at 'La Perfeccionada', in addition to the wage demand, they negotiated union recognition and the reinstatement of an unfairly dismissed worker.[25]

As far as the Constitutionalists were concerned, the strikes were not at all welcome, and far less so when they did not need the support of the unions and mutual associations in the clashes with the popular armies. Confrontation between the government and workers escalated with the general strike on 31 July 1916, sponsored by the *Federación de Sindicatos Obreros del Distrito Federal* (FSODF – Federation of Labour Unions of the Federal District), which since May had been demanding that workers be paid in gold, given the constant depreciation of paper currency, which reduced their meagre purchasing power yet further.

The government's attitude towards the strike was blunt: the COM was dissolved and orders were given for its leaders to be arrested, as well as instructions for strike breaking and the militarization of the railways. A telegram from Venustiano Carranza, the First Chief of the Constitutionalist Army, from Mexico City dated 11 August 1916, ratified the use of force: 'strikers arrested in this capital are being tried under the Law of January 25, 1862 for the crime of rebellion and treason by ordering suspension of work at the Necaxa plant'. For its part, the COM argued that right and reason were on the side of the workers, and that therefore those directly responsible for the strike were the capitalists; thus, the only thing was to 'avoid crimes such as those at Cananea and Rio Blanco'.[26]

Conclusion

The *Gran Círculo* was active for barely eleven years. Even so, this was long enough to develop comradeship amongst workers and extend its influence nationwide. It was also a vehicle for the secularization of public space and the formation of civil society, although it never completely managed to shake off state patronage; indeed, it never even raised the matter but constantly sought to recover the protection it had lost. The consolidation of the organization was never achieved both because of the limitations implicit in voluntary affiliation as well as the type of groups that amalgamated, many of which had no roots in the production process, but merely represented the addition of free and independent wills, united to provide relief and mutual aid. Its legal regulations worked in the same way: by limiting these groups to the civil sphere, they reduced their strength on the political level, which was indispensable in terms of handling workers' demands. Thus, they were trapped within the vagaries of daily politics, with the aggravating problem of acting in circumstances that were themselves full of conflict.

At the turn of the twentieth century, after two decades of peace in industrial relations, industrial workers created the first national unions, which put up stubborn resistance to foreign companies. And, during the armed struggle, associationism spread in the cities where the trades were reorganized, achieving successful wage negotiations, often with the mediation of the COM, which at first had a good relationship with the revolutionary governments. However, when the Constitutionalists defeated the Division del Norte, they got rid of their worker allies and behaved ruthlessly towards the general strike when it was triggered by the electricians of Mexico City. Despite their apparent hostility towards organized labour, the northern warlords used various resources to procure its loyalty, ranging from violence to the vision for a new legal and institutional framework for the world of work to attention to the most sensitive demands of labour. Even Carranza increased wages prior to the conflict with members of the FSODF, and Obregon pursued a policy of rapprochement and co-optation of the leaders, which took shape as the corporate pact upon which the postrevolutionary state was based. The *Confederación Regional Obrera Mexicana* (CROM – Regional Confederation of Mexican Workers), founded in May 1918, soon became the ubiquitous trade union arm of the regime, while the labour movement renounced direct action as a method of struggle.[27]

Notes

1. Anderson, 'Race and Social Stratification'; Pérez Toledo, *Población y estructura social de la Ciudad de México, 1790–1842*, pp. 165, 170.
2. Illades, *Estudios sobre el artesanado urbano del siglo xix*, pp. 103–4. In the same vein, albeit with questionable nuances, see Pérez Toledo, *Trabajado-*

res, espacio urbano y sociabilidad en la Ciudad de México 1790–1867, pp. 85–86. On the stagnation of the Mexican economy in the post-independence period, see Coatsworth, *Los orígenes del atraso*, pp. 116–17.

3. Illades, *Estudios sobre el artesanado urbano del siglo xix*, p. 171; Pérez Toledo, *Trabajadores, espacio urbano y sociabilidad en la Ciudad de México 1790–1867*, pp. 222 ff.; Illades, *Hacia la república del trabajo*, pp. 83 ff.

4. 'Origen de las sociedades mutualistas de la Ciudad de México' [The Origin of Mutual Societies in Mexico City], *La Convención Radical Obrera*, 15 December 1889, in *La Convención Radical*, p. 55.

5. 'Un triunfo más del sindicalismo' [Another Triumph for Trade Unionism], *Ariete*, 31 October 1915; 'Mitin de propaganda' [Propaganda Meeting], *Ariete*, 7 November 1915.

6. Illades, *Hacia la república del trabajo*, pp. 101 ff.

7. Ibid., pp. 94 ff.; Illades, *Estudios sobre el artesanado urbano del siglo xix*, p. 72.

8. On the topic of workers' congresses, more detail can be found in Illades, *Las otras ideas*, Chapter 8.

9. *El Socialista*, 31 May 1874. On the organization itself, see Villaseñor, 'El Gran Círculo de Obreros de México', pp. 28 ff.; Leal, *Del mutualismo al sindicalismo en México*, pp. 23 ff.; Illades, *Hacia la república del trabajo*, pp. 103 ff.

10. Tanck de Estrada, 'La abolición de los gremios', p. 325; 'Instalación de la junta directiva del Gran Círculo de Obreros que funcionará en 1873–1874' [Inauguration of the Board of the Great Circle of Workers to Be in Office from 1873 to 1874], *El Socialista*, 21 September 1873; 'Discurso pronunciado por el honorable Carlos Larrea, vicepresidente del Gran Círculo de Obreros, el 16 de septiembre, al recibirse la nueva mesa directiva' [Speech Made by the Honourable Carlos Larrea, Vice-President of the Great Circle of Workers, 16 September, Welcoming the New Board], *El Socialista*, 24 September 1877.

11. This is more extensively developed in Illades, 'Los trabajadores y la república', pp. 6 ff.

12. 'Los funerales de Juárez' [The Funerals of Juarez], *El Socialista*, 28 July 1872.

13. 'El Gran Círculo de Obreros. Guillermo Prieto' [The Great Circle of Workers. Guillermo Prieto], *El Socialista*, 27 July 1873; 'Juárez', *La Firmeza*, 15 July 1874.

14. 'Juárez y los obreros' [Juarez and the Workers], *El Socialista*, 23 July 1876; 'Benito Juárez', *El Socialista*, 23 July 1876.

15. 'Desconocimiento de la mesa del Gran Círculo Nacional de Obreros de México' [Repudiation of the Board of the National Great Circle of Workers of Mexico], *El Socialista*, 14 April 1879; 'El Gran Círculo Nacional de Obreros de México' [The National Great Circle of Workers of Mexico], *El Socialista*, 14 April 1879.

16. Walker, 'Porfirian Labor Politics', p. 264; Gutiérrez, *El mundo del trabajo y el poder político*, pp. 43 ff.

17. Arrom, '*Protesta popular en la Ciudad de México*' [*Popular Politics in Mexico City: The Parian Riot, 1828.*], p. 83; Teitelbaum, 'Asociación y protesta de los artesanos al despuntar la década de 1860', p. 68.
18. Illades, *Hacia la república del trabajo*, pp. 156 ff.
19. *El Imparcial*, 6 January 1912; *El Imparcial*, 21 January 1912; *El Diario*, 4 January 1913; *El Diario*, 8 January 1913; *El Diario*, 18 January 1913.
20. Ribera Carbó, *La Casa del Obrero Mundial*, p. 51; Lear, *Workers, Neighbors, and Citizens*, p. 158; Hart, *Anarchism and the Mexican Working Class, 1860–1931.*
21. 'Nuevos sindicatos' [New Trade Unions], *Ariete*, 5 December 1915.
22. 'Manifiesto del Centro de Estudios Sociales "Casa del Obrero Mundial" a los trabajadores de la región mexicana' [Manifesto of the Casa del Obrero Mundial's Centre for Social Studies to Workers in the Mexico City Region], ¡Luz!, 10 February 1920; 'Casa del Obrero Mundial', *El Sindicalista*, 31 January 1914; 'Huelga de panaderos' [Bakers' Strike], *Ariete*, 7 November 1915; 'Sindicato de Artes Gráficas' [Graphic Arts Union], *Ariete*, 21 November 1915, my emphasis; 'Se soluciona una huelga' [A Strike is Settled], *Ariete*, 5 December 1915. I cite the last three.
23. 'Sindicato de Carpinteros, Tallistas y Similares' [Union of Carpenters, Wood Carvers and Similar], *Ariete*, 12 December 1915.
24. 'Las obreras se sindican' [The Workers Unionize], *Ariete*, 21 November 1915; 'Sindicato de Taponeras' [Union of Cork Makers], *Ariete*, 12 December 1915; 'Sindicato de Obreras de Bonetería' [Union of Milliners], *Ariete*, 5 December 1915; 'Sindicato de Costureras' [Union of Seamstresses], *Ariete*, 12 December 1915. I cite the first.
25. 'Sindicato de Boneteras', *Ariete*, 12 December 1915; 'La huelga de "La Perfeccionada"' [The Strike at 'La Perfeccionada'], *Ariete*, 19 December 1915. I cite the former.
26. 'Julio Quintero, secretario general de la Casa del Obrero Mundial, al ciudadano presidente jefe Venustiano Carranza' (Tampico, 15 August 1916) [From Julio Quintero, General Secretary of the Casa del Obrero Mundial to Citizen President, First Chief Venustiano Carranza (Tampico, 15 August 1916)], *Tribuna Roja*, 1 September 1916.
27. González Casanova, *En el primer gobierno constitucional, 1917–1920*, pp. 21 ff.; Barbosa Cano, *La CROM, de Luis N. Morones a Antonio J. Hernández*, pp. 10–11.

Chapter 3

The 'Pueblos Unidos' Rebellion

In the second half of the nineteenth century, a large number of agrarian rebellions broke out in Mexico. Some of these were caused by the seizure of communal property, others by the expansion of the haciendas at the expense of the towns, by the threat to autonomy or by peasants' lack of social mobility. The state did very little to remedy the situation, partly because its links with landowners were very solid, but also because institutional and economic weakness made even the contemplation of action impossible.

Rebellions with socialist goals, such as that led by the young peasant Julio López, were nevertheless few in number. Tutored by Plotino Rhodakanaty, López took up arms against landowners in Chalco, State of Mexico, in 1868, proclaiming the 'Manifesto to all the oppressed and poor in the Universe'. Opposing human exploitation, this rejected all forms of government, churches and priests, seeking peace and order, the free use of land and the creation of agricultural societies, and aimed at achieving the 'Universal Republic of Harmony' and socialism.[1]

In addition to the restitution of land to the people and endowments of workable land to the soldiers of the revolutionary army, the rebels of the 'Pueblos Unidos' of the Sierra Gorda outlined a form of federal government, structured from the bottom up, in which officials were required to respond to the petitions at the base of the body politic. Like the 1868 Chalco Rebellion, the 1879 rebellion was related to the socialist nucleus Rhodakanaty had formed in Mexico City, but, unlike the former, occurred in a context where urban and rural workers were beginning to organize, so that it resonated considerably, so much that some liberal writers vilified it. Prison and public execution were the reward of those directly participating in rebellion. Even so, by incorporating the redistribution of land within its ideology and demanding the implementation of 'Agrarian Law', the first socialism would be injected into the Mexican Revolution of 1910, when this agrarian demand became very powerful.

The Mexican Socialist Confederation

Plotino Constantino Rhodakanaty was a Greek homeopath who, in 1871, formed 'La Social', an association 'for society's poor and underprivileged classes'. Its members, according to the press, were 'persons of both sexes, having the noble purpose of spreading teaching among themselves and disseminating it to the masses', giving 'great credit' to its founder, 'making him the centre of a multitude of citizens, who think of him as an apostle, who consult him as a guide and as a friend'.[2] Its 'inauguration and reinstallation' in May 1876, included the issuance of a regulation which consisted of a declaration of principles and basic rules under which the organization would proceed. The 'Central Organizing Committee' was in charge of direction, including, among other duties, presiding over the 'Great Assembly of Foreign Delegates or Representatives of the Towns' to which they could give 'discreet instructions'. Meanwhile, Rhodakanaty stressed the importance of agrarian law 'that will be so favourable to indigenous people and rural families in Mexico'.[3]

One year later, Francisco Zalacosta, editor of *La Internacional* and the most active of Rhodakanaty's disciples, travelled round the states of Mexico, Puebla, Tlaxcala and Hidalgo to bring communities closer to the organization, proclaim 'agrarian law' and organize, on 15 August 1877, an assembly of peasants in Mexico City to establish the *Gran Comité Central Comunero*, which also included the participation of Colonel Alberto Santa Fe, the Tetela political chief, appointed in 1872. Shortly before the end of the year, the Mayor of Texcatepec, Hidalgo, unleashed a campaign against the 'communists', in response to the federal mandate to 'hang all the troublemakers' and instructing the security forces to 'shoot anyone I think is a communist'.[4] Whether it was to define to or to bring them into disrepute, state governments and the press had dubbed several peasant rebellions 'socialist' in Ciudad del Maíz, in the Sierra Gorda – a complicated region bordering the states of Querétaro, Guanajuato, Hidalgo and San Luis Potosi – and other surrounding areas.[5]

Santa Fe, who would visit Victor Considérant in exile in Texas, published *Ley del Pueblo* in 1878, where he proposed abolishing haciendas and distributing rural property in small plots conceded to peasant families by the municipalities, which would be paid off over a period of ten years with an annual interest rate of 6 per cent, with inputs and draft animals provided. The expropriation 'for public utility' would be financed by the *Banco Agrícola e Industrial* through the issue of unconvertible currency notes (*billetes de curso forzoso*) up to a maximum of fifty thousand pesos in value. The bank would also offer soft loans to societies of artisans to install factories and workshops. Under no circumstances would water or forests remain in private hands, the entire community participating in their enjoyment. He also fought for economic protectionism and industrial development policies that would encourage the creation of arts and trades workshops in the states. He considered the removal of sales taxes and other barriers to internal trade, in addition to direct taxes on capital to strengthen public finances. He demanded free, compulsory primary education for both sexes, and free education at the middle and higher levels. He spoke in favour of severely punishing crime and establishing a policy of crime prevention. The army would be reduced to a minimum of five thousand men, leaving defence of the nation in the hands of the citizens themselves.[6]

At that time, the socialist press reported occasions of landowners stealing the lands of the peoples of central Mexico and even, from the remote state of Coahuila, came the warning that given 'the plight of the majority of the Mexican people … it appears that a deliberate effort is being made to thrust it towards socialism and the *commune*'.[7] It was not long after this wake-up call when, at the first meeting of the 'representatives of the *Liga de los Pueblos*' – we do not know if this was the 'Gran Asamblea de Delegados Foráneos o Representantes de los Pueblos' – a fiery orator expressed his sympathy for the Paris Commune[8] and municipalism, further noting that:

> With good governance and good principles, being those proclaimed by socialism, its march forward being based solely on equality and justice, and thus that which gives the best guarantee to the respect for all rights and, above all, that of property, not, as claimed by the enemies of the principle that it seeks to destroy it. In any event, so great a doctrine is based on science and not on empiricism, it is essentially scientific and essentially good. In Mexico, above all, its objective is to restore to the indigenous peoples the land that has been usurped from them, and impart to them, and also to the masses, the necessary instruction so that they will know at all times how to defend rights of which they have now been stripped.[9]

In February 1876, at a place known as 'Palo Huérfano' in Guanajuato, representatives of indigenous settlements on haciendas had assembled, seeking consensus on a strategy to banish the Spaniards, who, they believed, had seized the wealth of the republic. It was attended by representatives from Santa Catarina de las Cuevas, Santa Teresa de Jesús, San José de los Llanos Burras and San Miguel de los Naranjos y Calera.[10] The following year, they and representatives of dozens of towns from neighbouring states presented a document entitled *Defence of national land law raised by the Mexican people to the General National Congress, calling for the re-conquest of property in land so that it shall once again be distributed among all citizen-inhabitants of the Republic through agrarian laws and the general organization of work, by the series of protective laws having funds to create a National Bank of Loans.*

The document called for a distribution of land:

> Considering, that we still have resources and elements that we may dispose of, taking them out of stationary monopolization, so that the nation may take that path of civilization and intellectual, moral and physical advance, correctly organizing reconquered property interests, that have not yet had the opportunity to shake off the long unjust servitude, under an active and just general levelling, giving the true value that can itself represent our free land.[11]

Further, it proposed creating a loan bank to finance agricultural activities and establish schools of trades and sciences. One of its many signatories was Antonio Guevara from the town of San Francisco Buenavista (Querétaro), the leader of the 'Pueblos Unidos' Rebellion.[12]

In the same year (1877), the indigenous leader Juan Santiago began to occupy farms in Tamazunchale, in the Huasteca Potosina, keeping the forces of law and order pinned down for five years, though he was also skilful enough fight legal battles or negotiate with the federal government when necessary. In about August 1879, the Querétaro authorities reported the rising of 'five hundred men' in the neighbouring state and the mobilization of a hundred soldiers to cut off the 'rearguard of these gangs'.[13] By November, the exhaustion of Tamazunchale was such that:

> This force is currently under siege. General Juan Santiago is nearby, leading a crowd of armed indigenous men who will not allow food into the market. Panic in the town is generalized and hunger is setting in. Terrazas, the political boss, is only obeyed in the market. Juan Santiago, who issues decrees that are obeyed, dominates everywhere else.[14]

Before the end of 1881, Santiago, leading a force of over 2,000 peasants, attacked the town again. On this occasion, his militia bore a red banner with the slogan: 'Municipal Government and Agrarian Law.'[15]

In February 1879, in the district of Huejotzingo, Puebla, locals had taken up arms to obtain land and put an end to parish contributions, responsibility being attributed to Colonel Santa Fe, whose 'communist preaching has convinced some Indians that it is they who are the owners of the haciendas'. The Mexican Socialist Party – established in the city of Puebla in July 1878 and in which Santa Fe, Jesús A. Laguna and Manuel Serdán participated – tried to assist them, while the army tried to crush them at all costs. The army discovered Santa Fe asleep at the San Rafael ironworks at three o'clock in the morning on 8 May. Laguna and Gabino López Olivera were able to flee, but Santa Fe was not.[16]

Even so, the Pelagallinas rebellion followed its course despite Santa Fe's arrest. There is evidence of its link with the followers of the *Plan Socialista*, suggesting a degree of coordination between the *Partido Socialista*, *La Social*, the *Directorio Socialista* and the rebel movements, though we do not know how this worked. It may be that this was what was known as the *Confederación Mexicana Socialista*, which appears in various documents and is indicated in the emblem reproduced below, which includes a symbol of Freemasonry, the communist hammer and sickle, and an 'A' for anarchy. How this diverse mosaic of socialist ideas and images came to be formed and how it reached the almost impregnable Sierra Gorda are matters we are discovering only now and are trying to ascertain.

The Rebellion

On 1 June 1879, the *Socialist Plan proclaimed by the representatives of the towns of the states of Queretaro and Guanajuato* was issued at Santa Cruz Barranca, Guanajuato. It sought to restore land to indigenous people, protect the working classes from the abuses of the rich, protect national industry, create schools and hospitals, establish a lifetime pension for the relatives of the socialist fighters, and form 'agrarian committees' responsible for dealing with the restitution of land to the towns and the distribution of workable land among the soldiers of the revolutionary army (also known as 'popular phalanxes'), headed by the *Directorio Socialista*. All debts contracted by the movement would be paid off by the 'National Bank' at the end of the war, which would end with the occupation of Mexico City.[17]

The intellectuals at *La Libertad* demonized the plan, showing, like the positivists they were, that the masses should be directed by the guidelines of scientists and not by makeshift ideologues:

> When men of enlightened intelligence place themselves at the front
> of any movement of ideas and interests, however dangerous it may
> be, the evils that may result from such a movement will be vastly less

than if stupid men preach stupidities to a people, the vast majority of whom are still almost totally immersed in barbarism ... to activate five million Indians submerged in abject ignorance, all that is needed is for some ignorant individual to pull certain triggers of individual interest, triggers that are none other than plunder and the eviction of the owners.[18]

Shortly afterwards, the news spread: 'representatives of the united towns of the states of Querétaro and Guanajuato have accepted the political plan, with certain changes favourable to the cause they proclaim', that is, agrarian law, the defence of legitimately acquired property and the 'Social Democratic Republic'.[19]

Promulgated on 15 July 1879, this updated document, which incorporated the demands of General Miguel Negrete, who had also rebelled, is known as the *Plan Socialista* and contains three parts: a proposal for agrarian law, a second of political reform and a third of electoral law. The first made it illegal for haciendas to exact sums from their labourers, cancelled the debts that labourers and servants owed to the haciendas, and granted each worker ownership of the 'plot where he lived and the land he farmed', while the towns retained the communal and inalienable property of 'land sufficient to meet their social needs'. Political organization remained at the municipality, which would bring together political, social, educational and judicial functions. In state capitals, the municipal president would also be the state president, and in the federal capital, there would be a president. The armed population would be in charge of the security and defence of the nation. Electoral law would allow every town to choose its authorities freely and autonomously, applying the same procedure at the various levels of government. Elections would be held at a public assembly by direct and secret ballot. The document concluded with the slogan 'Land. Industry. Education. Weapons.' and is signed by Diego Hernández (president) and Luis Luna (first secretary):[20]

> In this manifesto, we find all the elements of agrarian socialism: a) all land and natural resources are the property of the nation and the plots and common lands are inalienable. Thus, social property is firmly established as the framework of private utilisation. b) land administration is placed in the hands of municipal governments (elected by the peasants themselves), and resources are placed in the hands of a direct democracy of workers and not a central state.[21]

On 12 September 1879, the political boss of the Jilotepec district, State of Mexico, reported to his superiors that seven armed and mounted individuals had been arrested at Villa del Carbón, admitting to being under the command of General Tiburcio Montiel and Colonel Santa Fe. They also acknowledged that Néstor del Oso and Félix Rodríguez (the latter being a member of *La Social*), both residents of this same district, were committed to this revolutionary movement. A document had been confiscated, signed by Rodríguez and addressed to Basilio Ramos, at that time a prisoner, and a 'socialist revolutionary', referring to 'General' Félix Rodríguez,[22] who proclaimed:

> For over three hundred years, most of the peoples of our beautiful Mexico has been lamenting the most infamous usurpation; this most iniquitous disinheritance, which by way of conquest and with no right whatsoever, the Spaniards inflicted on the Mexican race; on that humble and suffering indigenous race, the sacred, eternal and inalienable rights that the Supreme Creator of Heaven and Earth gave to man as his nature; to possess and enjoy the valuable fruits that our common mother who is the land provides to us in freedom, equality and justice. This malady of our unfortunate people was brought to this country because of the evil ambition of the race of conquerors…

He also encouraged distrust for:

> One of the most flattering political plans that has been seen in our country, to deceive the people, was that of the last revolution; the Plan of Tuxtepec, which offered complete regeneration to our nation. Therefore, making use of a right, in union with citizens who accompany me, I protest against and deny the revolution of Don Porfirio Díaz as President of Mexico, recognizing only the municipal or socialist government.[23]

Del Oso, accused of instigating a riot in the town of San Buenaventura, was arrested in early 1881 and placed at the disposal of the judge in Jilotepec. Prior to that, San Gregorio Mescapino, a town in that district, had signed a statement, which their representatives had sent to both the President of the Republic and the House of Representatives in 1878.[24] On the situation in the region, Tiburcio Montiel wrote:

> In the District of Jilotepec, an entire town was dispersed by the administrator of the estate who also holds office as mayor, being the hacienda of Don Miguel Rul on whose behalf such atrocities are perpetrated, preceded by violence, arson, despair and the weeping of the elderly, women and children, who were driven from their homes as if they were an infestation of vermin.[25]

Soon news of uprisings arrived from other parts of the mountainous region. In San Sebastián, a rumour grew of an imminent indigenous uprising 'in the communist sense' and, in Ixmiquilpan, also in the state of Hidalgo, there was news of two hundred armed indigenous people. Anticipating rebellion in Calpulalpan, Tlaxcala, the authorities apprehended twenty-one indigenous men, while in Villa del Carbón, State of Mexico, seven 'mounted and armed' individuals were captured with 'important documents relating to the revolution'. In the meantime, Fernando Ramírez, 'a distinguished soldier of the socialist army', in command of over two hundred horsemen and 'five hundred infantrymen', was able to repel forces of the government of Guanajuato from the fort of San Gregorio, who 'fled in terror and in complete disarray, suffering numerous desertions'. It was estimated that by then, the socialists numbered 'more than two thousand men'.[26]

During the following months, the 'Pueblos Unidos' Rebellion spread throughout the east of the State of Querétaro, while General Negrete concentrated his activities in the State of Puebla. In October, in an area between Bernal and Cadereyta, a party of thirty men pursued 'a band of criminals composed of twenty-six foot soldiers' armed with four rifles, one carbine, four bayonets, a sword, a box of dynamite and a machete. After six days, the *rurales* and landowners, in coordinated actions, with a 'public force of 100 men' were able to subdue 'the Communists' commanded by their 'leader' Félix Rodríguez and arrest nine (two of them wounded), while the forces of law and order lost one man. A proclamation was seized from the rebels, 'a notebook entitled *El revelador fidedigno*',[27] a manifesto, a tin, a big barrel of gunpowder, a dismantled carbine and rifle, a dagger, a bayonet, a small knife, a rope, a pair of cashmere summer trousers and white paper.[28]

Interrogated by the judicial authorities, the prisoners declared 'unanimously that they followed a political plan, that being socialism', which included 'the redistribution of land'. For that reason, said one of the detainees, 'they believed in some men who offered – if he went with them – to redistribute the land to the poor'. Another said that Félix Rodríguez 'compelled them to join and to obey by force'. Most said that they knew neither him nor other leaders of the movement; nevertheless, they were interned in Cadereyta prison on charges of being part of a 'gang of communists'.[29] Almost in the same terms, each one:

> was prosecuted on charges resulting from having joined Félix Rodríguez and his gang to support him in his revolutionary plan and having offered armed resistance to legitimately established authority, and for this crime being thereby deserving of the penalties indicated

by the law for offenders of their class, that which is to be imposed immediately as deserved.[30]

A little over one month later, José María Villarreal and Julio Muñoz were also apprehended in Cadereyta. There were several statements accusing Villarreal, identifying him as one of the instigators of the rebellion, though Félix Rodríguez was invariably identified as the leader and the person who awarded military rank within the insurgent group. Villarreal's record stated his place of birth as Huichapan, his age as forty, his profession as drover and that he was maimed. The still-fugitive Rodríguez was described by one of the detainees as a man 'of normal stature, yellow in colour, with a heavy black beard, 40-odd years old, average nose, average mouth' without 'any distinguishing marks'. The sentence for Villarreal was six years' imprisonment, for another prisoner named Felipe Lara who, according to the judicial authority, 'served as clerk to the leader Félix Rodríguez', one year and four months, and for the others, one year in prison, taking into account the coercion by the leaders of the rebellion.[31]

While outbreaks of rebellion were increasing in the mountains of Querétaro, on 14 December 1879 in Mexico City:

> at eleven, a huge crowd marched in the main streets of Mexico, with a large number of red flags fluttering above them. At the head of that crowd, a man of the people walked, brandishing a banner that bore in large letters the slogan: *La Social* – Great International League! Then followed another, equally red, saying: *Centro Socialista de la Confederación Mexicana!* and another in red and blue bearing: Indigenous Alliance – Agrarian Law! Then followed the others, all red, of the provincial branches of these associations ... among the multitude of artisans who formed the legion of workers, mingled the representatives of the indigenous peoples, demanding land, also having come long distances to take part in the celebration that took place.[32]

This was the preamble to the Second Workers' Congress, which was convened in the capital on 3 January 1880. *La Social* sent four delegates – Félix Riquelme, Benito Castro, José Rico and Juan O. Orellana – as well as town representatives – José Leon García (Ozumba), Juan Olvera (Ayapango), Jesús A. Laguna (Tepetlixpan), and Jesús Venegas (Zapotitlán) – a sign of their influence in some parts of the country where, it was said, it had sixty-two sections.[33]

The *Directorio Socialista,* which coordinated the rebellion in Querétaro, conferred titles and awards on the outstanding members of the popular phalanxes, appointments that included the responsibility to 'exploit all necessary means to carry out their mission and to organize phalanxes, demand weapons, ammunition, horses, saddles, money and other resources for the maintenance of their forces, naturally giving the necessary receipt to the people from whom they were making such requirements.'[34]

In addition, the *Directorio Socialista* called on all Mexicans to unite with the socialist cause, to leave 'slavery abolished forever, leaving liberated properties free of any rent, free from ... oppressors and the enemies of our race' and take back 'the lands that the Spanish had taken from them'. The documents typically concluded with slogans such as 'Independence and Social Freedom, Social Revolution, God and the Law of Freedom, Independence and Socialism', as well as the slogans 'The Workers and the Proletariat! The People of the Workers! Democratic and Social Republic!'[35]

A dispatch from the People's Army gives an account of the number of fighters, the weaponry at their disposal and the awkward Spanish of a lettered, indigenous man:

> On January 6, we moved and had at the same ranch Llervavuenas [*sic*] and arrived at that point at six thirty-four in the morning on that date we had four days at that point, on day nine we went down by way of the village of San Miguel Istla [*sic*] of the second border of the north we were fourteen armed men, it was a rifle gun and two musket; and all weapons were pistols two pistol with two shots and of the several shot ones nine pistols and then when we arrived in this town of San Miguel Ixtla there were already three person two were from Tepeji del Río and another was from Don Antonio Guevara ... and from there we got together ... twenty men and the three, two armed and one had a pistol.[36]

Another summons the 'chiefs, from captains up, involved in the social cause in the state under his command, to meet at the point known as "Puente del Roble", within eight days, without fail'.[37] In the same way, a general uprising scheduled for 25 December 1880 was also spoken of, which was finally thwarted 'as General Tiburcio Montiel did not arrive, who, after conquering from Salvatierra to the towns of Michoacán, should have, if the case arose, come to "place himself" at the head of the troops of the towns; but none of this happened, because so far as is known, Don Porfirio Díaz sent Mr. Montiel to the United States of the North'.[38]

There is evidence of the link between the movement and both the *Confederación Mexicana Socialista* and the various organizations that constituted it. A letter signed by Antonio Guevara and others complains about the roster of single men and widowers made by order of a 'Señor González, who claims to be the president of the republic' in order to evaluate the behaviour of farmworkers, addressed to Alberto Santa Fe, Señor Arellano, Félix Riquelme, to 'Mr. "Pill" [Rhodakanaty?] and all the other leaders of *La Socialidad* [*La Social?*]'.[39]

At the Congress of the International Workers' Association held in London in 1881, Eduardo Nathan Ganz spoke of the 'Pueblos Unidos' Rebellion. While he had never visited Mexico, he was aware of the situation in the country. He stressed its revolutionary tradition, especially in rural areas – similar to those in Russia and Ireland – and the depth of the agrarian conflict. He clearly considered Mexican tactics and political tendencies to be revolutionary, proof of this being the *Confederación Mexicana Socialista*, made up of 1,800 members divided into eighteen sections. He also reported that, in September 1879 in the capital of Querétaro, a contingent of forty men, which grew to seven hundred in under twelve hours, under the direction of Juan O. Orellana, 'one of our comrades', proclaimed the 'Communist and Anti-authoritarian Republic'.[40] In an unreliable story, Nathan Ganz claimed that these revolutionaries 'had not made the mistake of their predecessors by taking over the mayor's palace to proclaim a new government ... [but] the joy did not last', for in two days the army defeated the rebels, wounding twenty and leaving thirteen dead, while 'the rest retreated to the mountains'. However, recent research into state and local files has not found any evidence to confirm this.[41]

On 14 March 1881, the District of Querétaro Prefecture reported to the governor that they had recently captured Juan Díaz, Antonio Guevara, Ascensión Hernández, Anselmo de Jesús, Casimiro Jiménez, Justo Lira, José Jiménez, Gabriel Mendoza, Agustín Ramírez, Onofre Clemente and María Antonia Guevara, who were 'accused of belonging to an association formed to commit crimes against persons and their property, calling themselves "socialist"'. They had seized from Guevara: 'Proclamations to make the indigenous race rise in arms under a socialist plan, blank dispatches for chiefs and subordinates and tricolour flags, with a gold lettering reading: "Falanges Populares Socialistas".'[42]

The rebels were tried in the city of Querétaro. The trial records provide important information about the movement, about some of its key players and about the *Confederación Mexicana Socialista*. The prisoners were artisans and peasants who, with the exception of Guevara, declared themselves ignorant of the socialist organization and even that they were illiterate, and that therefore the officers' presumption with respect to their political affiliation was unfounded. While most witnesses stated that the arrested 'had always been model citizens', some incriminated Antonio Guevara; in addition, many of the documents of the *Directorio Socialista* carried his signature and others referred to him as either 'Colonel' or 'General'.

Antonio Guevara was a seventy-one-year-old farmworker born in the city of Querétaro. Ascensión Hernández, aged thirty-two, was a blacksmith from Tepeji del Río. Juan Díaz was a twenty-seven-year-old shoemaker from Celaya. Anselmo de Jesús was a twenty-five-year-old farmworker, originally from the San Antonio de la Punta neighbourhood in the city of Querétaro. María Antonia Guevara was a forty-eight-year-old domestic servant born in La Quinta and was the sister of the main prisoner. Casimiro Jiménez was a forty-two-year-old woodcutter from San Antonio de la Punta. Justo Lira was a fifty-three-year-old farmworker born in the same place. José Jiménez was a twenty-one-year-old farmworker from the same neighbourhood. Agustín Ramírez too was a fifty-one-year-old farmworker and Onofre Clemente was a twenty-two-year-old farmworker.[43]

Rómulo Alonso, a silversmith by trade, stated that he knew that Guevara 'wandered about the parishes of La Punta, Santa María, Carrillo, San Pablo and other places with flags, inviting people to join the association of those who preached the socialist plan'. He also characterized him as 'an individual with a bad nature who, with others of like mind, proclaims the Commune'. José Jiménez, one of the prisoners, said that: 'Guevara left a package at his home with contents that were unknown to him and he did not know if there were individuals going about proclaiming a plan.' The aforementioned package contained documents and 'two flags ... a little over a meter in length ... formed of three strips, approximately equal in width and size, ... with an inscription taking up the three mentioned strips and which reads horizontally "Municipal Government and Agrarian Law. Social Democratic Republic"'.[44]

Meanwhile, Guevara declared to the court:

> that these papers mean that the defendant and all of his race intend to create the momentum to claim their rights to Mexican land, because it is their property and they have an indubitable right to it. They can no longer so much as plant a quarter of corn, or cut a log, because landowners do not allow them to and do not even pay them for their work, but give them tokens and they cannot provide for their families with these tokens; that is why they claim their land and this claim is the objective of the socialist plan they proclaim.[45]

The *Directorio Socialista* had a colonel in charge of each town (a total of twenty-six in Querétaro). Guevara was listed as superior commander of cavalry in San Francisco de Buenavista, and José Jiménez was responsible for San Antonio de la Punta, but none of the other prisoners was listed as being militarily responsible for any town, hence the assumption that they were under the command of José Jiménez. Yet, Guevara absolved his comrades of guilt by stating that 'they had been given those documents in Mexico and that the person who presented them [had] died three years ago and was called Lorenzo Lancaster'.[46] At that time, the representatives of various indigenous peoples had attended the *Congreso de la Unión* to reveal the circumstances they lived in, which makes it plausible that it was there that Guevara came into contact with the Socialists. It is also to be noted that in February 1878, *La Social* held a meeting that discussed operating rules for when 'representatives of distant places were present'.[47] Prior to this possible meeting, the representatives of the towns – including Guevara – had gone to Mexico City for discussions with President Sebastián Lerdo de Tejada:

> not only from here in the state of Querétaro but from Guanajuato and all parts of the Republic to Mexico, to ask the President to give them possession of their towns and lands that had been awarded to the Spanish; that the said Señor Lerdo ordered the clerks to search the records in the General Archive of the Nation to decide on their request.[48]

In mid-1882, the rebel colonel and the other co-defendants were released on bail, given the colonel's health – 'who was found to be ill with rheumatism, given his advanced age and poor hygiene of the place where he was imprisoned' – and the lack of compelling evidence against his companions.[49]

However, their freedom did not last long: in the early morning of 19 October 1882, around thirty irregulars stormed the Tlacote El Bajo hacienda, seizing weapons, horses, money and goods. According to the court, 'their objective was to demolish the hacienda leaving only the town and that they must have been in alliance with the peons who aided them'. In the incident, the manager and the clerk were killed, and a granary keeper was badly injured. Subsequently, the guerrillas did the same thing at the El Zapote ranch in Obrajuelo, before disbanding in the mountains of Querétaro and Guanajuato.[50]

In late November, Guevara was 'arrested at home in the company of one of the individuals who had attacked the El Tlacote hacienda'. Others would be captured later on: 'the forces of the state were able to capture most of the bandits in the gang, recovering some of the stolen items from them and almost all the weapons and horses, which they had already ridden, were handed over to the judge'. However, the situation continued to worry the authorities, given 'the socialist gangs forming among indigenous persons and yet, these criminals were out on bail, having had the proclamations that these individuals call their dispatches returned to them, but which prove their guilt of communism'.[51]

In January 1883, the judge sentenced Guevara to death, as well as José Jiménez and Agustín Ramírez, who were 'imprisoned for robbery with violence and murder' and who were still to be tried 'for the crime of rebellion'. On this occasion, the witnesses said that he assumed command as 'conqueror of the towns that had been awarded to the Spanish or the traitors to the fatherland; that El Tlacote is not a hacienda but a village and its owner is therefore more of a thief than those who are prisoners'. On this occasion, Jiménez said that this 'is required by the law of socialism'. According to a local newspaper: 'He was the leader of the whole plan according to our exclusive reports.'[52] For the Querétaro papers:

> The executions of the Tlacote prisoners, whose summary and sentencing will be terrible, but necessarily just, for public vengeance must be satisfied; therefore, may the law in all its majesty proceed and the head rather than the heart decide what are the fitting consequences for public morality, of the death of these prisoners that society could not, nor can forgive. May God forgive them.[53]

Finally, the prisoners were hanged in the Alameda, in the city of Querétaro at 7 am on 16 June 1884.[54]

The end of the 'Pueblos Unidos' Rebellion put an end to the *Confederación Mexicana Socialista*, which in turn meant the decline of *La Social*. There is moreover no evidence that any of Rhodakanaty's followers kept up any activism in the Sierra Gorda region. According to a letter from Valadés to Max Nettlau, Zalacosta was arrested in Querétaro in 1880 and the authorities confiscated his correspondence with Rhodakanaty, placing it 'in the legal files of that state',[55] though after a review of the file, no evidence of this was found.

Although Rhodakanaty considered the federal system to be the most appropriate for society to best carry out its duties and the sovereign and independent 'commune' or 'free municipality' to be the fourth federal power, the 'Pueblos Unidos' Rebellion of the Sierra Gorda went beyond the postulates of the first socialism by setting in motion communalist Jacobinism and armed struggle, which also threatened a possible outbreak of 'indigenous savagery' if the legitimate demands of indigenous peoples were not met.[56]

In contrast, the *Cartilla Socialista-Republicana* (1883) would confirm Rhodakanaty's aversion to the revolutionary violence then demanded by anarchism:

> because, if it is true that these secret societies have socialist princi-ples as a general foundation, it is also true that, having the absurd pretention of violently changing the current social order via brute force, they have already abandoned rational socialist doctrine, which teaches that it is only possible to discretionally prepare the evolution that must necessarily transform human society, thereby imitating the harmonic and everlasting order of nature, which in every process is by slow and measured development, without jumps nor solution of continuity.[57]

Tired and sick, distanced from practical politics and attempting to deal with a precarious economic situation, Rhodakanaty, the Greek physician, may have dedicated his remaining life to this philosophical reflection.[58]

Conclusion

With the Second Workers' Congress and the 'Pueblos Unidos' Rebellion in the States of Querétaro and Guanajuato, both of which began in 1879, *La Social* was able to intervene in social movements and contrib-ute to the formulation of their demands. To the socialist demands for social regeneration and democratic social republic, agrarian rebellions added the autonomy of towns, vindication of the indigenous popula-tion, the recovery of lands confiscated by haciendas, and municipalism as an optimal form of community government. The conflict that it led to undoubtedly exceeded the doctrinaire guidelines of the first social-ism as it incorporated other elements of the socialist tradition, besides laying the foundations of agrarianism that would be developed during the Mexican Revolution. In terms of the history of land redistribution, along with the rebellion of Julio López in the valley of Chalco (1868), the 'Pueblos Unidos' Rebellion is its most important precursor, antici-pating the 1915 model of community autonomy in Zapatista Morelos. And as regards the vindication of indigenous peoples' rights, the 1879 rebellion forms part of a historical continuum of resistance and strug-gle that extends to the 1994 Lacandon uprising and right up to the present day.

Notes

1. Katz, 'Introducción: las revueltas rurales en México'; Tutino, *From Insurrection to Revolution in Mexico,* pp. 39–40; Illades, *Rhodakanaty y la formación del pensamiento socialista en México,* pp. 77–78.
2. Rhodakanaty and de Mata Rivera, *Pensamiento socialista del siglo xix,* p. 53; Rhodakanaty, *Obras,* p. 21.
3. Rhodakanaty y de Mata Rivera, *Pensamiento socialista del siglo xix,* pp. 61, 63; Rhodakanaty, *Obras,* pp. 50–51. In the socialist tradition, the demand for land distribution dates back to Gracchus Babeuf, who organized peasant resistance against taxation, and from 1791 fought for a 'land reform law' to redistribute land according to the model of the Gracchi brothers in ancient Rome. See Priestland, *The Red Flag.*
4. Valadés, *El socialismo libertario mexicano, siglo xix,* p. 116; Chávez Orozco, *Datos para la prehistoria del socialismo en México,* pp. 60–61.
5. 'Los socialistas' [The Socialists], *El Socialista,* 9 June 1879; Thomson and LaFrance, *Patriotism, Politics, and Popular Liberalism in Nineteenth Century Mexico*; 'Los liberales y el progreso' [Liberals and Progress], *La Voz de México,* 14 June 1879; José María Vigil, 'Boletín de *El Monitor*' [The *El Monitor* Bulletin], *El Monitor Republicano,* 19 June 1879; 'El plan socialista de Querétaro' [The Querétaro Socialist Plan], *La Libertad,* 20 June 1879; 'El plan socialista' [The Socialist Plan], *La Sombra de Arteaga,* 26 June 1879.
6. Considérant, *México. Cuatro cartas al mariscal Bazaine,* p. 37; 'Ley del Pueblo', p. 370. I cite the latter. By 1861, the Agrarian Law of Aguascalientes prepared the application of a tax on the owners of rural properties to finance the social policy of the municipalities. It also considered the purchase of land by municipalities for distribution among the poor. Reyes Heroles, *El liberalismo mexicano,* III [Mexican Liberalism], pp. 616–17.
7. Félix Riquelme, 'Indígenas y hacendados' [Indigenous People and Landowners], *La Internacional,* 11 August 1878; Félix Riquelme, 'La cuestión de "Bocas"' [The Question of the Estancia de Bocas Hacienda], *La Internacional,* 25 August 1878; 'Quejas que han elevado los representantes indígenas de los pueblos de la república al Congreso de la Unión' [Complaints that Indigenous Representatives of the Peoples of the Republic Have Raised to Congress], *El Socialista,* 9 February 1878; 'Síntomas de la revolución social: medios de precaverla' [Symptoms of Social Revolution: Ways of Guarding against it], *Periódico Oficial del Gobierno del Estado de Coahuila de Zaragoza,* 13 August 1878, my emphasis.
8. Rhodakanaty had published a biographical sketch of the principal leaders of the Commune. See 'Apuntes biográficos de los más célebres comunistas franceses' [Biographical Notes of the Most Famous French Communists], *El Socialista,* 11 November 1877; Rhodakanaty and de Mata Rivera, *Pensamiento socialista del siglo xix,* pp. 37–41.
9. 'La cuestión indígena' [The Indigenous Question], *El Hijo del Trabajo,* 1 June 1879.
10. Urbina Villagómez, 'Reconstrucción de una memoria negada', p. 154.

11. *Defensa del derecho territorial*, pp. 5–6.
12. Ibid., pp. 6, 109.
13. Reina, *Las rebeliones campesinas en México 1819–1906*, p. 271; AHEQ, Fondo Poder Ejecutivo, Sección Guerra, exp. 30. I cite the latter. According to *El Combate*, the rebels numbered 1,300. Rosales Suasti, 'Los socialistas libertarios', p. 4.
14. 'Tamazunchale', *El Hijo del Trabajo*, 9 November 1879. The lawyer Francisco Violante, an official responsible for the demarcation of land in the area, was accused of 'being the head of the revolutionary movement'. AGN, Seguridad Pública, sección segunda 879(13), caja 101, exps. 18, 64.
15. Cited in Reina, *Las rebeliones campesinas en México 1819–1906*, p. 277.
16. Thomson and LaFrance, *Patriotism, Politics, and Popular Liberalism in Nineteenth Century Mexico*; *El Hijo del Trabajo*, 11 and 15 May 1879; Valadés, *El socialismo libertario mexicano, siglo xix*, p. 124.
17. 'Plan de la Barranca' [The La Barranca Plan], *El Monitor Republicano*, 5 June 1879. According to Valadés, this was written by Zalacosta. Valadés, *El socialismo libertario mexicano, siglo xix*, p. 128.
18. 'El plan socialista de Querétaro'. *La Libertad*, 20 June 1879.
19. *La Voz de México*, 24 June 1879.
20. '*Plan Socialista*' [Socialist Plan], p. 71.
21. Semo, *México: del antiguo régimen a la modernidad*, p. 608.
22. AGN, Gobernación, Seguridad Pública: sección segunda 879(13), caja 101, exp. 75 and 881(8), caja 130, inventario de expedientes.
23. Félix Rodríguez, 'Proclama. "Hace más de 300 años que la mayoría de los pueblos de nuestro México ha tenido [y] lamentado la más infame usurpación"' [Proclamation. 'For more than 300 years most of the peoples of our Mexico have suffered [and] lamented the most notorious usurpation'] (15 September 1879). 'Causa instruida contra Felipe Lara y socios por el delito de rebelión' [Proceedings Instituted against Felipe Lara and Associates for the Crime of Rebellion], AHCCJEQ, Juzgado de Distrito de Querétaro (1879), fólder 63, caja 6, ff. 5–6.
24. AGN, Gobernación, Seguridad Pública: sección segunda 879(13), caja 101, exp. 75 y 881(8), caja 130, inventario de expedientes; *El Socialista*, 9 February 1879.
25. Tiburcio Montiel, 'Hoy', *El Socialista*, 11 July 1880.
26. AHEQ, Fondo Poder Ejecutivo, Sección Guerra (1879), exp. 39; AGN, Seguridad Pública, sección segunda 879(13), caja 101, exps. 183, 75, 61.
27. Its full title is *El revelador fidedigno o sean algunas razones de apoyo de la religión cristiana. Legitimidad del gobierno constitucional y Leyes de Reforma por un atempanense* [*The bona fide revelation, that is to say some reasons for supporting the Christian religion. Legitimacy of constitutional government and Reform Laws by a native of Atempan*] (Mexico, printed by Vicente García Torres, 1862).
28. CPD-UIA, legajo 005, caja 005, docs. 002614, 002644, 002274; 'El general Negrete' [General Negrete], *El Hijo del Trabajo*, 24 May 1880; 'Noticias sueltas' [Loose News], *El Hijo del Trabajo*, 10 October 1880; AHEQ, Fondo

Poder Ejecutivo, Sección Guerra (1879), exp. 58; 'Los comunistas' [The Communists], *La Sombra de Arteaga*, 2 November 1879; 'Causa instruida contra Felipe Lara y socios por el delito de rebelión', AHCCJEQ, Juzgado de Distrito de Querétaro (1879), fólder 63, caja 6, ff. 4, 3, 199. See also Illades, *Rhodakanaty y la formación del pensamiento socialista en México*, p. 120; Rosales Suasti, 'Los socialistas libertarios', p. 4; Rosales Suasti, *La rebelión campesina socialista queretana 1879–1884 y el congreso anarquista de Londres de 1881*, p. 9.

29. 'Causa instruida contra Felipe Lara y socios por el delito de rebelión', AHCCJEQ, Juzgado de Distrito de Querétaro (1879), fólder 63, caja 6, ff. s.n., 26, 32/2, 49/2, 53.
30. Ibid., fólder 63, caja 6, f. 66.
31. Ibid., fólder 63, caja 6, ff. 107, 113/5, 176, 199/2.
32. *La Revolución Social*, 18 December 1879.
33 Valadés, *El socialismo libertario mexicano, siglo xix*, p. 137; 'Congreso Obrero' [Workers' Congress], *El Socialista*, 18 December 1879; Hart, *Anarchism and the Mexican Working Class, 1860–1931*, p. 92.
34. 'Causa instruida contra Antonio Guevara y socios por el delito de rebelión' [Proceedings Instituted against Antonio Guevara and Associates for the Crime of Rebellion] (1881–90), AHCCJEQ, Ramo Penal, fólder 78, caja 7.
35. Ibid., fólder 12, caja 155.
36. Ibid., fólder 78, caja 7.
37. Ibid.
38. Ibid.
39. 'Carta de Antonio Guevara y otros a Alberto Santa Fe y otros' [Letter from Antonio Guevara and Others to Alberto Santa Fe and Others] (Santiago de Querétaro, 18 November 1880), in ibid., fólder 78, caja 7.
40. Lida, 'México y el internacionalismo clandestino del ochocientos', pp. 880–81; 'Rapport du Délégué de la Confédération méxicaine sur la Situation dans l'Amérique centrale et du Sud' [Report of the Delegate of the Mexican Confederation on the Situation in Central and South America], IISG, Collection Nettlau, Congress 1881, Rond AIT. I cite the latter. I should like to thank Professor Lida for having provided me with the transcript of this document.
41. Cited in Lida and Illades, 'El anarquismo europeo y sus primeras influencias en México después de la Comuna de París: 1871–1881'; Rosales Suasti, 'La rebelión campesina socialista queretana 1879–1884 y el congreso anarquista de Londres de 1881', p. 7.
42. AGN, Gobernación, Seguridad Pública: sección segunda 881(8), caja 130, exp. 178; *El Hijo del Trabajo*, 27 March 1881; 'Ejecución de justicia' [The Execution of Justice], *La Sombra de Arteaga*, 23 June 1884. The last two are those cited.
43. 'Causa instruida contra Antonio Guevara y socios por el delito de rebelión', fólder 78, caja 7.
44. Ibid.
45. Ibid.

46. Ibid.
47. 'Quejas que han elevado los representantes indígenas de los pueblos de la república al Congreso de la Unión'; 'La Social', *El Hijo del Trabajo*, 17 February 1878.
48. 'Causa instruida contra Antonio Guevara y socios por el delito de rebelión', fólder 78, caja 7.
49. Ibid.
50. Ibid.; Rosales Suasti, 'Los socialistas libertarios', p. 5. I cite the former.
51. 'Causa instruida contra Antonio Guevara y socios por el delito de rebelión', fólder 78, caja 7; Rosales Suasti, 'Los socialistas libertarios', p. 5. I cite the former.
52. Causa instruida contra Antonio Guevara y socios por el delito de rebelión', fólder 78, caja 7; 'Los sentenciados a muerte', *La Verdad*, 3 December 1882.
53. 'Castigo necesario' [Necessary Punishment], *La Sombra de Arteaga*, 14 June 1884.
54. 'Ejecución de justicia' [Execution of Justice], *La Sombra de Arteaga*, 23 June 1884; Rosales Suasti, 'Los socialistas libertarios', p. 5.
55. Nettlau, *Actividad anarquista en México*, p. 32.
56. Rhodakanaty, *Obras*, p. 263; Rhodakanaty and de Mata Rivera, *Pensamiento socialista del siglo xix*, pp. 94.
57. Rhodakanaty and de Mata Rivera, *Pensamiento socialista del siglo xix*, pp. 92–93.
58. 'Carta de Plotino Rhodakanaty a Porfirio Díaz' [Letter from Plotino Rhodakanaty to Porfirio Díaz] (Mexico City, 26 April 1886), CPD-UIA, leg. 011, caja 009, docto. 04145.

Chapter 4

Revolution and Xenophobia

During the Revolution, cracks surfaced in Mexican society. Ethnic and social factors often went hand in hand during the armed conflict, particularly when there was interaction between the popular armies and foreign colonies living in Mexico in the early twentieth century. Of these, the Spanish colony was the most numerous. They had accumulated their wealth in Mexico, occupied economic niches that the poor were very sensitive about, and had significant influence on the diplomacy of their country. However, the conflict with the revolutionary armies will be incomprehensible if we do not take into account the ideological burden that has always weighed down on this historical link. In order to understand this better, this chapter will begin by reviewing general aspects of the migration and colonization policies promoted under the liberal regime and will then go on to outline some of the economic and social characteristics of the colony resident in Mexico towards the end of the Porfiriato, focusing on the problems arising between it and the revolutionary forces, as well as noting some of the disputes arising from shortages and hunger in 1915. Finally, we will review the material losses suffered by the Spanish colony in Mexico City during the revolutionary crisis.[1]

The Centenary Celebrations

In 1910, the presidential election and commemoration of the Centenary of Independence occupied everyone's attention. The diplomatic corps accredited in Mexico joined in the celebrations. The Japanese embassy organized an art exhibition, good taste typifying the selection of its pieces, Kaiser Wilhelm II donated a statue of Alexander von Humboldt and the French government returned the Keys to Mexico City, which had symbolically been in its power since the Second Empire.

At the beginning of the year, the Spanish Central Centennial Commission was established, chaired by José Sánchez Ramos. As the widower of one of Juárez's daughters, a confidant of General Díaz and, at the time, President of the Casino Español, he was clearly the ideal person to head the organization of the celebrations to be held by his fellow countrymen. Throughout September, the Commission put on numerous balls, as well as an art exhibition. Several months earlier, Sánchez Ramos had organized a scheme to bring an equestrian statue of General Prim from Spain.

Flattered by the efforts of the Spanish community, by Alfonso XIII's decision to return Morelos' military uniform to Mexico (it had been stored in the Madrid Artillery Museum) and by their bestowing upon him the *Collar de Carlos III*, Porfirio Díaz responded gratefully to the Spanish government: he named a street in honour of Isabella the Catholic and had the foundation stone of a monument to her memory laid in Chapultepec Park. Some suggested raising a monument to Hernán Cortés, though that idea was eventually discarded. Díaz moreover provided a military escort for the Valencian journalists Joaquín Juliá and José Segarra so that they could follow Cortés' route to the great city of Tenochtitlán. Their arrival in Mexico City in early May 1910 caused tremendous excitement among the population and filled the front pages of the national press.

In the meantime, the Spanish government appointed Camilo García de Polavieja – hero of the colonial war in Cuba and brutal suppressor of the Cavite Mutiny in the Philippine Revolution[2] – as Ambassador Extraordinary for the centennial celebration. Upon his arrival at the port of Veracruz, the Mexican navy sent ships to meet him and, some hours later, at dawn on 7 September, the Marquis de Polavieja arrived in the capital, where the press reported that:

> Never has a bigger crowd been seen than the one yesterday at Buenavista Station … upon his arrival, General Polavieja received the most thunderous applause that has ever greeted any ambassador. It has been one of the few occasions when the Mexican public has spontaneously and enthusiastically cheered a foreigner as if he were one of the Republic's favourite sons.[3]

When the Marquis de Polavieja presented Morelos' uniform, an error of protocol made it impossible for him to decorate General Díaz at the same ceremony. It was on 19 September at the National Palace, on behalf of the King of Spain, that the Spanish ambassador presented the *Collar de Carlos III* to the aged dictator. The Ambassador Extraordinary pronounced a heartfelt speech in which he said that he would return to his country 'more enthusiastic about Mexico than ever, more convinced than ever of its vast and brilliant future, its indestructible autonomy and also more convinced of the immense labour that, like a providential artificer, you, as a statesman, have performed for the benefit of this noble people, who repay you with their love and veneration'.[4]

The Spanish Minority

Justo Sierra thought that 'colonization, strong arms, and capital [were indispensable] for exploiting our great wealth', echoing an assumption that had been in circulation since Mexico's early years as a nation. As for its origin, he preferred to 'attract European blood, which is the only one which we should seek to cross with that of our indigenous groups'.[5] From the first half of the nineteenth century onwards, colonization policies sought to increase the country's population and distribute it more evenly throughout the territory, based on the idea that this would trigger economic development. Based on this expectation, colonization projects were designed to populate the northern and coastal areas. However, by the middle of the century, the north and the country's coastlines remained virtually uninhabited, and total national population figures were not very promising. Estimates varied between the 7,853,395 inhabitants registered in the *Anales del Ministerio de Fomento* in 1854 and 8,287,413 recorded by Manuel Orozco y Berra three years later.[6] At that time, according to figures of the Ministry of Foreign Affairs, 9,234 were foreigners, although, as pointed out by Jesús Hermosa, 'it cannot be said that these represented the full tally of foreign residents in the republic because, despite provisions obliging them to take out or renew their papers, many do not fulfil this obligation'.[7]

The opportunity created by Ignacio Comonfort's government, following the alienation of the property of religious and civil corporations, the law on the alienation of vacant property issued by the Juárez administration, and the freedom of worship achieved in the Reform War, provided the state with new instruments for the colonization of the country. Incentives were increased to attract foreign immigration, such as the right to import, free of tax, tools, commercial inputs, personal belongings and household items, as well as allowing immigrants, alone or in partnership, to buy vacant land, even on a large scale. The government of Manuel González strengthened this policy by granting almost unlimited rights to colonizing companies, giving them uncultivated land to compensate them for the costs of developing the land they had previously acquired.[8]

At the beginning of the twentieth century, there were a little under 70,000 foreigners legally resident in Mexico. Clearly the colonization policies as regards immigration had not achieved the desired result. Nor were government expectations met as regards the preferred profile of immigration (white and from developed countries); those who came to Mexico were mainly Spanish, Chinese and Guatemalans. Moreover, the Spanish and Chinese immigrants abandoned the economic areas where they had been expected to go (mainly rural areas and productive activities), both moving into retail, with the Chinese in particular competing with Mexicans for work. However, what was achieved was the privatization of broad swathes of the country, the Chinese spreading throughout the cities of the Pacific and the north, and the Spanish in virtually every state of the republic. Both groups, because of their economic activities and geographical location, were to be particularly vulnerable once the armed struggle began.

By 1910, the numerically largest foreign minority was the Spanish, representing just over 25 per cent of all foreigners living legally in Mexico. If we are guided by the official data registered in population censuses, the number of legally resident Spaniards approached 30,000, with four males to every female, an insignificant number for a country with a population of some fifteen million.[9] Some authors who have attempted to quantify illegal immigration estimate that during the revolutionary period, the number of Spanish residents was between 40,000 and 50,000. However, these findings must be taken with caution as not one of them is supported by systematically developed statistical work.[10]

The favourite economic niches of Spanish immigrants were retailing, agriculture and services, though in certain places, such as Puebla and Mexico City, Spanish residents went into industry, mainly textiles.[11] Like Americans, but unlike other foreign minorities, they spread all over the country. Other foreign minorities mainly settled in Mexico City, or large provincial cities and capitals. The Spanish created spaces for socializing and consolidating their colony in urban centres.[12] Their shops, factories and farms, as we shall see below, were the most frequent locations for conflict between Mexican revolutionaries and Spanish immigrants.

From 1911 onwards, friction and tensions arose on innumerable occasions between Mexican revolutionary forces and foreign minorities. The Americans, Chinese and Spanish were the ones who suffered the greatest injuries as a result of the armed struggle, and sometimes paid with their property or even their lives for being in the wrong place. For example:

Andrés Fernández Alonso was travelling from Puebla to Tetela on July 4, 1914, on a passenger train which was blown up by Zapatistas revolutionaries. After the explosion, Mr. Fernández Alonso with a number of other people were taken to San Baltasar by these forces and was shot on the way there.[13]

A leading cause of the violence directed at Spanish immigrants was the connection some had with the Porfirio Díaz regime. The Spanish colony's close ties were obvious to contemporary observers.[14] However, some clarification and the explanation of certain nuances is necessary. First, Spanish residents had struck up a relationship with Díaz, either personally or through the representatives of their clubs and associations, most conspicuously through both the Casino Español and the Spanish Chamber of Commerce in Mexico. The links also operated at a local level. Retailers, speculators, industrialists, landowners and priests were prominent figures in provincial cities and therefore usually maintained a close relationship with the authorities and leading local figures. In the Yucatán peninsula, for example, there was a group, which prominently included several Spanish residents, known as the 'casta divina'. They controlled the production of henequen, the region's primary export, and ran the local government as they pleased. In places like Valle Nacional, as the American journalist John Kenneth Turner wrote, the most profitable crop was tobacco, which was controlled by landowners of Spanish origin. On his trip through this part of Oaxaca, what struck him was that the forced labourers were Mexican mestizos. The methods of coercion employed were even more severe than those he had seen in the Yucatán peninsula. Valle Nacional seemed him to be 'undoubtedly the worst slave hole in Mexico. Probably it is the worst in the world'.[15]

While the political ties that some segments of the Spanish colony had with the Porfirio Díaz regime helped to develop the conflict, at least three specific factors generated violence against the Spanish minority during the armed struggle: (1) the type of economic activities in which the Spanish were involved; (2) the cultural weight complicating the relationship between Mexicans and the Spanish; and (3) the militant anti-Madero position of some members of the Spanish colony. Being shopkeepers in times of scarcity and often prospering as a result,[16] or being landowners or overseers in times of agrarian insurrection were perilous activities for a foreign minority in revolutionary times. In Cuautla, there was a grocery store and cantina called 'Puerto Arturo'. It was owned by two brothers, Arturo and Rafael de la Borbolla Díaz, young Asturians who arrived in Mexico towards the end of the Porfiriato. The store was seriously damaged when Zapatista forces entered the city on 1 May 1914.[17] Another illustration of this can be seen in the incident suffered by Pedro Fernández, Mexico City resident and owner of the 'La Perla', a grocer's in Coyoacán:

> On February 28, 1915 Pedro Fernández was with Francisco Cárcoba, Alejandro Herrera and Florentino Rodríguez in Juan Garza's bakery on Avenida Hidalgo, when he received word that the above-mentioned shop was being plundered by Zapatista soldiers and they went to the place together to see the truth with their own eyes, because the soldiers and the people were taking everything in it, strewing goods all over the floor, as well as wines and spirits that were on a storage shelf in the store's warehouse, and though he begged them not to harm his property, as it was all he had, they took no notice of him, but instead threatened him with death if he got in the way.[18]

The fact that many Spanish immigrants were either owners or overseers of haciendas also made them targets for violence. They were the victims of ferocious violence in Morelos and Puebla. An example is the Zapatistas' attack against the Atencingo ranch in April 1911,[19] where the manager and six employees were killed, and two others were injured. Most of the victims were from Asturias, young, either single or married to Mexicans and, like José Yarazabal, were providing for 'his mother and three brothers in Spain'. In the poorest and most backward parts of the country, such as the Costa Grande region in Guerrero, where armed movements flourished in the 1920s, a revolutionary plan explicitly demanded the expulsion of Spaniards and the nationalization of their property because some of them monopolized trade, haciendas and transport in and around Acapulco. Sometime previously, the *Partido Obrero de Acapulco* (Acapulco Workers' Party) had taken steps against the Spaniards' monopoly.[20]

Another factor was that there were still reverberations from the old colonial relationship between Mexicans and Spaniards and, in the midst of a social crisis, deep-seated resentment and racist sentiment of every kind surfaced.[21] Thus, for example, in 1911, a group of Spanish immigrants complained that one of the frontline units of the *Ejército Libertador del Sur* (Emiliano Zapata's Liberation Army of the South) broke into a hacienda belonging to Spaniards, shouting 'Long live the Virgin of Guadalupe! Long live Madero! Death to Spaniards!', committed all sorts of outrages, venting their cruelty on the children '*for the simple fact of being Spanish*, forcing them to shout "Death to Spain" under threat of death'.[22] At the other end of the scale, the Spanish plenipotentiary in Mexico, in a damning verdict, attributed the revolutionary violence to the resurgence of 'atavistic instincts' among the 'indigenous classes':

Proving that four centuries have not changed their physiological and moral condition: they rob, pillage, destroy, kill and rape, far preferring this life, with its far greater risk of being shot than of disease, to peaceful effort and salary, which demonstrates that it is not only an agricultural but a cultural problem.[23]

The anti-Madero position, held by both prominent members of the Spanish colony of Mexico City and a section of large and small landowners in the states, led to numerous Spanish residents becoming the victims of violence.[24] Accordingly, in 1913 and 1914 in various parts of the country, revolutionary armies issued decrees for their expulsion. The places that they were forced to leave included Torreón, Chihuahua, Veracruz and San Luis Potosí.[25] In August 1914, in Salvatierra, Guanajuato, the garrison commander decreed that:

> Spanish residents in this district being *personas non grata*, I hereby inform them that within *three days* of this date, they must leave this district; those who contravene this decree will be judged by court martial. And so that individuals to which this order refers may not claim *ignorance*, a copy of this decree will be sent to them and they shall acknowledge receipt.[26]

After the fall of Victoriano Huerta, using the anti-Maderismo of some members of the Spanish minority as an argument, in the 'Draft Law on the Confiscation of Property of Supporters of the Usurping Government' written in 1914 by the constitutionalists Eduardo Fuentes and Rodrigo Gomez, it was decided to confiscate the property of Spaniards who had opposed the revolution. This was the situation for Iñigo Noriega, who had, by 1915, already lost many of his properties.[27] The División del Norte treated the Spanish colony with extreme brutality. The capture of Torreón by the forces of Francisco Villa in late 1913 is still remembered for the violence perpetrated against the Spanish. A letter sent from Mexico to a Santander newspaper provides information on the violence that occurred:

> The revolutionaries or bandits released a manifesto saying that every *gachupín* [Spanish immigrant] found in the enemy camp would be shot; and as the enemy camp was Torreón, they had no choice but to leave with the defeated troops ...

> Of the Spaniards remaining in Torreón, eight have already been shot, and a few days before the rebels took the town, they had shot nine others at a ranch, forcing them to dig their own grave. A 12-year-old child was among them.[28]

Events in the Torreón region left their mark on the claims brought by Spanish citizens in the following decades. The murders of Spaniards were often mentioned and their relatives demanded compensation. An example is the case of the relatives of Sergio Fernández, who was shot by Villa's forces at the *Palo Blanco* hacienda near Torreón, and also that of Juan José Rosillo, a resident of Torreón, who on 7 October 1913 was 'taken by car to the [Torreón] cemetery with other Spaniards by the revolutionary troops and, by order of General Villa ... shot that same day'.[29]

Sometimes the violence against Spanish citizens – especially against moneylenders and shopkeepers – was unrestrained and irrational. A case in point is that of Juan Pría, the owner of a pawnshop. In 1914, a group of people 'dressed in the uniforms of Zapatista soldiers' came in looking for weapons; finding none, one of the men shouted 'bastard *gachupín*' while shooting the moneylender. A similar fate awaited Ramón Cots Prat, who sold basic goods and, after being robbed on the highway, 'was shot in the head, but the bullet only went through the back of his skull ... [and] as a result of such a serious injury, he became completely deaf, subject to nervous attacks, and was completely unable to work'.[30]

Although in general there were no major armed clashes in Mexico City, as the country's political centre and the seat of federal power, it was involved in the conflict and it suffered from the shortages caused by the war. Both situations affected the conduct of the Spanish colony and its relationships with both the revolutionary forces and the city's population. The first major conflict between revolutionary groups and the Spanish colony in Mexico City centred on Íñigo Noriega, who in 1911 was accused of meddling in the country's internal affairs by participating in the presidential campaign of General Bernardo Reyes, and was also accused of stealing land belonging to rural communities in Xochimilco, near the capital. The tension rose to a peak at the end of 1911, when a demonstration in the streets of the capital demanded that Noriega and other Spaniards and foreigners be expelled from Mexico. Noriega had to leave the country three years later and, by the beginning of 1915, the government had confiscated his most important agricultural and industrial properties.[31]

Another cause of the confrontation between the Spanish in Mexico City and the revolutionary forces was the participation of a still-undetermined number of Spanish citizens in the coup that overthrew President Francisco I. Madero in February 1913. Based on this supposition, an anonymous letter was sent to the Spanish plenipotentiary minister in Mexico, accusing members of the Spanish colony of having helped to 'breach the peace during the terrible Ten Tragic Days'. The Spanish colony in Mexico City itself acknowledged that some Spaniards took part in the bloody events when the following statement in *El Correo Español* was published in December 1913: 'It is said that 500 Spaniards took part in the Ciudadela Pronouncement. The number was in fact 14 and to suggest that our colony is in sympathy with these events is the height of folly.'[32] By the following year, in a letter sent from the Mexican representation in Madrid, there was talk of two participants:

> Subject to court martial [several of those involved in the coup d'état] were sentenced to death, but there being two Spanish subjects, those named Barrada and Fragoso, among the detainees, holding executive power, the First Chief of the Constitutionalist Army [Venustiano Carranza] resolved to pardon them, as a sign of extreme and exceptional consideration to the Spanish flag.[33]

Retail establishments, in particular grocery stores, were the main locus of conflict between the Spanish minority and the Mexico City poor. While the civil war divided the country, a ruthless battle between the urban crowd and their independent proprietors was waged in their shops. This battle, like so many, often had tragic episodes. The time of greatest conflict was in 1914 and 1915, the years when the armies of Zapata and Villa occupied the city and when supplying the city was severely hampered by the war, causing shortages of food and other necessities.

Known as the 'year of hunger', 1915 was particularly serious in Mexico City. Towards the middle of the year, the capital was undergoing a dreadful crisis. It was common to see women walking from one closed city market to another. With the population in despair, Spanish shopkeepers took advantage of the situation. They raised the price of sugar from fifty cents a kilo to eight pesos, while a kilo of butter, which had cost one peso in January 1915, went up to eight pesos in Spanish shops in August. Faced by famine and rising prices, the capital city's poor began to attack the grocery shops. At that time, there were regularly confirmed events like those of 25 June 1915 at *Los Tres Leones*, property of José González, and *La India*, owned by Nicolás Alonso. José González, 'being ... in his shop, saw a crowd of about two thousand people assemble at the door'; a moment later, they forced their way into the store and 'seized all the goods'.[34] The same thing happened at *La India*, where:

> A large group of men and women, led by General Barona in a car, demanded maize at the door of the establishment while, at the same time, he incited them to ransack it, which they did, taking all existing

stocks to a value of no less than $14,700. Mr. Alonso promptly and repeatedly asked the authorities and nearby barracks for help, but no help was provided, leading to the successful looting of the property.[35]

The economic difficulties, the shortages and the inflation did not only affect Spanish shops; the *Casa del Obrero* supported work stoppages at workshops and small factories. Reports from the workers' press in 1915 record a number of strikes in Mexico City. Given the difficult situation, the local government was forced to implement a number of extraordinary measures to overcome the shortage of basic goods, control prices and avoid chaos.[36]

The attacks on Spanish residents and their properties reverberated in the Spanish press. Newspapers of the time often published complaints, such as the following one in *El Correo de Asturias* on 12 November 1913 by 'a Spaniard recently returned from Mexico':

> In Mexico, the life and property of all foreigners is in danger, especially the Spanish, currently bereft of solid support.
>
> Other nations, almost all, have a warship in Mexican waters to safeguard their subjects and those under their flags, should the occasion arise …
>
> Spain has a bounden duty to protect her own, by sending a ship from her navy to Mexico. Not one more victim more can be added to those we mourn.[37]

The possibility of sending of a warship to Mexico was discussed at the Spanish State Department on several occasions. However, the Spanish ambassador in Mexico, Bernardo Jacinto de Cólogan y Cólogan, rejected the plan, not wishing to aggravate 'the enormous touchiness of this people'.[38] Yet, when it became clear that the government of Victoriano Huerta would not last long, the *Carlos V* docked off the Mexican coast to assist in the withdrawal of Spanish residents who wished to go. Against the wishes of the ship's commander, the Spanish plenipotentiary rejected his offer to supply the area around the legation with artillery.[39]

Despite the problems faced by Spanish immigrants during the revolution, there was no massive return to their country of origin as the news stories seemed to indicate. Between 1911 and 1914, the most difficult period for them, the number of those leaving the country was similar to those entering.[40] The correspondence exchanged in 1915 between Luis Simón y Simón, a Spanish citizen, and Juan Sánchez Azcona, a representative of the Venustiano Carranza government in Spain, is illustrative. The former, the owner of the textile factory in Querétaro[41] and 'commissioner and representative of foreign firms', asked the diplomat:

> Today, once I have finished my affairs here [in Spain] I wish to re-
> turn to Mexico. Would Don Juan allow me to ask his opinion of my
> returning to Mexico? Does the minister think that I would find no
> difficulty disembarking? ... I have never meddled in political matters
> nor of any other kind in your beautiful and hospitable country.[42]

The Mexican diplomat blamed the forces of Francisco Villa for the disorder and violence towards foreigners and said 'given that you have had no involvement in the political movements that have developed in my country, I think you may return to it without fear'. Comforted, the Spanish citizen replied that on 'the 19th inst. I will take passage to Veracruz on the steamship Alfonso XII, and I am most entirely at your service for anything you might wish to order'.[43] In conclusion, Sánchez Azcona added:

> I wish you a very happy voyage and beg you that you will do as much
> as you may, once back in my homeland, to erase the misunderstand-
> ings that have tended to arise between our party and the honourable
> Spanish colony, for as you very well know, the esteem in which Mexi-
> cans hold the industrious Spanish is sincere and when there has been
> friction, this has been due to the lack of tact of a very small number.[44]

With the defeat of the popular armies and once the armed phase of the revolution had come to a close, the numbers of violent incidents against Spaniards fell, largely because President Carranza wanted to minimize diplomatic tension with foreign governments and clear the way for their recognition of his. Nevertheless, in the post-revolution-ary period, Hispanophobia had new legal instruments at its disposal for channelling this latent conflict. Article 33 of the 1917 Constitution allowed for the expulsion of unwanted foreigners and was repeatedly used to get rid of people who were in the way. Rightly or wrongly, a significant number of Spaniards had to leave the country. The social conflict, fuelled daily by inequality and an unresolved ethnic conflict, had found a new means of expression.[45]

The Demands

As mentioned above, Spain had had a good relationship with the Díaz regime and regarded the triumph of the movement led by Madero with scepticism. Although Spain maintained diplomatic representation in Mexico after the fall of Díaz, when the presidency of Madero weakened, the Spanish legation contributed to his downfall. It is well known that it was Cólogan y Cólogan who, on behalf of the foreign diplomats, suggested to Madero that he should resign.[46] Moreover, the Spanish government supported the de facto government of Victoriano Huerta from start to finish. Once deposed, Huerta lived in exile in Barcelona for several months. On this topic, one constitutionalist diplomat commented:

> Spain is overrun with old *Huertistas* and, to the best of my ability, I try to find out what their purposes are, but very few still seem to hope for a reaction, they are very divided among themselves and the majority complain that Huerta has abandoned them. He lives in glory in Barcelona, drinking constantly.[47]

Notwithstanding the scant sympathy for the Mexican Revolution on the other side of the Atlantic, when the victory of Constitutionalist forces was in fact imminent, both the Spanish government and the Constitutionalists themselves sought a rapprochement that culminated in November 1915 in Spanish recognition of the Carranza's de facto government. A key consideration for Alfonso XIII's recognition of the Carranza government was his commitment to discuss and, if necessary, compensate for the losses suffered by Spanish residents as a result of the civil war. There was a background to this commitment. The interim President, Francisco León de la Barra, had formed the *Comisión Consultiva de Indemnizaciones* (Advisory Committee on Compensation Claims) in 1911, charged with discovering and processing claims from Mexicans and foreigners for losses caused by the armed struggle. When Carranza took up arms against Huerta in 1913, he recognized the right of all foreigners to claim for losses suffered as the result of war.[48] In 1925, this decree provided the basis for the governments of both countries to form the *Comisión Mixta Hispano Mexicana de Reclamaciones* (Joint Hispano-Mexican Claims Commission) to take action and resolve claims. Five years later, they decided to extend its work.

From the outset, Carranza was far more careful than either Villa or Zapata when dealing with foreign minorities. Regarding Spanish immigrants, he issued express orders that priests should not be disturbed during the American occupation of Veracruz. In 1916, he returned many of the haciendas that Villa had seized in northern Mexico and in subsequent years made finance widely available to coffee exporters.[49] A note published in *El Correo de Asturias* comments on the growing détente and the change in Spanish public opinion regarding the Mexican Revolution:

If we consider that Mexico is an extension of Spanish soil (which are two like-minded races entwined by feelings and family ties), that Spanish is better spoken in Mexico than in many parts of Spain, and a thousand times better than anywhere else on the American continent, we should feel exceedingly proud and pleased that we know one other, to broaden our relationships in business and in thought. It is therefore essential that men of goodwill, of enterprising and progressive spirit, concern themselves with studying Mexico's economic vigour, as it will undoubtedly be the country with the most promising future for capital investment and the establishment of large industries.[50]

The gradual pacification of the country, the First World War, diplomatic skill[51] and a healthy dose of pragmatism from both governments helped smooth things over and settle differences. However, from 1925 onwards, Spanish immigrants demanded restitution from the Mexican government for damages unpaid since the war. More than a thousand lawsuits were filed before the Joint Hispano-Mexican Claims Commission. Although obviously many were concentrated in the areas of greatest conflict, what is striking is the range of places they came from. In even the remotest areas of the country, Spanish demands were to be heard because, as indicated above, they were distributed across the length and breadth of the country. Looting of grocery stores, damage to and confiscation of property, seizure of arms and horses, and murders were the main types of complaint presented to the commission.[52] A large proportion of the claims were made by people from Asturias, Galicia and Cantabria. From the owner of a large hacienda or factory in Puebla to the owner of a grocer's in Mexico City or Cuautla, their demand was for the payment of damages resulting from the armed struggle. In relation to this, a Spanish citizen said in 1928:

> So, thank goodness, finally, let's save those unlucky compatriots who lost their capital and until today had no hope; let's also put aside any who ask without justification; let's all proceed to do our part as far as is humanly possible so that Mexico can pay these unfortunate men; yet always proceed with our heart half in Mexico, half in Spain.[53]

Of the over one thousand demands presented by Spanish citizens, nearly five hundred fulfilled the legal requirements and were settled by the Joint Hispano-Mexican Claims Commission. A review of these records provides a sketch of the conflict between the Spanish colony and the revolutionary armies.

As shown in Table 4.1, with the exception of the State of Colima and the territory of Baja California, Spanish immigrants in every state declared that they had suffered losses. The highest number of settled

Table 4.1 Spanish Immigrants' Claims for Damages*

State	Number	%
Aguascalientes	1	0.22
Campeche	1	0.22
Chiapas	14	3.08
Chihuahua	30	6.60
Coahuila	32	7.03
Distrito Federal	57	12.53
Durango	23^	5.05
Guanajuato	29	6.37
Guerrero	9	1.98
Hidalgo	4	0.88
Jalisco	4	0.88
Michoacán	12*	2.64
Morelos	17	3.78
Nayarit	3	0.66
Nuevo León	7	1.54
Oaxaca	8	1.76
Puebla	51	11.21
Querétaro	1	0.22
Quintana Roo	2	0.44
San Luis Potosí	26	5.71
Sinaloa	1	0.22
Sonora	2	0.44
State of Mexico	28	6.15
Tabasco	19	4.18
Tamaulipas	14	3.08
Tlaxcala	8	1.76
Veracruz	46	10.11
Yucatán	3	0.66
Zacatecas	3	0.66
Total	455	

* The statistics are of the total of settled claims, and not the claims presented at the Joint Hispano-Mexican Claims Commission.
^ Includes a claim for losses at an event between Durango and Coahuila.
+ Includes a claim for losses at an event between Michoacán and Jalisco.

Source: AHEEM, CMHMR, cajas 1–93.

claims were from Spanish citizens resident in Mexico City, Puebla, Veracruz, Coahuila and Chihuahua.

In 1910, the largest numbers of Spaniards lived in Mexico City, Veracruz, Yucatán, Puebla and Coahuila. If we ignore the case of Yucatán, where the revolution started late, we can confirm a direct relationship between the number of claims for damages and the size of the colony in each state. Finally, if we focus on the areas where the various revolutionary armies operated, it is clear that the largest number of conflicts with the Spanish minority occurred in areas under the Zapatistas (Morelos, Mexico State, Puebla, Guerrero, Tlaxcala and Mexico City) and the followers of Pancho Villa (mainly Chihuahua, Coahuila and Durango), since more than half of the settled claims correspond to these states.

The settled claims of Spanish citizens in Mexico City indicate that most had come to Mexico during the Porfiriato and that they were usually very young and single. The most numerically significant group came from Asturias, followed by Galicia and Santander. The next most numerous groups came from Catalonia, the Basque Country, León and Extremadura, and the fewest from Castile and Navarre. Hardly any of them had been shopkeepers in their homeland, but went into retail once they arrived in Mexico. According to the general population census of 1910, Spaniards living in the capital accounted for more than 40 per cent of all Spanish immigrants. The data available for the Porfiriato indicate that the vast majority were shopkeepers, around 85 per cent, far fewer being employees and artisans.[54]

As is shown in Table 4.2, in relative terms, the largest number of losses suffered by the Spanish population in Mexico City took place at grocery stores and, in general, presented similar characteristics to those described above, though owners sometimes tried to repel the crowd with gunfire.[55] Theft of livestock, robbery and occupation of private houses were usually associated with the revolutionary armies' need to avail themselves of horses, food, feed and quarters when they occupied the capital. Attacks on pawnshops and lending businesses, partly carried out by the abovementioned forces, were carried out in the search for weapons, and additionally channelled the population's resentment towards moneylenders mentioned earlier.

Based on the testimonies of those affected, the Zapatista forces, and to a lesser extent the Constitutionalists, were those responsible for the crimes committed against Spanish citizens. While this is certainly broadly true, it must be taken with some caution because, to city inhabitants, any peasant with a big hat and a gun was a Zapatista soldier. Based on this 'certainty', Miguel Solares, owner of the 'Colón' shop and

Table **4.2** Categories of Spanish Immigrants' Losses in Mexico City*

Type of Loss	Number	%
Robbery at pawnshops	7	11.48
Burglary of private houses	8	13.11
Murder	6^	9.84
Accidental damages	1	1.64
Theft of livestock	9	14.75
Sacking of grocery stores	23	37.70
Other	7	11.48
TOTAL	61+	

* The statistics correspond with the total of settled claims (57) for losses suffered in Mexico City.
^ Includes the case of a prisoner who was shot for meddling in the internal affairs of the nation.
+ The difference of 4 is because in these cases, the deaths of the owners were caused by the action.

Source: AHEEM, CMHMR, cajas 1–93.

cantina, stated that on 11 March 1915, a group of Zapatista soldiers broke down the door of his cantina 'and, once inside, began to eat a six-kilo aged cheese and other goods', while on 15 August, Clementina Núñez, owner of a shop and cantina on the streets of Imprenta and Palomas, presented an accusation for the theft of bottles of cognac, sherry and eggnog to the tune of 400 pesos.[56]

Conclusion

The economic niches occupied by Spanish citizens in the countryside and the city, their numerical importance in relation to the size of other foreign colonies and their distribution throughout the country placed them in situations where friction with the revolutionary groups and the urban crowd was constant and intense, and conflict was impossible to avoid. Another element complicating the relationship between the Spanish and Mexicans was the open wound of three centuries of colonial domination, which, while this was not decisive for the behaviour of the revolutionary armies and the urban poor, did provide an additional ingredient to the violence committed against the Spanish minority, and sometimes it was merely a rationalization for brutality or mere plunder.

At the political level, the reason for the conflict was the link between some segments of the Spanish colony, particularly the wealthier immigrants, and the Porfirio Díaz regime, their subsequent rejection of the Madero government and their participation in its destabilization. This intervention had effects at the diplomatic level, as it contributed to Spanish support for the Huerta regime. With the triumph of the Constitutionalists, there was a détente between Mexicans and Spaniards: Spanish public opinion viewed the Mexican Revolution more indulgently, diplomatic reconciliation was achieved and, in the 1920s, claims for damages resulting from the Revolution were negotiated. However, the social dispute, being ethnic and even one of identity, endured using legal procedures in many cases, though it went in new directions.

Notes

1. On this subject and its effect on diplomatic relations between Spain and Mexico, see: González Loscertales, 'Los españoles en la vida social y económica de Méjico, 1910–1930'; Fuentes Mares, *Historia de dos orgullos*; Illades, *México y España durante la Revolución mexicana*; Illades, *Presencia española en la Revolución mexicana, 1910–1915*; Illades, 'Reclamaciones españolas: índice de expedientes fallados'; Mac Gregor, *México y España del porfiriato a la revolución*; Illades, 'Los propietarios españoles y la Revolución mexicana'; Flores Torres, *Revolución mexicana y diplomacia española*; Zuloaga Rada, 'La diplomacia española en la época de Carranza'; Cerutti and Flores, *Españoles en el norte de México*; Meyer Cosío, *El cactus y el olivo*; Mac Gregor, *Revolución y diplomacia*; Moreno Lázaro, 'La otra España'; Delgado Larios, *La Revolución mexicana vista desde España 1910–1931*; Pérez Acevedo and Rivera Reynaldos, 'Propietarias españolas en México ante los efectos de la Revolución'.
2. On Polavieja's iniquitous career, see Anderson, *Under Three Flags*.
3. Embajada de España en México, *Relaciones diplomáticas hispano-mexicanas (1826–1917)*, caja 277, leg. 2, carp. 1.
4. Ibid.
5. Sierra, *México su evolución social*, III, pp. 416, 434.
6. Olveda, 'Proyectos de colonización en la primera mitad del siglo xix', p. 43; Davies, 'Tendencias demográficas y urbanas durante el siglo xix en México', p. 483. I cite the first.
7. Hermosa, *Manual de geografía y estadística de la República Mexicana*, p. 29.
8. For a review of the relevant legislation, see Illades, 'Poblamiento y colonización', pp. 134 ff.
9. Pla Brugat, 'Españoles en México (1895–1980)', pp. 111, 117; Lida, 'Los españoles en México. Del porfiriato a la post-revolución', pp. 322–23.
10. González Loscertales, 'Bases para el análisis socioeconómico de la colonia española de México en 1910', p. 267; Richmond, 'Confrontation and Reconciliation', p. 216.

11. Pérez Herrero, 'Algunas hipótesis de trabajo sobre la inmigración española a México: los comerciantes', pp. 120–23; González Loscertales, *El empresario español en Puebla, 1880–1916*; Moreno Lázaro, 'La otra España', p. 119. For the most complete study on Puebla, see Gamboa Ojeda, *Los empresarios de ayer*. In Morelos, owners often brought in Spanish immigrants to run their farms: Womack, Jr., *Zapata and the Mexican Revolution*, p. 42.
12. Kenny, *Inmigrantes y refugiados españoles en México (siglo xx)*, pp. 42, 81.
13. 'España en nombre de Andrés Fernández Alonso, hoy sus herederos, contra los Estados Unidos Mexicanos' [Spain on behalf of Andrés Fernández Alonso, today his heirs, against the United Mexican States] (1932), AHEEM, CMHMR, caja 40.
14. On this topic, Ramón del Valle-Inclan's description in his *Tirano Banderas* speaks for itself.
15. Paoli Bolio y Montalvo Ortega, *El socialismo olvidado de Yucatán*, p. 41; Turner, *Barbarous Mexico*. I cite the latter.
16. Richmond, 'Confrontation and Reconciliation', pp. 222–23. Of all the economic activities engaged in by the Spanish minority in Mexico City, retailing concentrated the highest percentage of its assets. By 1914, this amounted to 27,192.70 pesos oro. Moreno Lázaro, 'La otra España', p. 119.
17. 'España en nombre de Antonio y Rafael de la Borbolla contra los Estados Unidos Mexicanos', AHEEM, CMHMR, caja 4.
18. Ibid., caja 43.
19. González Loscertales, 'La colonia española de México durante la revolución maderista, 1911–1913', pp. 349–50.
20. 'España en nombre de Nicanor Amiela, hoy sus herederos, contra los Estados Unidos Mexicanos' [Spain on behalf of Nicanor Amiela, today his heirs, against the United Mexican States] (1932), AHEEM, CMHMR, caja 4. On this subject, see Chapter 5 below.
21. Since the revolution, 'while xenophobia was accentuated, there emerged a new and almost mythical indigenous ethnophilia'. Lida, 'La inmigración española en México: un modelo cualitativo', p. 209.
22. AHEEM, caja 280, leg. 1, No. 2, emphasis in original.
23. AHEEM, caja 291, leg. 4, No. 5.
24. It is worth mentioning that this kind of behaviour was not widespread among the Spanish minority. We should recall the participation of some immigrants in the formation, during the years of the revolution, of the *Casa del Obrero Mundial* and that others joined the Zapatista army. This was the case of two Catalans, Salvador Alcalde, who held the rank of major, and Jaime Marimón, who held the rank lieutenant, who were ordered to withdraw from the *Orfeó Català* as its statutes banned participation in politics. Martí Soler, *L'Orfeó Català de Mèxic, 1906–1986*, pp. 33–34.
25. AHEEM, caja 298, leg. 1, No. 30; Richmond, 'Confrontation and Reconciliation', p. 219; Illades, *Presencia española en la Revolución mexicana, 1910–1915*, p. 88.
26. Illades, *México y España durante la Revolución mexicana*, p. 38. My emphasis.
27. AHEEM, caja 298, leg. 2, No. 22. For the case of Nuevo León, see Flores Torres, 'Revolución mexicana y diplomacia española'. Josefina Mac Gregor

argues that Hispanophobic action was marginal: 'without discounting the fact that some individuals did express animosity or contempt for the Spanish, and putting the outbursts of the *Villistas* to one side, no revolutionary group, not even the Zapatistas, included the destruction or departure of the Spaniards from Mexico in their ideological outline, nor did they implement systematic actions against them'. Mac Gregor, 'Villa y los españoles: una relación difícil en tiempos difíciles', p. 402. For the opposing view, see Yankelevich, 'Denuncias e investigaciones contra españoles'.

28. *El Cantábrico* (6 December 1913).
29. 'España en nombre de Sergio Fernández, hoy sus herederos, contra los Estados Unidos Mexicanos' [Spain on behalf of Andrés Fernández Alonso, today his heirs, against the United Mexican States] (1931); 'España en nombre de Juan José Rosillo contra los Estados Unidos Mexicanos' [Spain on behalf of Juan José Rosillo against the United Mexican States] (1932), AHEEM, CMHMR, caja 41.
30. 'España en nombre de Juan Pría Álvarez contra los Estados Unidos Mexicanos' [Spain on behalf of Juan Pría Álvarez against the United Mexican States] (undated); 'España en nombre de Ramón Cots Prat contra los Estados Unidos Mexicanos' [Spain on behalf of Ramón Cots Prat against the United Mexican States] (1932), AHEEM, CMHMR, cajas 135 and 12, respectively.
31. AHEEM, caja 281, leg. 1 and caja 311, leg. 13.
32. AHEEM, caja 292, leg. 1.
33. Illades, *México y España durante la Revolución mexicana*, p. 40.
34. Richmond, 'Confrontation and Reconciliation', p. 222; 'España en nombre de José González Alonso contra los Estados Unidos Mexicanos' [Spain on behalf of José González Alonso against the United Mexican States] (1932), AHEEM, CMHMR, caja 44.
35. 'España en nombre de Nicolás Alonso contra los Estados Unidos Mexicanos' [Spain on behalf of Nicolás Alonso against the United Mexican States] (1931), AHEEM, CMHMR, caja 31.
36. Illades, *Las otras ideas*, p. 261; Rodríguez Kuri, 'Desabasto, hambre y respuesta política [Shortages, Hunger and Political Response, 1915], 1915', pp. 150 ff.
37. Illades, *México y España durante la Revolución mexicana*, pp. 174–75.
38. AHEEM, caja 281, leg. 1, No. 29.
39. Illades, *Presencia española en la Revolución mexicana, 1910–1915*, pp. 129–30.
40. Bojórquez, *La inmigración española en México* [Spanish Immigration into Mexico], p. 15. The figure given is 209 Spaniards killed during the Mexican Revolution. González Navarro, *Población y sociedad en México (1900–1970)*, II, p. 79.
41. Carta de Luis Simón y Simón a Juan Sánchez Azcona [Letter from Luis Simón y Simón to Juan Sánchez Azcona] (Ezcaray, 9 March 1915), AREM, serie Embamex España, s.c.
42. Simón y Simón a Sánchez Azcona [Simón y Simón to Sánchez Azcona] (Ezcaray, 29 May 1915), AREM, serie Embamex España, s.c.

43. Sánchez Azcona a Simón y Simón [Sánchez Azcona to Simón y Simón] (Madrid, 11 March 1915); Sánchez Azcona a Simón y Simón [Sánchez Azcona to Simón y Simón] (Madrid, 1 June 1915); Simón y Simón a Sánchez Azcona [Simón y Simón to Sánchez Azcona] (Ezcaray, 4 June 1915), AREM, serie Embamex España, s.c.
44. Sánchez Azcona a Simón y Simón [Sánchez Azcona to Simón y Simón] (Madrid, 7 June 1915), AREM, serie Embamex España, s.c.
45. Yankelevich, 'Denuncias e investigaciones contra españoles', p. 436.
46. Katz, *La guerra secreta en México*, I, p. 125.
47. AHEEM, caja 298, leg. 1, No. 36.
48. Illades, *Presencia española en la Revolución mexicana, 1910–1915*, p. 140; Luquín Romo, *La política internacional de la Revolución constitucionalista*, p. 24.
49. Cumberland, *Mexican Revolution*; Richmond, 'Confrontation and Reconciliation', pp. 210 ff.
50. M. Suárez Díaz, 'Nuevas relaciones comerciales entre España y Méjico' [New Commercial Relations between Spain and Mexico], newspaper article in *El Correo de Asturias*, Oviedo, May 1917.
51. On the Spanish diplomatic negotiations of with revolutionary groups, see Mac Gregor, 'España entre dos caminos: Villa y Carranza'; Mac Gregor, 'Agentes confidenciales en México'.
52. The ninety-seven claims brought by women refer to losses mainly in trade, industry, and rural and urban properties. Pérez Acevedo and Rivera Reynaldos, 'Propietarias españolas en México ante los efectos de la Revolución', p. 780.
53. Posada Noriega, *México ante el derecho internacional*, p. 55. For an evaluation of these, see Illades, 'Reclamaciones españolas: índice de expedientes fallados'.
54. Pla Brugat, 'Españoles en México (1895–1980). Un recuento', p. 119; Jarquín, 'La población española en la Ciudad de México según el Padrón General de 1882', pp. 197–98.
55. Fuentes Mares, *Historia de dos orgullos*, p. 55.
56. 'España en nombre de Miguel Solares contra los Estados Unidos Mexicanos' [Spain on behalf of Miguel Solares against the United Mexican States] (1931), AHEEM, CMHMR, caja 72; Piccato, City of Suspects, p. 226. I cite the former.

Chapter 5

The Circle of Violence

In the second half of the twentieth century, many movements claimed basic civil liberties (expression, association and assembly) and simultaneously fundamental social rights (decent wages, employment, land ownership, education and health). The state's usual response to this was repression, forcing some movements towards armed violence, one of the forms of 'coordinated destruction' directed towards objects and people.[1] These movements nonetheless re-emerged and presented democratic demands only to find, once again, that state authoritarianism had shut the doors.

I hypothesize that, at crucial locations in Mexico's geography, the cycle of violence began in periods when social movements (both rural and urban) were on the rise. The authoritarian state – with its local base in *cacicazgos*, areas controlled by local political bosses, and its national base in the 'sectors' – then responded either by co-opting the leaders of these movements or using repression (broad-based or specific, as the case may be). The movement would then develop a permanent organization and, under certain circumstances, adopt forms of self-defence that sometimes morphed into a guerrilla movement. In these circumstances, the strength and intensity of the government's response increased, with the objective of eradicating the armed groups and dismantling the social movement. The ones that were able to overcome this onslaught regrouped and began a new cycle that also culminated in violence.

This is precisely what happened in the State of Guerrero, which is the focus of this chapter: from 1920 to 1923, with the socialist municipality of Acapulco, the murder of Juan Ranulfo Escudero and the armed uprising of the Vidales brothers; in 1960, with the movement in Chilpancingo, repression and the guerrilla, (the Partido de los Pobres – Party of the Poor); and in 1995, with the relaunch of the popular movement, the Aguas Blancas massacre and the reappearance of armed movements, the Ejército Popular Revolucionario (EPR – Popular Revolutionary Army). The novelty that accompanied the alternation between the presidencies of the Partido Revolucionario Institucional (PRI – Institutional Revolutionary Party) and the Partido Acción Nacional (PAN – National Action Party) is not the interruption of this cycle, but the diversification of the actors who participate in, perpetrate and suffer violence, interrelating their various types (social, political or criminal actors), which makes it difficult to distinguish between them for heuristic purposes. In the same way, the communities' armed response took the form of *autodefensas* (citizen self-defence groups), that is, a social entity not only focused on achieving power (such as the guerrillas), but on assuming certain state functions (security and justice), given the state's obvious inability to fulfil them.

The Socialist City Council

Since its founding in 1849, the state of Guerrero has been poor, isolated, socially unequal, run by *caciques* and politically unstable. It is also multicultural, rich in natural resources and biodiversity; it is hard to control and has a strong tradition of popular organization. Of the 3,338,778 inhabitants registered in the national population census of 2010, the indigenous population accounts for almost 15 per cent and lives in the La Montaña and Costa Chica regions. Guerrero contributes only 1.5 per cent to national GDP and it shares with Oaxaca and Chiapas the lowest social indicators in the country. Besides being one of the world's leading opium producers, its strategic position for shipping drugs means it is in a much worse situation than either Oaxaca or Chiapas, particularly as regards criminal violence.

Historically, popular movements in Guerrero have arisen on the coasts and in the mountains. It was in the Costa Grande that the Partido Obrero de Acapulco (POA) was founded by Juan R. Escudero and a small group of artisans and port stevedores in 1919. Escudero, their candidate, won the municipal elections the following year with a limited platform that called for: (1) fair payment for a day's work; (2) the protection of individual rights; (3) the exclusion of corrupt elements from the government; (4) participation in elections; (5) an eight-hour workday; (6) land for peasants; (7) the extension of education; (8) arranging for the construction of the Mexico–Acapulco highway; and (9) a campaign to fight disease. The POA supported Álvaro Obregón for the position of president and Rodolfo Neri for that of governor. Intervention in state and national politics enabled it to promote its programme along the full length of the coast and to call for the formation of agricultural committees.[2]

Following his re-election in the municipal elections of December 1921, attacks on Escudero by local powerbrokers (several of them merchants of Spanish descent) became increasingly virulent. In March the following year, military forces stormed the city council offices. Wounded during the violence, Escudero was left partially paralysed and with a speech impediment, although he did not give up his political activities. Following a partial recovery, he was elected federal deputy for the first district of Acapulco and the POA also won the local elections. Meanwhile, in neighbouring Tecpan de Galeana, a primary school teacher called Valente de la Cruz presided over the agrarian committee, having founded the Partido Obrero de Tecpan on Escudero's instructions. The de la Huerta revolt, led by Rómulo Figueroa in Guerrero, brought the socialist municipality of Acapulco to an end when rebel soldiers trapped Escudero and his brothers at the San Diego fort: they shot them at point-blank range nearby. The same fate befell the other municipalities won by the POA along the Costa Grande: their mayors were deposed one by one.[3]

Amadeo S. Vidales, Mayor of Tecpan, Baldomero Vidales and Feliciano Radilla Ruiz, a member of the Liga de Campesinos de Atoyac (Atoyac Peasants' League), accompanied the Escudero brothers during the de la Huerta revolt and then led a guerrilla movement in Atoyac, the Movimiento Libertario de Regeneración Económica Mexicana (Libertarian Movement for Mexican Economic Regeneration), whose social programme, announced on 6 May 1926, was known as the Plan del Veladero. This plan attributed Mexico's problems to the Spanish, emphasized the Zapatista agrarian struggle and the socialist direction taken by the 1910 revolutionary movement. It called for the disavowal of the chapter in the Plan de Iguala that guaranteed the life and property of the citizens of 'the [Spanish] monarchy', and for the strengthening of the principles of the 1917 Constitution; accordingly, it considered it essential to expel the Spaniards, nationalize their assets and turn these over to the municipalities for management. It furthermore called for the promotion of education, the introduction of technology into agriculture and the modernization of its methods. It demanded the restoration of the lands usurped from villages and the redistribution of large landholdings. It warned that during revolutionary activities, the lives of foreigners should be respected, damages should be paid to them and their property should be protected, unless they were Spanish, as well as contemplating the indemnification of the disabled, orphans and widows for losses caused by the armed struggle. It also called for the expropriation of mining companies and the control of industries, along with urging the administration of shipping and taking control of the means of transport, in addition to nationalizing livestock and banks.

In 1929, after a bloody military campaign against the Vidalistas, which included murder, arson and extortion of the wealthy of the coast, Amadeo Vidales and his principal followers surrendered; as a consequence, President Emilio Portes Gil granted them amnesty and gave them land in Cacalutla near Atoyac. At the beginning of the following year, the pardoned guerrillas established the Juan R. Escudero agricultural colony.[4]

The organization and mobilization of the peasants on the Costa Grande made it possible for land reform under the Cardenas government to be generous in this region and even in other parts of the state (Costa Chica and the north) where the majority of the large landholdings were located. Between 1935 and 1940, 534,897 hectares in Guerrero were handed over to 51,207 peasants. Although the lands were not very fertile and the *ejido* endowment policy did not include resources and technology to make them more productive, they were adequate for growing coconut palms, coffee plants and traditional crops. In any event, this was not sufficient to eradicate agrarian violence, which, by 1938, had resulted in a total of twenty-six murdered peasant leaders.[5]

Land distribution reduced pressures and tempered the conflict in the Guerrero countryside for two generations. In addition, the development of tourism during the Miguel Alemán presidency caused a major exodus from rural areas into Acapulco, with an estimated average of 3,000 immigrants arriving in the port annually between 1950 and 1960. However, pressure on land[6] and a resulting increase in popular movements towards the late 1950s again threatened the *caciques'* control over the population. The *cacicazgos* and the subordination of the population to them lies at the origin of Guerrero as a state and a federal entity.[7]

From Popular Movement to Guerrilla Movement

In October 1960, the dispute between the state governor, General Raúl Caballero Aburto, and the Mayor of Acapulco, Jorge Joseph Piedra, both members of the PRI, catalysed the silent discontent with Guerrero's authoritarian state executive. The governor ordered that the vaults of Acapulco's municipal treasury be closed as the local Congress accused the mayor of embezzling public funds. For his part, the mayor accused the governor of numerous crimes, dispossession and Guerrero's massive treasury debt, claimed that Aburto had sent him death threats, and had bribed and intimidated representatives in an attempt to force his resignation. In support of the governor, a contingent commanded by Alfredo López Cisneros (known as '"King" Lopitos') of approximately 3,000 residents who lived illegally in the Colonia La Laja, a ring of poverty surrounding Acapulco, attacked the mayor's private residence. In support of the deposed mayor, a demonstration involving some 2,000 people took to the streets in the port. Meanwhile, the Comité Cívico Guerrerense (CCG – Guerrero Civic Committee), which had been formed only the previous year, demanded that the powers of the state be suspended and the governor prosecuted under the Law of Political Accountability.[8]

A few days later, a student strike broke out in Chilpancingo, demanding university autonomy, the removal of the dean, reforms to the Organic Law of the Colegio del Estado de Guerrero and increased subsidies for higher education. Various sectors in the state capital supported the students and a large demonstration in the city culminated in the formation of the Coalición de Organizaciones Populares. In November, 10,000 people took the protest to the main streets of Chilpancingo, the state capital. On the morning of 25 November, security forces evicted students and citizens from the Alameda Francisco Granados Maldonado, resulting in several injuries and arrests. Church bells rang and factory sirens wailed to rally the population, who were arming themselves with whatever they could find en route. The city was practically under siege by state and federal security forces. Meanwhile, taxpayers declared they would suspend tax payments, the local bureaucracy went on strike, small traders stopped work and, in the streets near the university, Mexican flags and banners bearing the Virgin of Guadalupe flew.

The mayor of Tierra Colorada led a demonstration on December 27 demanding the impeachment of the governor. In Taxco, students took the town hall with, apparently, the consent of the municipal authorities. And the town halls of Chilpancingo, Tixtla, Chilapa, Zumpango del Río, Taxco, Apango, Huitzuco and Tenango del Río repudiated the administration of General Caballero Aburto who, on 30 November, ordered the police to attack the population of Chilpancingo. Half an hour later, thirteen or more were dead and thirty-seven lay seriously wounded, almost all of them civilians, though two soldiers also perished in the eviction. Less than one week into the new year, the federal Senate declared the powers of the state of Guerrero suspended and removed the governor from office. Meanwhile, in various parts of the state, the population took the town halls, expelling the General's forces.[9]

The CCG became part of the Asociación Cívica Guerrerense (ACG) in 1962 and participated in state elections that culminated in the dubious legal victory of the PRI candidate Raymundo Abarca Alarcón. The *cívicos*, as they were known, countered with demonstrations in the major cities of Guerrero, and the government in turn responded with a brutal crackdown that cost the lives of eight people in Iguala. To the ACG, this was proof that the electoral route was blocked, so it made a strategic change of direction, becoming a national organization, the Asociación Cívica Nacional Revolucionaria (ACNR), and outlined a political programme that proposed the formation of a coalition government with urban workers, peasants, students and 'progressive' elements of society. In order to take power, as soon as the organization achieved adequate preparation and sufficient penetration of the popular movement, it would resort to arms. In accordance with its political ideology, the new administration would employ economic planning, redistribute large landholdings, bail out mining and grant the freedom to unionize.

In 1966, the police arrested Genaro Vázquez Rojas, one of the leaders of the 1960 movement. Two years later, an armed commando unit freed him from prison in Iguala and he went underground. By this time, there was a guerrilla nucleus in the Guerrero mountains. Via its Comandos Armados de Liberación (Armed Liberation Commandos), the *Vicente Guerrero*, the *Juan Álvarez* and the *Emiliano Zapata*, the organization obtained resources by kidnapping wealthy local individuals. At the same time, the security agencies responded with the forced disappearance of activists and guerrilla bases.[10]

In Atoyac de Álvarez in May 1967, the motorized police attacked teachers and parents protesting outside the Juan N. Álvarez School because of the injustice, mismanagement of economic resources and arrogance of the school's principal.[11] Giving the motorized police a free hand, the municipal police remained in their stations following the orders of the state prosecutor, who ordered the motorized police to take charge of 'security' in Atoyac, a municipality of just over 30,000 inhabitants at the time. The immediate cost in human lives was eleven civilian deaths, a modest anticipation of the enormous toll that would be left by the military strategy employed to wipe out the guerrilla movement. In the midst of the panic, shooting and corpses, as the documentary novel *Guerra en el Paraíso* narrates, the leader of the teachers, Lucio Cabañas Barrientos, who was by then actively participating in the organization of teachers and *ejidatarios*:

started running, in the middle of the men and women who covered him. When they got round the church, it seemed to Lucio that the streets were empty, that nothing had happened in them, that not a shadow seemed to understand the sweat and blood he was stained with, the heat with which he was running, the fury and the haste with which he saw the stones of those streets as if receiving him, telling him that this was safe ground, free.[12]

Within days, there were 2,000 soldiers occupying Atoyac, the gateway between Costa Grande and the mountains with their important water and forest resources, to prevent further bloodshed because 'peasants have been coming down from the coffee plantations, the ones who have always been considered extremely dangerous'. In August, the assembly of the Asociación de Copreros (copra farmers) in Acapulco, who were attempting to bring about the democratic appointment of their leaders, was broken up by the gunfire of the state judicial police, during which the forces of law and order murdered twenty-seven unarmed peasants.[13]

After the events in Atoyac, Lucio Cabañas abandoned his civilian life as a rural teacher and went underground, assembling a peasant guerrilla movement in the Sierra de Atoyac. In 1970, he formed the Partido de los Pobres (PdlP), whose armed wing was known as the Brigada Campesina de Ajusticiamiento (Peasant Justice Brigade). This did not aim at a proletarian revolution in the Leninist sense, but articulated a set of primary claims for the poor in plain language: the overthrow of the 'wealthy class' by society's 'poor class'; the expropriation of privately held large industrial and agricultural properties; universal access to education at all levels, similarly to health, culture and leisure; effective rights and decent wages for industrial workers and agricultural labourers; treatment without discrimination for all Mexicans, irrespective of race or origin; and to ending American colonialism in Mexican territory.[14]

According to the FBI, the PdlP financed its activities through kidnappings. Its 150 troops acquired army weapons via successful ambushes.[15] After several attacks on the armed forces, the Secretaría de la Defensa Nacional increased its military presence in Guerrero, wiped out whole villages, repeatedly violating their inhabitants' human rights, as well as controlling the flow of information on the conflict, a task that was made considerably easier by the fact that the press and the television stations were obedient to the authoritarian regime. A telegram from General Hermenegildo Cuenca Diaz, Secretary of National Defence, to the military commanders of Guerrero sent in December 1971 gave the following orders:

Order ratified. – [In the] sense [of] increasing activities [to] locate, harass, capture or exterminate gangs [that] operate in this region and must use [to the] maximum measures [of] security and good treatment [towards] civilian population, coordinating activities with all [the] government agencies and related individuals. – Avoid demonstrations of force [that] alarm civilian population.[16]

On 2 December 1974, Cabañas' column was located by the army in El Otatal in the municipality of Tecpan de Galeana. According to the war report, the guerrilla leader and his men died in combat. A U.S. intelligence document assessed the political consequences of this military success:

> Army will of course receive merited accolades for having finally eliminated the only terrorist known by name to the Mexican public. It should be recalled, however, that Cabanas's activity was geographically restricted, to extent that terrorist activity in Mexico represents threat to political stability, (and we believe it minimal) the anonymous violence of urban terrorist groups is cause for greater concern than Cabanas ever was.[17]

The armed outbreak having been averted, the federal government instigated a strategy with various facets to eradicate the guerrillas. Through the Plan de Desarrollo Integral del Estado de Guerrero (Integrated Development Plan for the State of Guerrero), it channelled substantial economic resources into the villages of the Sierra for health, education, electrification, drinking water, roads and economic development, allocating 446 million pesos to the *ejidatarios* of Atoyac in the 1975 budgetary year.[18] It also carried out a dirty war against the cadres of armed groups and their bases, and established a legal amnesty that some guerrillas took advantage of. Finally, it enacted political reform that allowed the opposition into Congress, providing an opportunity for left-wing groups to take part in the electoral process. Guerrero was militarily occupied for the rest of the decade. However, as discussed below, this was not sufficient to eradicate the armed movements in either Guerrero or in other parts of the country because, as we know, the crux of their demands was not focused on democracy, and far less liberal democracy, but social justice, which was the fundamental reason for their recurrence.

Reorganization and Repression

The political reform brought Guerrero's left-wing opposition back into mainstream politics after two decades when the government had been working in the opposite direction. In 1980, the Partido Comunista Mexicano (PCM) won in the local elections in Alcozauca en la Montaña and, from thereon in, consolidated its position within the state. But it was not until the civilian revolt of Cuauhtémoc Cárdenas that the electoral map in Guerrero dramatically changed. Although not reflected by the official result, it has been estimated that on election day (6 July 1988), Cuauhtémoc Cárdenas won Guerrero. Despite the scandalous fraud that occurred in the municipal elections of December the following year, the population turned out massively under the banner of the Partido de la Revolución Democrática (PRD), only to be swindled out of victories that seemed incontrovertible. Dissent led to the taking of town halls all over Guerrero, the establishment of popular town councils in some of them, and in a resistance movement up and down the coast that lasted for three months without the state agreeing to correct the election. Instead, as is usual in the south, the state resorted to expedient repression. Of the approximately 300 members of the PRD killed during the presidency of Carlos Salinas de Gortari, many were inhabitants of Guerrero; between July 1988 and January 1990 alone, fifty-six members of the PRD were killed in Guerrero, which was governed at the time by José Francisco Ruiz Massieu:

> For the presentation of the Government Report on 8th February, 2,500 army troops with 20 light tanks and 40 military police convoys are patrolling Chilpancingo. The document is being read by Ruiz Massieu from behind a thick wall of soldiers because at dawn that day two local PRD deputies were kidnapped and 3,000 angry supporters of the party took to the streets ready to censure the governor.[19]

Civil society in Guerrero took on specific fights, whether in favour of protecting natural resources on community lands or against the frenetic alienation of public land for high-cost housing developments (such as Punta Diamante) or the assignment of public spaces to business interests. The mobilization of the Consejo de los Pueblos Nahuas del Alto Balsas (CNPNAB) to prevent the construction of a hydroelectric plant in San Juan Tetelcingo, and the defence of the Ignacio Manuel Altamirano (Papagayo) ecological reserve and recreation park (a section of which Governor Ruiz Massieu was kind enough to hand over to a businessman who intended to build a shopping centre) are examples of these struggles.[20]

The 1993 election brought the Figueroa clan to power for the third time in a century (Francisco Figueroa, Rubén Figueroa Figueroa and Rubén Figueroa Alcocer). With an extremely high abstention rate (66 per cent) and a total vote of only 200,000, Figueroa Alcocer won the governorship, while the left-wing opposition won 27.4 per cent of the vote according to the scarcely credible official figures. In the absence of consensus, there was coercion. For the second time in twenty years, two historical enemies would face one another: the *caciques* of Huitzuco and the peasant guerrillas, based in Atoyac.

In January 1994, the Organización Campesina de la Sierra del Sur (OCSS – South Mountain Range Peasant Organization) was established in Tepetixtla, a small town in the municipality of Coyuca de Benítez, adjoining Atoyac and rich in forest resources. The organization brought together men and women who mainly worked in agriculture; from the day of its foundation, it was characterized by its use of radical methods (blocking roads, taking town halls) in order to obtain services and resources (schools, construction materials, fertilizers, hospitals, etc.) for the extremely poor population of the region; it also aimed at protecting the forests and natural resources of the region, and demanded that the state return alive all those who had disappeared in the dirty war of the 1970s. One of the first things the OCSS did was to expel the motorized police from Tepetixtla. During the administration of Rubén Figueroa Alcocer (the son of Rubén Figueroa Figueroa, who had been kidnapped by the Partido de los Pobres in 1974 when running as the PRI's candidate for governor), this police force had been responsible for several murders and forced disappearances of the social leaders from the mountain regions.

On the morning of 28 June 1995, approximately 400 members of the Guerrero judicial police intercepted a contingent of about 60 people, some carrying machetes, at the ford of the Las Hamacas river near Aguas Blancas. They were members of the OCSS heading to a rally in Atoyac in an open truck to demand the release of one of their fellow members, as well as the building materials and fertilizer promised by the state government. After an incident, the details of which are unclear, the police shot at point-blank range, killing seventeen and wounding twenty-one, later placing weapons on the corpses to simulate a confrontation. The government secretary and director of the state judicial police supervised the crime scene from a helicopter.

The resonance of the case in the media and the indignation it provoked in civil society brought it to the attention of the Comisión Nacional de Derechos Humanos (CNDH – National Human Rights Commission), which then discovered sufficient evidence to attribute guilt, while the Supreme Court of Justice of the Nation determined that the governor was responsible. Forced by the circumstances, Figueroa Alcocer requested a leave of absence on 12 March 1996. In July 1997, the Third Criminal Court, based in Acapulco, gave final judgment against the policemen involved in the massacre and against certain minor officials linked to the bloodshed: thirty-nine people were tried and sentenced, although they were only in prison until 1999.[21]

After being virtually wiped out in 1974, it took the rural guerrillas a generation to restructure themselves. Two main currents converged in the EPR, one being the remnants of Lucio Cabañas' PdlP, and the other the Unión del Pueblo founded in Oaxaca in 1971 by the former Guatemalan guerrilla José María Ignacio Ortiz Vides. The union of these two would lead to the creation of the PROCUP-PdlP, the Partido Revolucionario Obrero Clandestino Unión del Pueblo (PROCUP – Clandestine Revolutionary Workers' Party Union of the People) with the PdlP, umbrella organizations for the fourteen organizations that formed the EPR in 1994.[22]

The commemoration of the first anniversary of the Aguas Blancas massacre provided the context for the first presentation of the EPR in public. According to the newspaper report, 'about 100 men and women armed with AK-47 and AR-15 rifles, soldiers in olive green, hooded and booted, with the initials EPR in red badges on their sleeves, came down from the mountains'. One of them read the *Aguas Blancas Manifesto*, which was interrupted several times by a chorus of 'Justice! Justice! Justice!', which a young woman then summarized in Nahuatl. Subsequently, an armed escort laid a floral wreath – a reference to the fact that the victims were peasants – then rendered honours to the Mexican flag (which was placed next to that of the EPR) by firing seventeen volleys in memory of the seventeen fallen on 28 June 1995. 'The young soldiers, some with an indigenous accent, were at the ford for 20 minutes'; one of them confided that the EPR had 500 fighters deployed throughout the state.[23]

The guerrillas made five declarations: (1) the overthrow of the anti-popular and anti-democratic government; (2) the restoration of popular sovereignty and human rights; (3) the solution of the demands and immediate needs of the people; (4) the establishment of fair relations with the international community; and (5) the punishment of those responsible for political oppression. They also added that they would no longer stand by 'defenceless while repression and death snatch our lives away with impunity'. For them:

> Repression, persecution, imprisonment, murders, massacres, torture and disappearances continue as the government's policy, a similar situation to the one that in 1967 and 1968 led Commanders Lucio Cabañas Barrientos and Genaro Vázquez Rojas to take up arms against exploitation and oppression; that experience, the unjust cur-

rent situation and the revolutionary spirit that motivated them in-spire the struggle of the Mexican people once again.[24]

The presence of the new (or old) guerrillas was not limited to the epi-centre in Atoyac, but developed small groupings in Oaxaca, Puebla, Veracruz, Chiapas, Hidalgo, San Luis Potosi, Chihuahua, Morelos, Mexico State and Mexico City. However, unlike the PdlP, the EPR was internally less cohesive because of the difficulties involved in unifying so many groups, each with their respective leaders, rules and politi-cal expectations. In January 1998, there was the first major secession with the separation of the faction that would give rise to the Ejército Revolucionario del Pueblo Insurgente (EPRI – Revolutionary Army of the Insurgent People), citing the 'top-down nature' and 'dogmatism' of the way in which the EPR worked, further criticising the 'loss of objectivity', 'spirit of self-criticism', 'relationship with the people' and 'revolutionary spirit' on the part of the party leadership. On this ba-sis, the segment that disagreed, 'virtually the whole of the structure in Guerrero', where '60 per cent of the country's existing columns' were located, 'decided to separate from the rest of the structure because of political differences unresolved for over a year'. The EPRI was prepar-ing a national uprising for the year 2000, given that 'it is possible today to incorporate thousands of Mexicans into the fight and it will soon be possible to include millions, but this cannot be done without establish-ing military strategy and tactics, based on deepening our thinking and our military studies'.[25]

After the schism within the EPR, on 7 June 1998, the army extraju-dicially executed ten Mixtecs and a student of the Universidad Nacio-nal Autónoma de México (UNAM – National Autonomous University of Mexico), as well as wounding others in the community of El Charco in the municipality of Ayutla de los Libres (Costa Chica) based on the assumption that they belonged to the EPRI. The survivors stated that:

> the federal army surrounded the place, then burst in, shooting and throwing in two fragmentation grenades, which caused 11 deaths and 5 wounded, who were arrested along with 22 others, who were taken (contrary to the provisions of the law) to the Base of the Ninth Military Region, in Cumbres de Llano Largo, where they were held and tortured for two days. Among these were 5 minors, who were transferred to the Hostel for Juvenile Delinquents in Chilpancingo on June 9, except for a child who was wounded and remained in the naval hospital for one month.[26]

It is surmised that some of the victims were administered a coup de grace.[27]

Autodefensas and Criminal Violence

The offensive against the neo-Zapatista and EPR guerrillas during the Ernesto Zedillo presidency led to the deployment of the army in different areas of the country, including the mountains of Guerrero. As in the 1970s, military occupation led to abuses against civilians, abuses of human rights, the strengthening of local *caciques* and looting. To tackle the situation, and with the important precursor in 1992 of the Consejo Guerrerense 500 Años de Resistencia (Guerrero Council 500 Years of Resistance), community police forces were established in 1995 among the *Na'Savi* (Mixtec) and *Me'Phaa* (Tlapanecos), two of the poorest and most isolated indigenous groups living in one of the most remote and marginalized states in the country.[28]

This form of security organization and administration of local justice, based on the community's 'customs and traditions' recognized by Convention No. 169 of the International Labour Organization (ILO), quickly spread to other parts of Guerrero in the north and the Costa Chica area, leading to the establishment of the Coordinadora Regional de Autoridades Comunitarias-Policía Comunitaria (CRAC-PC – Regional Coordinator of Community Authorities-Community Police) in 1998, making it possible to 'repel the criminals that filled our homes, our roads and our communities with grief'. These policemen, with unmasked faces and either unarmed or equipped with small-bore weapons registered with the appropriate authorities, were appointed by the communities themselves, the office being honorary and providing a basic level of police training.[29]

Political change came to the state in the constitutional election of 2005, consolidating the upward trend of left-wing opposition that began in 1980 and was advancing in spite of the deficient and biased local elections and the repression of their activism. Within a virtual two-party system, the PRI was losing positions in a state where the blue of the PAN has never been seen. By a margin of just 14,000 votes, the PRI's René Juárez Cisneros beat the PRD candidate in the 1999 election. However, by 2003, the PRD beat the PRI for the first time in the election of federal deputies, setting a benchmark for the 2005 election for governor and the 2006 presidential election. With the highest voter turnout on record (60.3 per cent), the PRD's Carlos Zeferino Torreblanca Galindo received 589,074 votes (48 per cent of the total votes cast).[30]

In any event, social violence did not stop and the fragmentation of the guerrillas continued. In July 2005, the hitherto unknown Comando Popular Revolucionario 'La Patria es Primero' (CPR-LPEP) assassinated José Rubén Robles Catalán, one of the masterminds of the Aguas Blancas massacre, in Acapulco when he was Government Secretary in the Figueroa Alcocer administration. According to the guerrillas' statement, 'at 8:38 a.m. on July 6 this year, José Rubén Robles Catalán was condemned and executed, his escort also being killed. As is known, execution of the remaining sentences is still pending', referring to Figueroa and other members of his political circle. Another guerrilla group held Torreblanca Galindo responsible for having made a pact with Figueroísmo and included its representatives in his cabinet: 'the PRD's Zeferino has made a commitment to the former PRI governor, currently barred from regional power, helping him to keep certain enclaves of regional power allowing him to continue exercising repression and looting natural resources'.[31]

The origins of the CPR-LPEP fell into doubt given the 'execution', in September 2005, of Miguel Ángel Mesino, son of Hilario Mesino, founder of the OCSS and brother of Rocío Mesino, the PRD Mayor of Atoyac. The former political prisoner, linked to the EPR, was shot in the back in broad daylight just 100 metres from the police headquarters. The murder was carried out by three unidentified individuals using the high-calibre weapons (AK-47s) that are a feature of organized crime.[32]

According to the CPR-LPEP, Mesino had become the ally 'of drug gangs, military intelligence and paramilitaries' and committed all kinds of excesses and crimes, even focusing 'his actions on the murder of social activists':

> All the foregoing – in recognition that the criminal practices that this person and his group had been carrying out, in addition to the fact that constant threats against various social activists have placed the democratic movement in the state of Guerrero at risk (disguising these activities behind his masquerade as a social activist) – obliged us to put an end to the subject's criminal career.[33]

The authorities never offered a convincing explanation for the murder. During the commemoration of the second anniversary of Mesino's death, his sister Rocío assured the paramilitary groups operating in Guerrero that they 'will never disable our movement because in between there is the fighting spirit and courage of our comrades'.[34]

In addition to the structural violence suffered in Guerrero, which pitted communities and social organizations against *caciques* (with their links to the state and criminal organizations), overwhelming criminal violence surged during the government of Felipe Calderón, although its origins were in the dirty war against the guerrillas. Regional *caci-*

ques and state structures rife with corruption are currently the best channels available to organized crime. Within the huge trafficking in national, *ejido* and community assets brought about by neoliberal globalization, both mediums have been the spearhead for private capital (whether legal or criminal) to acquire possession of forests. A guerrilla group therefore warned that 'if they ever want to, they can find Bernardino Bautista, in San Luis de la Loma, municipality of Tecpan, before his paramilitaries or those of Rogaciano Alba Álvarez, murder more environmentalists and social activists of the Sierra de Petatlán, of Tecpan and of José Azueta'.[35]

Guerrero's strategic location for drug trafficking and poppy production in the highlands (occupied by the army after the annihilation of the guerrillas of Lucio Cabañas) similarly increased the relative power of *caciques* and corrupt officials. Its long coastline, significant production of opium poppies (which are crucial in the global opiates market) and high-quality marijuana in the mountains (highly sought after in the United States), the crisis in traditional crops, extreme poverty, precarious justice and government corruption paved the way for the expansion of organized crime in Guerrero. In alliance with regional *caciques,* organized crime encroaches upon the economy and politics significantly in a way that leads to both groups becoming stronger. As regards winning elections, this symbiosis is highly functional: one group brings the 'masses' and others bring the resources to mobilize them. It is therefore unsurprising that Rogaciano Alba Álvarez, PRI mayor and President of the Unión Ganadera de Petatlán (Petatlan Cattlemen's Association), linked to both Rubén Figueroa and El Chapo Guzmán, should launch a fierce pursuit of the ecologists Rodolfo Montiel and Teodoro Cabrera – prominent activists of the Organización Ecologista de la Sierra (Environmentalist Organization of the Sierra) – for having protected the forest against excessive logging by the American company Boise Cascade, to which Figueroa Alcocer had granted a disproportionately generous concession in 1995.[36] According to the Consejo Ciudadano de Seguridad Pública (Citizens' Council for Public Security), 'the breakdown takes in the bulk of the local political class. It includes senators, federal deputies, local deputies, leaders of political parties and, of course, Ángel Aguirre and his collaborators', the same suspicion that hangs 'over most politicians who aspire to the governorship'.[37]

During the Torreblanca Galindo administration, coinciding with the war on organized crime launched by President Calderón, violence in the state grew exponentially – from 2007, the rate of homicide in Guerrero soared considerably. In addition, there were notorious political crimes, such the killing of Armando Chavarría Becerra in August

2009, the First Secretary of the government, president of the local Congress and the PRD's best prospect for the governorship. Many voices blamed Torreblanca, who supported another candidate. The situation got even worse in the second administration of Ángel Aguirre Rivero, who had served as interim governor of the state when Figueroa Alcocer was deposed: the break-up of the Beltrán Leyva cartel, after the execution of Arturo Beltrán Leyva in Cuernavaca in 2009, led to the group splintering into smaller subgroups that either retained the territories or fought for them in a perpetual war throughout the state, in which at least twenty-two organized crime gangs operate. Incessant crime in Chilpancingo, Iguala and Acapulco led to the latter, the 'jewel' that dates back to the corruption of the Miguel Alemán era, becoming the most dangerous city in the country. With Iguala, it was among the municipalities with the largest number of disappearances in 2014.[38]

The outbreak of criminal violence hindered the activities of social movements as hostilities towards their leaders increased. If impunity has been the common currency of dealings between the three levels of government and the citizens of Guerrero, with the wanton violence of recent years, the aggrieved population's demands for justice and the effective rule of law that works for all, and not merely to promote the interests of big business, seems as urgent as it is unfeasible in the short to medium term. To offer just one example from the many possible choices, in July 2011, Isabel Ayala Nava, widow of Lucio Cabañas, and her sister Reyna

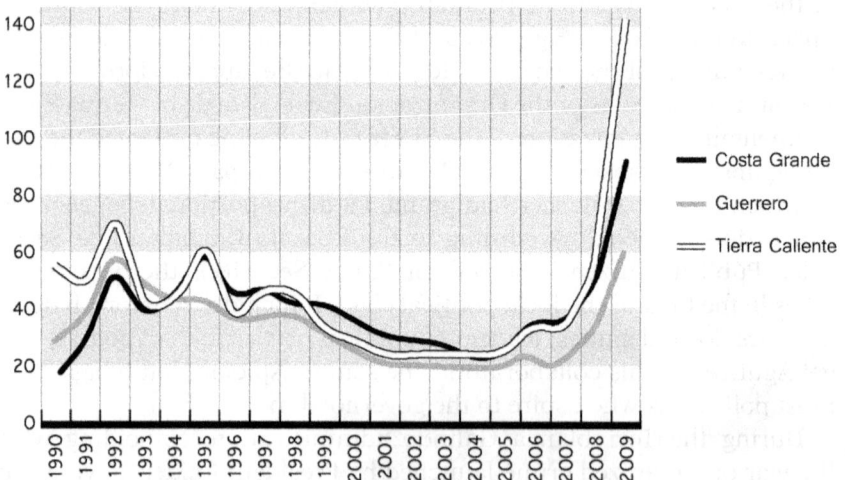

Figure 5.1 Homicide Rate in Guerrero, 1990–2009

Source: Escalante Gonzalbo, 'Homicidios 2008–2009', p. 47/Instituto Nacional de Estadística y Geografía (INEGI)

Ayala were shot outside a church in Xaltianguis. According to the press release, 'gunmen shot the two women from a passing blue car and then one of them got out and seized the victims' mobile phones'. Micaela Cabañas, daughter of Lucio Cabañas, the guerrilla leader, and Isabel, attributed her mother's murder to her participation in an organization for the relatives of those who disappeared during the dirty war.[39]

In May 2013, three agriculturalists of the Unión Popular Emiliano Zapata (UPEZ – Emiliano Zapata Popular Union) were shot near Iguala. According to a witness, the city's mayor, José Luis Abarca, personally executed Arturo Hernández Carmona, who was also a member of the PRD and had been responsible for blocking the road into the city demanding fertilizer. Abarca, who is alleged to have said, 'Stop fucking with me because I have people who will handle the job', is currently imprisoned, accused of being responsible for the murder of six civilians and the forced disappearance of forty-three students. Further, in Mexcaltepec in October 2013, a gunman shot Rocío Mesino, the aforementioned leader of the OCSS, at close range with a high-calibre weapon in the 'nape of the neck' and the 'back'.[40]

For the fourth time since the end of the 1910 Revolution, violence against citizens, towns, communities and social groups – now perpetrated by criminal organizations and in addition to the historical violence of the *caciques* and state organizations – led to a violent response from society via the armed self-defence groups (*autodefensas*) that started to be set up in 2012, when the towns of Olinalá, Huamuxtitlán, Culac and Xochihuehuetlán, on the borders of the state of Puebla, set up community police forces equipped with high-powered weapons. They set up checkpoints, suspended school lessons and established a partial curfew to protect themselves from criminal gangs. The *autodefensas* subsequently spread to San Marcos (Costa Chica), several towns in Tixtla (near Chilpancingo) and Florencio Villarreal (Costa Chica), as well as Cuautepec, Coyuca de Benítez, Tierra Colorada, Xaltianguis and Tecpan de Galeana (Costa Grande). The *autodefensas* occupied eight communities between Chilpancingo and Acapulco.[41] In Ayutla de los Libres, they even took prisoners:

> Members of the citizens' armed *autodefensa* movement of the Costa Chica region agreed – with some citizens protesting – to hand over only some of the 54 persons they have held for over a month for their alleged ties to organized crime.

> Although they did not specify the number of people who will be handed over to state authorities, members of the movement said they are considered highly dangerous prisoners.[42]

It has been noted that there are *autodefensa* groups (seven) or community police (forty-one) in others of the eighty-one municipalities of the state. Along the coast, they range from Tecpan de Galeana to Cuajinicuilapa; they are also in Acapulco, Chilpancingo, Iguala and Taxco, as far as Tlapa de Comonfort, Metlatónoc, Zapotitlán Tablas and other parts of La Montaña.[43]

The 'forced disappearance' in Iguala of forty-three students from the Raúl Isidro Burgos rural teacher training college in Ayotzinapa on 26 September 2014, the murder of six other people plus another twenty-five wounded, presumably at the hands of the municipal police, mark an extreme situation not only in terms of public security but also of human rights, which has led to growing social outrage, focusing the attention of the mass media and international pressure on this increase and a state apparatus that at best does nothing when not the actual accomplice of organized crime. These events show how local power is being shaped in a number of regions where crime and politics are closely intertwined and democratic representation has been taken over by criminal organizations.[44]

However, the situation is not limited to this. Social unrest is at a very high level in Guerrero (the 2013 teachers' demonstrations can be given as an example), there have been guerrilla cores there for fifty years and *autodefensa* groups have proliferated all over the state. The EPRI announced the formation of the Brigada Popular de Ajusticiamiento 26 de Septiembre (26 September Popular Justice Brigade) to confront the Guerreros Unidos drug cartel, which is blamed for the disappearance of the Ayotzinapa students, once again reactivating the cycle of social violence.[45] If we add the natural disasters of 2013 to this and the dismal performance of the state government before, during and after these calamities, it is clear why Ángel Aguirre Rivero joined the ranks of governors of Guerrero who did not complete their term, whether through repression or ineptitude. Whether it is irony or farce, it remains the case that the man who concluded Figueroa Alcocer's constitutional period did not end his own, although it remains to be seen whether his possible collusion with organized crime is investigated seriously by the federal government.

Conclusion

With or without the changeover between PRI and PAN presidencies, Guerrero has suffered from civil violence, with electoral democracy, always precarious in the south, being insufficient to contain it. Extreme social inequality and rampant injustice, being more acute here than in the rest of the country (with the exceptions of Oaxaca and Chiapas), feed it daily, while migration (approximately one million people from Guerrero live in the United States and Canada, and Guerrero is also in first place as regards internal migration in Mexico), resistance and rebellion have been recurrent tendencies. This does not mean that civil society will not turn to democratic methods to promote the objective of social justice; what it means above all is that, seeing its demands unmet or its activists imprisoned and persecuted, it will opt for radical forms of social mobilization and political action. However, there has been no democratic opening sufficient to channel this discontent via the ballot box.

The sequence of mobilization – repression – self-defence has completed several cycles in Guerrero since the Revolution, though the characteristic it currently presents is that social self-defence does not adopt the guerrilla form exclusively, but rather community policing (in La Montaña and Costa Chica) and citizens' *autodefensa* groups in the rest of the state, with significant differences between one another that are beyond the scope of this study. In any event, it should be noted that the criminal violence spread outside social boundaries and that the poor are not the only victims; however, they continue to suffer from the structural violence (poverty, social inequality, injustice, discrimination, repression and forced disappearance) generated daily by Mexican society.

Nor were democratic legitimation mechanisms sufficient to delimit the role of *cacicazgos* as intermediaries between society and the state. On the contrary, not only have these obstructed the direct link between citizens and public power (the liberal ideal), but they were reinforced by the deployment of criminal networks throughout the state. Today, the *caciques* have more instruments at their disposal to subdue the population and greater resources for trafficking the citizens' vote. Instead of modernising, politics in Guerrero re-energized its archaic mechanisms, meaning that violence (whether social, political and criminal) surges and the three branches of the state lack a minimally credible strategy to confront it.

Notes

1. Tilly, *The Politics of Collective Violence*, pp. 104, 109–10; Tarrow, *Power in Movement*.
2. Gill, 'Los Escudero de Acapulco'], p. 297; Taibo II and Vizcaíno, *Las dos muertes de Juan R. Escudero*, p. 28.

3. Illades, *Guerrero*, p. 119; Taibo II and Vizcaíno, *Las dos muertes de Juan R. Escudero*, pp. 82–83; Bartra, *Guerrero bronco*, p. 48.
4. Gomezjara. *María de la O y Benita Galeana*, pp. 35 ff.; Bartra, *Guerrero bronco*, p. 58.
5. Bustamante Álvarez, 'Periodo 1934–1940', p. 397; Ávila Coronel, 'Problemas para el estudio de la guerrilla del Partido de los Pobres (PdlP)', p. 13; Bartra, *Guerrero bronco*, p. 73.
6. In Atoyac, for example, according to the 1950 Census of Agriculture, Livestock and *Ejidal* (1950), *ejido* community members represented 25 per cent of the economically active population of the municipality, agricultural workers (35 per cent) and relatives of the *ejidatarios* (40 per cent) making up the remaining 75 per cent. Ávila Coronel, 'Problemas para el estudio de la guerrilla del Partido de los Pobres (PdlP)', p. 15.
7. Bellingeri, *Del agrarismo armado a la guerra de los pobres, 1940–1974*, pp. 116–17; Bartra, *Guerrero bronco*, pp. 22 ff.
8. Illades, *Guerrero*, pp. 132–33.
9. Ibid., pp. 133 ff.
10. Castellanos, *México armado 1943–1981*, pp. 114, 123; Rangel Lozano and Sánchez Serrano, 'La guerra sucia en los setenta y las guerrillas de Genaro Vázquez y Lucio Cabañas en Guerrero', pp. 508 ff.; Macías Cervantes, *Genaro Vázquez, Lucio Cabañas y las guerrillas en México entre 1960 y 1974*, p. 58.
11. Montemayor, *La violencia de Estado en México*, pp. 190–91; Ávila Coronel, 'Problemas para el estudio de la guerrilla del Partido de los Pobres (PdlP)', p. 29; Bartra, *Guerrero bronco*, p. 108.
12. Montemayor, *Guerra en el Paraíso*, p. 23.
13. 'Aparente calma en Atoyac, donde patrulla la tropa' [Apparent Calm in Atoyac Where Troops are on Patrol], *Excélsior*, 20 May 1967; Montemayor, *La violencia de Estado en México*, p. 191. I cite the first. By the 1960s, Guerrero was the largest producer of copra in the country and the Costa Grande contributed 90 per cent of state production. Bartra, *Guerrero bronco*, p. 77.
14. Macías Cervantes, *Genaro Vázquez, Lucio Cabañas y las guerrillas en México entre 1960 y 1974*, pp. 78–80, 84.
15. AGMS-UACM, Fondo General Francisco Gallardo, 'Characterization of Mexican Revolutionary, Terrorist and Guerrilla Groups', Poor People Party (Partido de los Pobres (PLP), Re Legat, Mexico City letter to Bureau, 3 June 1974.
16. 'Ordenó la Sedena exterminio en 1971' [Defence Ministry Ordered Extermination in 1971], *El Universal*, 26 January 2015.
17. AGMS-UACM, Fondo General Francisco Gallardo, 'Death of Lucio Cabañas Barrientos' From Embassy Mexico to Department of State, 4 December 1974.
18. Rangel Lozano and Sánchez Serrano, 'La guerra sucia en los setenta y las guerrillas de Genaro Vázquez y Lucio Cabañas en Guerrero', pp. 521–22.
19. Bartra, *Guerrero bronco*, p. 152.
20. Quintero Romero and Rodríguez Herrera, 'Organizaciones sociales', p. 40. The irresponsibility, shortsightedness and greed of the authorities here would have a significant effect on the enormous costs to Acapulco and

other cities resulting from Hurricane Paulina (1999) and Tropical Storm Manuel (2013).
21. Illades, *Guerrero*, pp. 154–55.
22. Lofredo, 'La otra guerrilla mexicana', p. 233.
23. Cited in 'Irrumpe grupo armado en Aguas Blancas' [Aguas Blancas: Armed Group Bursts in], *La Jornada*, 29 June 1996.
24. Ibid.
25. Cited in Carlos Marín, 'Diferencias de carácter político, de estrategia, táctica y visión terminaron en la escisión del EPR' [Differences in Politics, Strategy, Tactics and Vision Led to Division in the EPR], *Proceso*, 29 June 1998; ERPI, 'Poder popular, partido y ejército de masas', 1999. After the EPRI split off, there followed splits with the Fuerzas Armadas Revolucionarias del Pueblo (FARP – Revolutionary Armed Forces of the People), in 1998; the Ejército Villista Revolucionario del Pueblo (EVRP – Villista People's Revolutionary Army) in 1999; and the Tendencia Democrática Revolucionaria (TDR – Democratic Revolutionary Tendency), also in 1999. Two years later, the FARP, the EVRP and the Comité Clandestino Revolucionario de los Pobres-Comando Justiciero 28 de Junio (CJ-28 – Clandestine Revolutionary Committee of the Poor-Justice Command 28 June), a group that split from the EPRI, formed the Coordinadora Guerrillera Nacional José María Morelos (National Guerrilla Coordination 'José María Morelos'). Lofredo, 'La otra guerrilla mexicana', p. 233.
26. LIMEDDH, 'Informe sobre la masacre de El Charco'.
27. Ibid.
28. Gasparello, 'Policía Comunitaria de Guerrero, investigación y autonomía', pp. 66–67; International Crisis Group, 'Justice at the Barrel of a Gun', p. 9.
29. CRAC-PC, 'Comunicado de las comunidades fundadoras de la Coordinadora Regional de Autoridades Comunitarias-Policía Comunitaria'.
30. Illades, *Guerrero*, p. 158.
31. CPR-LPEP, 'Comunicado guerrillero núm. 3'; MRLCB, 'Comunicado núm. 5'.
32. 'Asesinan a Miguel Ángel Mesino, hijo del líder fundador de la OCSS' [Miguel Ángel Mesino, Son of the Founding Leader of the OCSS, is Murdered], *La Jornada*, 20 September 2005.
33. CPR-LPEP, 'Comunicado guerrillero núm. 3'.
34. Cited in 'A dos años del asesinato de Miguel Ángel Mesino, exige la OCSS castigar a los responsables' [Two Years after the Murder of Miguel Ángel Mesino, the OCSS Demands Punishment of Those Responsible], *La Jornada Guerrero*, 19 September 2007.
35. MRLCB, 'Comunicado núm. 5'.
36. Alba Álvarez was arrested in Guadalajara in 2010 for his links to organized crime.
37. Cited in 'Ayotzinapa, fruto de la colusión de 10 años de la clase política con el narco, dice informe' [Ayotzinapa the Result of Ten Years' Collusion between the Political Class and the Narco, Says Report], *El Sur*, 3 December 2014.
38. Guerrero Gutiérrez, 'El estallido de Iguala', p. 46; Merino, Zarkin and Fierro, 'Desaparecidos', p. 16.

39. 'Matan a la viuda de Lucio Cabañas en Guerrero' [Widow of Lucio Cabañas Murdered in Guerrero], *El Universal*, 3 July 2011; 'La hija de Cabañas pide asilo a Obama' [Cabañas' Daughter Asks Obama for Asylum], *El Universal*, 4 December 2014. I cite the former.

40. 'Desde 2013 se denunció que el alcalde era un asesino pero lo dejaron suelto' [Mayor Accused of Murder since 2013, But Allowed to Go Free], *La Jornada*, 7 October 2014; 'Asesinan a dirigente de la OCSS Rocío Mesino' [OCSS Leader Rocío Mesino Murdered], *Milenio*, 19 October 2013.

41. Illades and Santiago, *Estado de guerra*, p. 147.

42. Ezequiel Flores Contreras, 'Grupos de autodefensa de Ayutla inicia entrega de reos' [Ayutla Self-Defence Groups Begin Handing over Prisoners], *Proceso*, 8 February 2013.

43. Guerrero Gutiérrez, 'La inseguridad 2013–2015', p. 46; *El Universal*, 5 February 2014.

44. The events of Iguala and its immediate background are covered in Illades, Esteban, *La noche más triste*, 2015.

45. '43 Missing Students, a Mass Grave and a Suspect: Mexico's Police', *New York Times*, 6 October 2014; 'Llama el ERPI a crear una brigada de ajusticiamiento contra Guerreros Unidos' [EPRI Calls for the Formation of a Justice Brigade against Guerreros Unidos], *La Jornada*, 10 October 2014. For some, the undercurrent of violence against the Ayotzinapa students would be the state's fear regarding 'a threat or a promise of popular or community organization'. Bosteels, 'Detrás de Ayotzinapa', p. 17. In Chapter 8, I discuss the social mobilization caused by the events in Iguala.

Chapter 6

Taking the Streets

Social movements emerged in the mid-eighteenth century in order to petition the state with respect to specific collective demands. While from the outset they incorporated public meetings, organization, propaganda and group demonstrations of will and commitment, it was not until a century later that the demonstration triumphed as a means of protest, particularly for the working class when they demanded better working conditions and political rights. In the twentieth century, the number of actors applying collective action multiplied. Moreover, as Charles Tilly points out, social movements flourished in democratic countries, becoming established as a legitimate form of popular politics, while in authoritarian states, they were usually more constrained.[1]

Public protest is a current practice that, among Mexico City artisans, emerged in the mid-nineteenth century and grew noticeably during the democratic transition from PRI to PAN. However, it would be misleading to think that it had previously been banned by the postrevolutionary regime and is currently allowed under democracy. After the student movement of 1968, the state was fairly tolerant of opposition demonstrations in Mexico City so long as they did not finish in the Plaza de la Constitución (the 'Zócalo'), which was reserved for the exclusive use of the PRI's 'sectors' for public statements of solidarity with the regime or for civic commemorations. Nevertheless, since 2000, the police have occasionally been tasked with dealing with road blocks or arresting demonstrators when acts of vandalism break out, which has even involved fatalities. In provincial towns and rural areas, there was less tolerance for protest. This brings into play a hypothesis that is complementary to that of Tilly, which points towards increasing public demonstrations as an expression of crisis in politics and representative institutions, institutions which incidentally are decidedly underappreciated by young Mexicans.[2]

Many very large mass rallies have taken to the streets of Mexico City since the year 2000, from the arrival of neo-Zapatista contingent demanding the recognition of the rights of indigenous people to demonstrations demanding that the forty-three Ayotzinapa students be brought back alive. Between these, there have been: the *ejidatarios* of Atenco, the 'white' march against the lack of security, the protests against the *desafuero* of the Head of Government of the Federal District as then known, teachers' demonstrations, the electricians' conflict, Javier Sicilia's Movimiento por la Paz con Justicia y Dignidad (MPJD – Movement for Peace with Justice and Dignity) and the demonstration at the Estela de Luz convened by the #YoSoy132 movement. There have also been many others that derived from these or from less important issues, not taking into account the rallies held outside Mexico City, the largest of these being the 2006 Asamblea Popular de los Pueblos de Oaxaca (APPO – Popular Assembly of the Peoples of Oaxaca).

We can start with the intended audience of social mobilization. With the exception of the 'white' march and the #YoSoy132 movement, all of the other demonstrations were directed at the federal government. The 'white' march blamed the capital's administration for inefficiency in fighting crime and kidnapping in particular, while #YoSoy132 exposed the bias in private television's news coverage, which favoured the PRI during the 2012 election campaign. The federal government was the subject of demands that aimed to ensure the recognition of the autonomy and culture of indigenous peoples (2001), to reverse the expropriation of *ejido* land in San Mateo Atenco, which had been seized to build an airport (2001), to restore the political rights of the PRD's popular presidential candidate (2005), to cancel the alliance for education (2008) and to prevent educational reform (2013), to reverse the liquidation of power company Luz y Fuerza del Centro (2009), to compensate victims of the war against organized crime (2011) and to demand that the forty-three students who went missing in Iguala be returned alive (2014).

In addition to marching through the streets, occupations and caravans, as well as blocking roads, protest became international by bringing in activists from other countries (neo-Zapatistas) and incorporated new forms of action into the repertoire of protest (the Atenco horseback marches and the machete *performance*), indefinite and relay occupations (the post-election conflict in 2006, teachers), the intensive use of social networks (the neo-Zapatista and #YoSoy132 movements) and through violent groups acting as shock troops (the neo-anarchists). Although some of these received the direct attention of the federal powers (the neo-Zapatista caravans and the MPJD), their demands were handled so unsatisfactorily that collective action continued, albeit with reduced intensity. After a lengthy confrontation, the Sindicato Mexicano de Electricistas (SME – Mexican Electricians Union) did agree to a settlement with federal authorities, and while it did not reinstate the former state enterprise, it did allow unionized workers who rejected the company's winding up to form a private company servicing the sector.

We will now look at the most important manifestations of each of these movements in greater detail, focusing on its participants, demands, repertoire and the collective energy deployed, its social resonance and the state's response, focusing above all on the question of whether being 'in the context of democracy' changed the government's attitude towards social movements and improved its responsiveness to their demands. Furthermore, we will explore the hypothesis suggested above: whether the increase in the number and magnitude of the protests is indicative of institutional dysfunction and the inability of the public sphere to express social plurality.

In Fifteen Minutes

On 11 March 2001, just three months after Vicente Fox took office, the 'Marcha de la Dignidad Indígena' (March for Indigenous Dignity) arrived in Mexico City, familiarly known as the *Zapatour*. Three years previously, the Ejército Zapatista de Liberación Nacional (EZLN – Zapatista Army of National Liberation) had published the *Quinta Declaración de la Selva Lacandona* (*Fifth Declaration of the Lacandon Jungle*), a document containing a programme that defined its perspective with respect to constitutional reform on indigenous issues, warning that 'any reform that seeks to break the bonds of historical and cultural solidarity between indigenous peoples is doomed to failure and is, simply, an injustice and an historical denial'. In the future, the expectation of an indigenous law directed neo-Zapatista action. With his usual arrogance, Fox said it would only take '15 minutes' to solve the Chiapas problem.[3]

Starting from San Cristóbal de las Casas, the *Zapatour* held mass rallies in the capitals of Oaxaca and Puebla, in Ixmiquilpan and Nurio (spending several days in Nurio to participate in the Tercer Congreso Nacional Indígena (Third National Indigenous Congress)), then in Iguala, Milpa Alta and Mexico City. The route from Cuautla to Mexico City followed the historic route of Emiliano Zapata (1914), entering the city via Xochimilco. While it traced an imaginary historical continuity with Emiliano Zapata's Ejército Libertador del Sur (Liberation Army of the South), the neo-Zapatista contingent encouraged foreign activists to accompany them in order to underline the international nature of the movement and its involvement in the cycle of collective action that began in Seattle (1999), better known as alter-globalism.[4] The 'Monos Blancos' (White Monkeys) attracted attention because of their white overalls, their decisive attitudes ('White monkeys have big balls!') and their security cordon around the EZLN leadership that was so efficient that certain journalists complained about their aggressive behaviour and urged the application of Article 33 of the Constitution to compel the daring Italians to abandon the country.[5]

According to the press, around 200,000 people gathered in the Zócalo and the surrounding streets at the event, which concluded a seven-year struggle. Approval of the legal initiative, which had been drafted by the Comisión de Concordia y Pacificación (COCOPA – Commission of Concord and Pacification) and accepted at the Indigenous Congress in Nurío, seemed at hand, according to the representative of the Consejo Nacional Indígena (CNI – National Indigenous Council). The neo-Zapatista caravan and its discourse sought to convince society of the justice of its demands, to create sympathy for it and to shift public opinion in its favour,[6] to that end using the media resources available to it with great skill. It even came to be known as the 'guerrilla war on paper'. At the political heart of the republic, Subcomandante Marcos stated that the EZLN had no intention of seizing power, but wished to democratize society 'on all floors', building a counterhegemony from the bottom up. And, using the 'mask' metaphor to which he so often resorted, he said that the state had rendered indigenous people invisible, while the neo-Zapatista leadership had somehow supplanted them: 'We should not be here ... those who should be here are the indigenous Zapatista communities.'[7]

Two weeks later, Comandante Esther spoke in Congress, where there had previously been an intense debate about whether it was fitting[8] to give the Zapatistas the floor in the house of national representation, given that 'the population' was represented by legislators (as argued by the PAN) or were the indigenous people mobilized by the EZLN (as the PRD argued) – in other words, the abstract population of liberalism versus the actual population of romantic socialism, though we do not know if lawmakers realized that this is what it was. In the end, the August 2001 constitutional reform on indigenous rights and culture did not incorporate autonomy, the neo-Zapatista movement's fundamental demand.

The conflict in San Salvador Atenco began when Vicente Fox tried to build an alternative to Mexico City's Benito Juárez Airport on *ejido* property in Texcoco, offering risible compensation for the expropriated land (7.20 pesos per square metre for seasonal land and 20 pesos for irrigated land). The *ejidatarios* responded by creating the Frente de Pueblos en Defensa de la Tierra (FPDF – Community Front for the Defence of Land) and immediately mobilizing its forces. At the same time, the EZLN expressed its support, leading to a lasting alliance between the two organizations. The Atenco community, having pre-Hispanic roots, had adopted Nezahualcóyotl, the cultivated and prudent fifteenth-century warrior poet and ruler of Texcoco, as their patron, regarding themselves as the heirs of warriors, artists and scholars. Furthermore, at least in the collective imaginary, they had a record of resistance against the French intervention, the community having also united with the popular armies during the Revolution.[9]

In November 2001, the FPDF marched to Mexico City in order to put pressure on the federal authorities:

> At about 9 a.m., more than 1,500 ejidatarios from Atenco set off on foot, on horses, tractors, carts and trucks for Mexico City's main square to protest against the expropriation of their lands. At the head of the column, they carried the town's patron saint, San Salvador Atenco. The inhabitants followed the Lechería-Texcoco highway, then the Mexico-Puebla highway as far as the junction with Calzada Ignacio Zaragoza, with not one single incident while in the state of Mexico. However, on arrival in the Federal District they were intercepted by a group of riot police, at the junction of Calzada Ignacio Zaragoza and Avenida Francisco Morazán, which led to the confrontation.[10]

Five people were injured in the clash. A policeman's hand was wounded with a machete. There were also arrests, in retaliation the *ejidatarios* blocked the Lechería-Texcoco road, demanding the release of their comrades. After several violent episodes, on 1 August 2002, the president accepted the greatest defeat of his term in office by cancelling the project and reversing the expropriation. But the affront would not be borne in silence. On 3 May 2006, a near seven-hour operation involving state and federal forces to dislodge a road block in Atenco ended in the arrest of over 200 people and the deaths of two youths. Police tactics combined *performance* (an impressive police mobilization closing all roads into the town), surprise (the attack at dawn), excessive force (searches of homes, threats, beatings, mass arrests and torture) and the booty of war (plunder and rape). The leader of the *ejidatarios* was imprisoned in the Altiplano penitentiary to serve a 112-year prison sentence, and the custodial sentences given to his comrades arrested by the police ranged from twelve to thirty-one years. They would remain in detention for just over four years.[11]

Using a different repertoire from that of normal protest, the Atenco mobilization, which did not budge during the Fox presidency, brought the country into the city with the intimidating image of the popular armies entering Mexico City in 1914. The screech of machetes being dragged along the road surface, broad-brimmed hats and horses running around the streets brought confusion to the inhabitants and the federal government, which found the tolerance shown by the PRD's Mexico City government to be excessive. Unlike the neo-Zapatistas, the FPDF protest was not intended to convince, but to intimidate. They did not seek the recognition of their rights, but respect for them. Their message was summarized by the fierce, resolute appearance of the marchers.

Two years earlier, on 28 June 2004, an impressive human column, over one kilometre in length, had walked down the Paseo de la Reforma:

> Men, women and children, dressed in black and white, marched in silence towards the Zócalo in the heart of Mexico City. Some carried banners saying 'Stop kidnappings' and 'Let's rescue Mexico' and many gave accounts of kidnapping, their own or those of relatives and acquaintances. Also, some demanded the death penalty for kidnappers.[12]

It was organized by a civil association founded in 1998, México Unido contra la Delincuencia (Mexico United against Crime), the Consejo Ciudadano de Seguridad Pública (Citizen Council for Public Security), an alias of the semi-clandestine 'Yunque' organization, business corporations and major radio and television stations. This was the right-wing that normally shunned street protest,[13] bursting in on the scene, criticizing the Mexico City government for its ineffectiveness in combating the wave of kidnappings that had grown exponentially in recent years. Overwhelming those who had called the march, a contingent of mothers of young women murdered in Ciudad Juárez joined the vanguard, giving it a more plural bias. At the gates of the National Palace, some shouted 'You can see it, you can feel it: there is no president!', which at least distributed public responsibility. Indeed, the various rival groups all sang the national anthem together. Deliberately downplaying the meaning of the demands, the Head of Government dismissed it as reflecting the perverse interests of business and political groups in discrediting his administration, even using the unfortunate expression 'noise' to define the protest,[14] the result being that he exposed a new flank in the political dispute that was then raging. Would he govern for all or only for the lower classes?

In any event, voter intention in 2005 for the next presidential election indicated a consistent advantage for Andrés Manuel López Obrador.[15] The enemy to beat was the prospect of 'populism'. That was how President Fox understood it, and he was someone who, judging from his hypersimplified view of reality and propensity to demagoguery, could be described as populist himself.[16]

In an attempt to make it impossible for López Obrador to stand for election, rather than enforce the law, on 7 April 2005, a majority vote of the PRI and the PAN in the Chamber of Deputies stripped him of his *fuero* (judicial immunity) so that he would face trial for expropriating land in order to build a road. Hours before the trial instructed by Congress, thousands of people came together in the Zócalo, packing the nearby subway stations in his support (he was still Head of Government). It was not a uniform crowd; it went beyond the usual base of hardcore PRD supporters and included 'young and old, professionals and peasants, more popular classes than middle classes'. They stayed all morning, following the live broadcast of the trial, repeatedly shouting 'Get out!' 'Liar!' 'Arsehole!' during the summary of the special prosecutor from the Procuraduría General de Justicia (PGR – Attorney General's Office), Carlos Javier Vega Memije from Chilpancingo. When López Obrador's turn came, the crowd became festive, 'with thunderous clapping, shouts of "Be hard on them!" and howls of laughter'.[17] Given the immense political cost it represented, which had been underestimated when the decision was made, the Fox administration withdrew the criminal action and restored political rights to the Tabasco-born López Obrador, though not his position as Head of Government.

Lord of War

The year of the election coincided with growing social unrest (the miners of Lázaro Cárdenas and the uprising in Atenco) and the presidential election itself occurred in the middle of the largest urban insurrection in contemporary Mexico, the 'Oaxaca commune'. When, after six months, the commune's end came on 29 October 2006, it required the intervention of 4,500 federal police. In the attack, federal forces used armoured cars and guns, tear gas and water cannons, but even so, it took them ten hours to dismantle the barricades and retake the old Antequera district in the historic centre of the city of Oaxaca. Once the ground had been cleared, over the next few days, the murderous gangs of Governor Ulises Ruiz – comprising state police and gunmen – were allowed to go after the protesters, killing twenty-six people.[18]

Alleging that the decision of the people had not been respected, the left did not accept the official result of the July 2006 presidential election, which gave a narrow victory to PAN candidate Felipe de Jesús Calderón Hinojosa, a margin of barely 250,000 votes (0.56 per cent of the vote) over the tally of the PRD candidate, Andrés Manuel López Obrador. Four percentage points below, the PRI suffered its worst result ever. While district committees were conducting the final count, López Obrador called an 'informative meeting' on 8 April. This concluded the march that had begun at the Anthropology Museum, continuing down Reforma before turning into Juárez and ending in the Zócalo:

> Chanting 'No to fraud, no to fraud!' for several minutes, the crowd that stretched away from the Zócalo, the Plaza de la Constitución, spread like a large yellow stain into the streets that converge there, from Avenida Veinte de Noviembre to Izazaga, and from Avenida Cinco de Mayo, Avenida Juárez and Tacuba, to the Eje Central …
>
> A cheer erupted when the candidate said that if the count were done vote by vote the official IFE result would be reversed …
>
> Opposite the platform … a monumental white cardboard dove (four and a half metres high by five wide) had been installed with a message on its chest: 'Everyone for peace and respect for the vote.' At the far end, there was an equally enormous rooster, made of brightly coloured cellophane.[19]

The obvious implication was that the legal route would be followed. Invariably careful in his dealings with the army, López Obrador requested it to not allow 'any interference at the district headquarters where the ballot boxes are being held'. Two marches were planned for the next few days. At the third informative meeting on 30 July, the PRD candidate 'called on his followers to maintain a permanent occupation, from the Zócalo to the Paseo de la Reforma, for an indefinite time': to be exact, forty-eight days.[20] Although the PRD candidate argued that the blockade responded to the urgent need to provide an outlet for the anger of his followers via orderly and peaceful action, the fact remains that it held the attention of the media, the implicit goal of every street demonstration. The occupation of public spaces recalls Tiananmen Square (Beijing, 1989), Tahrir (Cairo, 2011), Gezi Park (Istanbul, 2013) and Maidan (Kiev, 2014). But the regime did not crack, nor was there a massive repression that would detonate a popular uprising. Instead, a segment of the middle class and businessmen who did business under the protection of the López Obrador administration distanced themselves from him, subsequently punishing him in the 2012 presidential race.[21]

In the eyes of President-elect Calderón, the blockade of Reforma and the 'Oaxaca commune' were an expression of chaos, of a fratricidal struggle resulting from 'a violent past'. The leader of 'the peaceful', as he then called himself with unintentional irony, began to outline a discourse based on order, that issue so beloved by the right, abandoning the issue of employment that he had emphasized in the campaign. Both his desire to legitimize himself after a tight election that was called into question by a third of the population and his determination to be heavy-handed towards out-of-control social movements influenced his decision to militarize the country.[22] In fact, street protests declined substantially in the first two years of the second PAN presidency, increasing again when he took the first steps in what would later be called structural reforms, in principle affecting the teachers' and electricians' unions.

Through the 2008 strike, dissident teachers expressed powerful resistance to Calderón's attempt to regulate the teaching profession known as the 'Alianza por la Calidad Educativa' (Alliance for Quality Education), in relation to which he had signed an agreement with Elba Esther Gordillo, the leader of the teachers' union and a strategic ally of the PAN during the 2006 presidential campaign. The teachers' movement gained strength in Morelos, where they staged a mass demonstration in Cuernavaca on 23 August. The strike, which had begun some days earlier, went on for a couple of months. In October, several sections of the Coordinadora Nacional de Trabajadores de la Educación (CNTE – National Coordinator of Educational Workers) occupied downtown Mexico City, seeking an annulment of that agreement. Adopting the repertoire of Oaxaca's Section 22 of the CNTE, dissident teachers blocked traffic in the streets of República de Brasil, Luis González Obregón and República de Venezuela, in addition to erecting tents for the night.[23] The dissident teachers did not manage to get rid of the 'Alianza por la Calidad Educativa', but they did manage to neutralize it in states where they were strong.

At midnight on 10 October 2009, military and federal police occupied the offices of Luz y Fuerza del Centro one hour before the *Diario Oficial* published the decree that wound up the state company, using the argument that it was financially unsustainable. The electrician's union was an experienced campaigner. Founded in 1914, the SME was party to the collective contract, a fact that foreshadowed a long conflict. Less than a week passed before the union organized a large demonstration. It started at the Diana Cazadora roundabout, proceeded along Reforma and ended up in the Zócalo. López Obrador took part. The Head of Government Marcelo Ebrard offered to help resolve the conflict by facilitating communication between the parties:

> 'Can you sleep, Calderón? We can't. My father has been made redundant.' 'Felipe, do your children know how many children you have made go hungry?' 'Felipe, president of unemployment.' 'Calderón, you came like a vile thief in the night and left us without food.' 'It's not influenza that kills us, but Calderón' were the slogans on some of the thousands of banners that accompanied the demonstration.[24]

From then on, over the following six years, the SME held countless protest rallies in the streets of the capital, occupations and road blocks, as well as perhaps, though this was never proven, sabotaging the decrepit power grid. Faced by the impossibility of Luz y Fuerza del Centro resuming operations, the nearly 17,000 workers who did not accept the settlement of the total of 41,000 who worked for the state-owned company, sought work elsewhere in the industry. In August 2015, they signed an agreement with the Portuguese firm Mota-Engil to offer specialized services to the electricity sector.[25]

The title of Javier Sicilia's open letter to 'politicians and criminals', 'Estamos hasta la madre' ('We've had it up to here'), reverberated around the country in 2011, the year when criminal violence, exacerbated by the strategy chosen to combat it, reached its highest peak.[26] With that resounding expression of being fed up, the MPJD focused on the monstrous human cost that the war on drugs had on society, on whose behalf Calderón had decided to wage it, berating him for precisely that at the 8 May rally in the Zócalo:

> Speaking to the thousands of participants in the movement that began on Thursday in Cuernavaca, Morelos. Sicilia asked, 'Why was the president of the republic allowed to put the army into the streets in an absurd war that has cost us 40,000 victims, with millions of Mexicans left in fear and uncertainty?'[27]

In a clear and forceful speech, the poet minutely analysed the elements of complicity between the worlds of money and the politics behind the drug business, Congress's omission in not holding President Calderón to account for waging a war without their authorization, the deafness of politicians who did not listen to the claims of a wounded and aggrieved society, and American hypocrisy expressed in forcing the war on Mexico, but benefiting economically from it via money laundering and arms trafficking. Sicilia also observed that every political party had been penetrated by organized crime and stated that narcotics consumption should be dealt with as a public health issue rather than by militarizing the country, which, instead of resolving the problem, made its citizens victims twice over. It was the voice of a man of faith who questioned an obsessed Catholic's 'holy war'. Reading out testimonials of the atrocious damage that the war had inflicted on the population and the words of other victims of government absurdities (the fire at the Guardería ABC, where 49 children died and 106 were injured), he was accompanied at one point by the release of white balloons in memoriam of the victims and the tolling of the cathedral bells.[28] The event, and the caravan itself, called for the expression of pain, but, above all, of reflection.

Despite the great expectations generated by the June 2011 meeting at Chapultepec Castle, described on Calderón's Twitter account as an 'intense learning experience',[29] it did not actually provide any lessons to the federal government. There was no substantial change in the strategy for tackling organized crime and the PAN administration was not even able to provide a reliable figure of the number of casualties (those killed, missing, displaced, etc.). Although the MPJD forced the 2013 enactment of a law on this matter, it has not made much difference. However, the real importance of the coordinated public outcry orchestrated by the MPJD lay in the fact that it was the phrase 'enough is enough' that sensitized consciences when the atrocities at Tlatlaya, Tanhuato, Apatzingán and Iguala occurred.

'To Move Mexico'

For generations, the massacre at the Plaza de las Tres Culturas defined the image that young university students would have of the regime (authoritarian, repressive, corrupt and ineffective) and identified the visible objective of collective action. The Mexican 'Leviathan' was both responsible for the problems and simultaneously was the only actor able to solve them. Both its ability and willingness was in enormous doubt, though that did not preclude demands for specific results. Nor was it allowed to forget the massacre. Shortly before losing the presidency, the PRI government had had to deal with the student strike that paralysed the UNAM for nearly a year. For their part, the PAN administrations did not face significant student protests, although it did confront important social movements, the most powerful left-wing opposition in living memory and peaceful protest by the relatives of victims of the insane drug war that Calderón launched without any sensible calculation of its consequences.

At a seemingly routine campaign event, speaking to a usually doc- ile audience, Enrique Peña Nieto, the leading candidate in the 2012 presidential election, slipped furtively away from the campus of the Universidad Iberoamericana after being heckled by students about re- pression at Atenco, with the students shouting: 'Coward! The Ibero does not want you!' TV stations edited out the shocking moments of the event and as a result outrage spread among students when they contrasted what had actually happened in the morning with what had been shown on television at night and the description of the incident as a 'staged riot'. Faced with an accusation from PRI headquarters say- ing that they were 'thugs' and 'had been shipped in', a total of 131 students made a video displaying their university IDs and stating their names and registration numbers. By nightfall, 'the hashtag "#131stu- dents of the Ibero" had become a trending topic worldwide'.[30] Thus, the #YoSoy132 movement was born.

The movement was short-lived, in part because of its horizontality, limited structuring and the unlimited autonomy of each of the local assemblies, prompting each to speak for itself, but interpreted as if it were speaking for the whole (in any event, they were all #YoSoy132). This confused the public and made the group's messages seem less effective. Furthermore, because its scope was limited to the 2012 pres- idential election, it had no proposal for the day after. It did at least brighten up a lacklustre contest in which the PRI was expected to emerge victorious. Moreover, for the first time, the students of pub- lic and private universities marched together. According to a newspa- per report, in the demonstration that took place on 24 May: 'Reforma Avenue was filled with banners where students of the Tecnológico de Monterrey, the Universidad Autónoma Metropolitana, the Instituto Politécnico Nacional and even universities of other states spoke out against the media monopoly.' Various stops outside corporate offices emphasized the protestors' conviction that television companies were manipulating the news, leading to the emergence of the slogan: 'Turn the telly off and turn the truth on.'[31]

The poor coordination of the movement, almost non-existent con- trol over the bases and the lack of a core of (unquestionably represen- tative) averagely professionalized activists made it possible for radical groups to take over the movement, being better organized than the students, who were taking a position in the public space for the first time. The election result mobilized those groups that had been pres- ent at the 7 July march. In spite of the large number of participants, the march nonetheless demonstrated the fragmentation of the student movement. While #YoSoy132 distanced themselves from the convocation in advance, 'considering it to be an attempt to use them for personal and party purposes', there was still a large amount of propaganda with their name attached to it circulating on social networks and posted at subway stations. 'We want democracy, not soap operas' stated one banner, while a young man protested by climbing the Estela de Luz.[32]

With the arrival of radicals on the scene, referring to themselves as 'anarchists', the social protest that had originally been aimed against Peña Nieto taking power assumed an anti-state dimension that also challenged economic power. However, the new emphasis became confused in the muddle of events that occurred on 2 December and the multiple interpretations that actors and the media offered: accusations, denials and evidence (objective or fabricated) abounded. There is, however, absolute certainty about the incompetence and brutality of the police, as well as the presence 'of several groups of masked individuals wearing gas masks and bandanas, who attempted to tear down the barricades set up the previous week on Avenida Eduardo Molina'. Hours later, 'clashes between police and anarchists spread to the corner of Reforma and Bucareli, where a dense group of people with their faces masked destroyed cash machines, the windows of a Bancomer building and the alternate offices of *El Universal*'. Apart from the dozens injured and arbitrary arrests, one activist suffered a fatal wound from a rubber bullet fired by law enforcement officers.[33]

The 2012 Educational Reform was a contest of strength between the CNTE and the new PRI government. Of all the measures in its package of structural reforms, this was the one that encountered the greatest resistance, perhaps because this particular adversary was steeled for the fight and had a strong union cohesion – a mixture of authoritarian practices, handouts and the genuine loyalty of its base. The aim of education reform was for the Ministry of Education to regain control of education management by introducing mechanisms for evaluating teachers. The imposition of reform was achieved through the acquiescence of the Sindicato Nacional de Trabajadores de la Educación (SNTE – National Union of Education Workers), who had been subdued by the imprisonment of its lifetime president, though it faced strong opposition from the CNTE, especially in the states of Oaxaca, Guerrero, Chiapas and Michoacán.[34] Receiving insignificant support from other areas, the teachers' sections in these states kept the population of Mexico City on edge for four months, and the populations of their respective states indefinitely.

At the start of the 2013–14 school year, the teachers' strike left about two million pupils in primary and secondary education without classes in the four states mentioned above. In Oaxaca alone, the figure was around 1,300,000 and, in addition to the repeal of educational reform, the Oaxaca CNTE's Section 22 demanded the same thing for labour reform, as well as the criminal prosecution of Ulises Ruiz for the murders carried out in 2006. A few days later, the protesting teachers blocked access to Mexico City International Airport and threatened a sit-in at the Zócalo, which it had occupied since 9 May, during the September national festivities. Red lights went off at both the federal government and the capital's government, which set up a police operation to 'clean up' the Zócalo. After the recovery of this public space – now forever lost to social movements because of the CNTE's intransigence – 'groups of masked individuals, teachers' supporters, and the so-called "anarchists" confronted elements of the federal police'.[35]

There remains to the date of writing a camp at the Monument to the Revolution that functions as the teachers' embassy in the capital. Rather than gaining the sympathy and trust of society, absorbed in their union politics, the basic strategy of the teachers was to challenge the state, blocking main roads or sabotaging the elections. The result, when the government counter-offensive came after the 2015 midterm elections, was that support for the CNTE from other social sectors was virtually non-existent.

The murder of six people and the disappearance of forty-three students in Iguala on the night of 26 September 2014 revealed that the boundary between crime and the state could be erased.[36] If the MPJD made the civilian victims of war visible, Iguala revealed that they were also unarmed. This was not an isolated event, but was an extreme one, and thus gave meaning to the fragmentary experiences of many. Simultaneity, the product of the era of globalization, meant that the Ayotzinapa forty-three were known throughout the world. Meanwhile, demonstrations began in Chilpancingo on 29 September and in Mexico City on 8 October. In Guerrero, dissident teachers quickly came to dominate the protests, while in Mexico City there were many varied collective actions. On 20 November, huge contingents marched to the Zócalo from three different points of the city: the Ángel de la Independencia, Tlatelolco and the Monument to the Revolution:

> At first, they only shouted one slogan, counting to 43 and demanding justice. Cries of 'They were taken alive; we want them back alive' was the echo at later demonstrations.

But as the march progressed, the shouting changed: together the thousands of demonstrators shouted, 'Peña Out!', and moving into Insurgentes and Reforma, the chorus was 'the Senate is running the narco-state'. Something had changed from previous occasions, the shout of 'It was the state' was replaced by a longer but more articulate sentence: 'Now, now, now. Now, it is indispensable ... bring them back alive, punish those responsible!'

And another slogan, 'Gaviota, ratota, ¡devuelve la casota!' ('Gaviota! Thief! Give back the mansion!') thundered in the Hemiciclo a Juárez[37] ('Gaviota' refers to Peña Nieto's wife).

The contingent starting from the Ángel, with the parents of the missing students at their head, were marchers who brought together all the cultural and political diversity of a complex society: from the hardcore CETEG from Guerrero (grouped according to their SEP administrative units), to guerrillas, Greenpeace environmentalists, artists from the Faro Oriente, pro-marijuana activists, feminist groups, organized cyclists, an association of Masons, a group of the blind, whole families and citizens with no collective affiliation. The universities set off from Tlatelolco: the experienced ones – the Universidad Nacional Autónoma de México (UNAM – National Autonomous University of Mexico), the Universidad Autónoma Metropolitana (UAM – Metropolitan Autonomous University) and the Instituto Politécnico Nacional – and the novices – the Instituto Tecnológico Autónomo de México (ITAM – Mexico Autonomous Institute of Technology), the Centro de Investigación y Docencia Económicas (CIDE – Centre for Research and Teaching in Economics), the Libre de Derecho and the Tecnológico de Monterrey. The unions and social organizations started at the Monument to the Revolution. It was clear that the geography of the march also made historical references, now united by the continuous human flow towards the Zócalo. Each had its own locus referring to symbols and past struggles; civil organizations, students and union members adopted the common cause of human rights, the universal reference that gave meaning to the public demonstration, preventing it from being reduced to a sectoral or identity protest. As one mother said: 'I came because I think we should put a stop to the situation we are living through ... I am also here because I have two children and, when they are doing their degrees and making this kind of protest, I wouldn't want the same thing to happen to them.'[38]

The collective action, the compassion it generated in other countries and the cycle of protests that started in the second period of the

Calderón administration, intensifying with the return of the PRI to Los Pinos, increased the scope of the event. Silenced massacres were a thing of the past, but the authorities did not understand; they reacted late and badly, to the point that it will now be virtually impossible for them to offer a convincing version of what happened that night in Iguala. The protest died away, taking with it a chunk of the government's already scant credibility.[39]

Conclusion

As a form of popular politics, social movements question power, particularly the state, presenting a structured set of demands that they think should be addressed. When this dialogue is fluid and the claims are legitimate – that is, they do not generate privileges for one single group within society, but extend the rights of all – they strengthen the democratic life of societies, especially now that the unequal distribution of resources and information leads to *de-democratization*, where, as Étienne Balibar states, the 'normalised construct of majorities is merely the government of the "oligarchic minority"'.[40]

Public outcry clearly increased during the democratic transition from the PRI to the PAN not because guarantees increased for those who mobilized – for better or worse, they were also respected before 2000 – but because political society is as unreceptive to claims arising in civil society, as it had been before the democratic transition. With this change in relation to who held power, political competition developed, but communication with society continued to be very poor. The faulty connection between the government and the governed remains unchanged. Yet, at the same time, social movements have not generated political forms that will allow them to win spaces in the public sphere, and their explicit rejection of politics (identifying it with parties) weakens them when the mobilization recedes. In this way, despite the intense collective action in the fifteen years since the changeover, changes have been minimal and wear and tear on the regime on the rise.

Public protest has nonetheless served to generate a broad consensus on human rights, placing a spotlight on the demands of indigenous peoples and those of the victims of the war on organized crime, as well as demanding transparency and plurality in the mass media. As regards union claims, the electricians regained a little of what they had lost with the liquidation of Luz y Fuerza del Centro, but the teachers, with their all-or-nothing policy, retreated. With the exception of the teachers, where it is debatable whether sectoral interests should come before the general interest, all the other social movements that we have mentioned not only concern the construction of Mexican democracy but also urge the state to fulfil its basic obligations, such as protecting citizens and respecting (and enforcing the respect of) human rights throughout the country. The #YoSoy132 movement brought the relationship between the media (especially television) and politics into the discussion, as well as the need to open the media up to public debate, allowing a plurality of opinions to be expressed, which is an indispensable condition for the rational solution of conflict or the management of conflict by peaceful means. This is not to mention the social responses to insecurity or in defence of the population's basic rights, a demand that is not only genuine but is also a necessary condition for society's normal functioning. However, what is striking is that the fight against corruption (both political and economic) has not yet been included in the agenda of social movements, which, somewhat resigned, remain on the outside of this fundamental demand of contemporary struggles.

Notes

1. Tilly and Wood, *Social Movements, 1768–2008*.
2. Fillieule and Tartakowsky, *La manifestation*.
3. Comité Clandestino Revolucionario Indígena-Comandancia General del EZLN [Clandestine Indigenous Revolutionary Committee-General Command of the EZLN], *Quinta Declaración de la Selva Lacandona* [Fifth Declaration of the Lacandon Jungle], 1998. Retrieved 12 October 2016 from http://es.wikisource.org/wiki/Quinta_Declaraci%C3%B3n_de_la_Selva_Lacandona; '15 minutos para pacificar Chiapas' [15 Minutes to Pacify Chiapas], *El País*, 15 July 2000. I cite the former.
4. We take a cycle of collective action to be a set of social movements that last for months or years, extend to various places and countries, and are synthesized as if they amounted to a single event. See Tarrow, *Power in Movement*.
5. '*Monos blancos*, fruto del desempleo en Europa' [White Monkeys, Fruit of Unemployment in Europe', *La Jornada*, 14 March 2001; 'Los *Monos blancos* italianos' [The Italian White Monkeys], *Reuters*, 18 March 2001. I cite the former. There were also twenty-five Spaniards in the caravan and around '500 co-operators from all around the world'. Manuel Vázquez Montalbán, 'Y *Marcos* entró en México D.F.' [And Marcos Came to Mexico City], *Interviú*, 12 March 2001.
6. I am here following the general approach of Fillieule and Tartakowsky, *La manifestation*.
7. Cited in 'No somos quienes aspiran a hacerse en el poder, dice Marcos en el Zócalo' [We are Not Those Who Aspire to Power, Says Marcos in the Zócalo], *La Jornada*, 12 March 2001.

8. 'Determina el Congreso de la Unión aceptar el diálogo directo con el Ejército Zapatista' [Congress Decides to Accept Direct Dialogue with the Zapatista Army]. Retrieved 12 October 2016 from http://www.margen.org/marcha/8-03-02d.htm.
9. Zamora Lomelí, 'Conflicto and violencia entre el Estado and los actores colectivos', pp. 31 ff.
10. 'Chocan ejidatarios and granaderos' [Ejidatarios and Riot Police Clash, *El Universal*, 15 November 2001.
11. Ibid.; 'PFP asegura que desarticuló el movimiento de Atenco' [PFP Asserts that it Has Dismantled the Atenco Movement], *El Universal*, 5 May 2006. I cite the former.
12. 'Gigantesca marcha contra los secuestros en México' [Gigantic March against Kidnappings in Mexico], *La Nación*, 28 June 2004.
13. This tendency is also observed in European countries. See Fillieule and Tartakowsky, *La manifestation*.
14. Tamayo, 'Dinámica de la movilización', p. 255; 'Rebasó a los organizadores el reclamo de miles contra la inseguridad' [The Demand of Thousands against Insecurity Overwhelmed Organizers], *La Jornada*, 28 June 2004; 'Gigantesca marcha contra los secuestros en México' [Massive March against Kidnappings in Mexico], *La Nación*, 28 June 2004.
15. The figures are as follows: 36.1 per cent López Obrador (PRD); 8.2 per cent Santiago Creel (PAN); 4.9 per cent Roberto Madrazo (PRI); 4.4 per cent Arturo Montiel (PRI); 1.8 per cent Cuauhtémoc Cárdenas (PRD); 1.6 per cent Felipe Calderón (PAN); 0.8 per cent Jorge G. Castañeda (independent). Andrés Manuel López Obrador is often known by his initials, AMLO.)
16. D'Eramo, 'Populism and the New Oligarchy'. The Italian political scientist forcefully demonstrates how populism has become an empty concept.
17. Cited in 'Un Zócalo a reventar y una larga lista de agravios individuales and colectivos' [Zócalo Full to Bursting Point and a Long List of Individual and Collective Grievances], *La Jornada*, 8 April 2005. According to a survey conducted in August 2004, 65 per cent of Mexico City inhabitants disagreed with the *desafuero*, while 28 per cent thought the opposite. Nationally, 40 per cent rejected it, while 29 per cent approved of the decision. Parametría, *El desafuero de López Obrador*, p. 3.
18. Sotelo Marbán, *Oaxaca*, p. 147; Gibler, 'Afán de impunidad', p. 165; Osorno, *Oaxaca sitiada*, p. 289; Illades and Santiago, *Estado de guerra*, p. 77.
19. Cited in 'Convoca AMLO a marcha nacional por la democracia' [AMLO Summons National March for Democracy], *La Jornada*, 9 July 2006.
20. 'Confirma AMLO plantón por tiempo indefinido' [AMLO Confirms Occupation to Last Indefinitely], *El Universal*, 31 July 2006. Some authors argue that the selection of the streets where the camp was set up meant a historical reappropriation of public space. See Tamayo, 'Dinámica de la movilización', pp. 459 ff.
21. 'El plantón de 2006 evitó que hubiera muertos: AMLO' [The 2006 Occupation Prevented Deaths: AMLO], *La Jornada*, 20 December 2011; 'El fantasma del plantón de Reforma persigue a AMLO en reunión con empresarios' [Ghost of the Reforma Occupation Haunts AMLO in Meeting

with Businessmen], Proceso.com, 20 March 2012. According to experts, the protest camp (occupation) is substantively incorporated into the repertoire of protest in Mexico. Fillieule and Tartakowsky, *La manifestation.*

22. 'Felipe festeja su triunfo sobre "México del caos"' [Felipe Celebrates His Victory over 'Chaotic Mexico'], *El Universal,* 11 September 2006; Aguilar and Castañeda, *El narco,* p. 13; Illades and Santiago, *Estado de Guerra,* p. 154.

23. 'Marchan 20 mil maestros contra la alianza educativa en Morelos' [20,000 Teachers March against the Education Alliance in Morelos], *La Jornada,* 23 August 2008; 'Deja plantón de maestros pérdidas de mil 500 millones de pesos en Morelos' [Teachers' Occupation Causes Losses of 1,500 Million Pesos in Morelos], *El Universal,* 10 October 2008; 'Bloquea plantón tránsito en las inmediaciones de la SEP' [Occupation Blocks Traffic around Education Ministry], *El Universal,* 9 October 2008.

24. Cited in 'Megamarcha del SME rebasa toda previsión' [SME Megamarch Exceeds All Expectations], *La Jornada,* 16 October 2009.

25. 'Explotan mufas en el centro histórico; un lesionado' [Electricity Service Access Explodes Downtown; One Hurt], *El Universal,* 23 December 2009; 'SME firma contrato de trabajo con Mota-Engil' [SME Signs Employment Contract with Mota-Engil], *El Financiero,* 21 August 2015.

26. Guerrero Gutiérrez, 'La inseguridad 2013–2015', pp. 41–42.

27. Cited in '"No más muertes: que renuncia García Luna a la SSP": Sicilia' ('No more deaths: García Luna Must Resign as Minister for Public Security': Sicilia), *La Jornada,* 9 May 2011.

28. Ibid.

29. Sicilia, *Estamos hasta la madre,* p. 159; 'Diálogo con Sicilia, "intenso and aleccionador": Calderón' [Dialogue with Sicilia, 'Intense and Instructive': Calderon], *Proceso,* 24 June 2011.

30. 'La Ibero no te quiere' [Translator's note. This translates as both 'The Ibero Does Not Want You' and 'The Ibero Does Not Love You'], *Reporte Índigo,* 11 May 2012; cited in Estrada Saavedra, 'Sistema de protesta', p. 93; 'No somos porros ni acarreados, responden alumnos de la Ibero que increparon a Peña' [We are Not Thugs Nor Shipped-in Respond Ibero Students Who Heckled Peña], *La Jornada,* 15 May 2012; De Mauleón, 'De la red a las calles', p. 40. According to the Network Society theorist, Castells, 'la autocomunicación de masas proporciona la plataforma tecnológica para la construcción de la autonomía del actor social...' (auto-communication of the masses provides the technological platform for the construction of the autonomy of the social actor ...) Castells, *Redes de indignación and esperanza,* p. 24.

31. 'Marcha YoSoy132 toma las calles de México' [The #YoSoy132 March Takes Mexico's Streets], *El Economista,* 24 May 2012; '#YoSoy132 pide "apagar la tv y encender la verdad"' [#YoSoy132 Says 'Turn off the Telly and Turn on the Truth'], *La Jornada,* 14 June 2012. It should be noted that the first mention of a march against Peña Nieto was made in a tweet on 1 May. De Mauleón, 'De la red a las calles', p. 35. In contrast, the Gay Pride marches, which began in 1979, have suffered growing depoliticization, in part due to the 'normalization' of the gay community in globalization via

consumption, and also as a result of having decoupled from other protest movements (workers, migrants, etc.), focusing on the construction of
identity, that is, looking inwards. If anything, politicization is now reduced
to transgression. Voegtli, '¿Cómo manifestar la diversidad?', p. 490.

32. 'Protestan contra la "imposición"' [Protest against 'Imposition'], *El Univer-sal*, 8 July 2012; 'Miles de personas protestan contra Peña Nieto en mega marcha' (Thousands protest against Peña Nieto in mega march), *El Econ-omista*, 7 July 2012.

33. 'Enfrentamientos dejan 121 heridos' [Clashes Leave 121 Injured], *El Uni-versal*, 2 December 2012; 'Muere el activista Kuykendall, herido en el oper-ativo policiaco del 1 December 2012' [The Activist Kuykendall, Wounded in the 1 December 2012 Police Operation, Dies], *La Jornada*, 26 January 2014. For more on these groups, see Chapter 7.

34. Following the adoption of educational reform by the Guerrero Congress on 24 April 2013, enraged teachers destroyed the Chilpancingo headquar-ters of the PAN, the PRD and the PRI. In the morning, about two thousand teachers from the Coordinadora Estatal de Trabajadores de la Educación de Guerrero (CETEG – State Coordinating Committee of Guerrero Edu-cation Workers) attacked the local PAN headquarters with 'stones, pipes and sticks'. The PRD offices, which had been attacked previously, was the target of 'Molotov cocktails' and was partially set on fire. At the PRI build-ing at about 3 p.m., dissident teachers 'destroyed everything in their path, including computer equipment, then sprayed gasoline and set fire to the place'. 'Incendian Guerrero; destruyen sedes locales de partidos políticos' [Guerrero Torched; Local Headquarters of Political Parties Destroyed], *Excélsior*, 24 April 2013. In the case of Michoacán, union mechanisms – just as corporate as their SNTE nemesis – are explained clearly in Rivera Velázquez, 'El abismo Michoacáno', pp. 47–48.

35. 'Mega paro magisterial: dos millones de niños sin clases en cuatro estados' [Mega Teachers' Strike: No Classes for Two Million Children], *Proceso*, 19 August 2013; 'Maestros bloquean inmediaciones del aeropuerto del DF' [Teachers Blockade Environs of Mexico City Airport], *El Universal*, 23 Au-gust 2013; 'Detienen federales a 31 tras el desalojo' [Federal Police Arrest 31 after the Eviction], *El Universal*, 14 September 2013.

36. The best-documented reports are given in Illades, Esteban, *La noche más triste*; González Rodríguez, *Los 43 de Iguala*, 2015.

37. Illades, Moreno and Millares, 'México se mueve'.

38. Ibid.

39. See Chapter 8.

40. Tilly and Wood, *Social Movements, 1768–2008*, p. 268; Balibar, 'El comu-nismo como compromiso, imaginación y política', p. 39.

Chapter 7

Violence and Public Protest

◦━━━◦

According to the French psychologist Gustave Le Bon, the individual member of the group (which, following Spencer, he called a whole with new features) abandons rational behaviour, a thesis that the Norwegian historian George Rudé demolished by convincingly demonstrating that the crowd's actions had specific goals: restoring the social pact broken by governments, the ruling classes or by market laws. This was what E.P. Thompson termed 'the moral economy', the most famous of his historical categories. Violence, when it occurred in preindustrial society, was directed at things and occasionally at people. Smashed windows, wrecked machines and burned barns were the principal targets of popular anger because 'far from being "blind" the crowd was often disciplined, had clear objectives, knew how to negotiate with authority, and above all brought its strength swiftly to bear'.[1]

The working class turned the street demonstration into the space for its collective expression because it lacked political rights and also because, in the nineteenth century, the public sphere was under the control of the propertied classes. Although violent episodes prompted by state repression did occur, the collective protest of a class disciplined by work in a factory was generally orderly, had clear demands and was capable of containing any violent responses by subordinates.[2] Even though in the second half of the twentieth century, other groups began to join social movements (pacifists, students, women and minorities), the reference point continued to be the labour movement. In fact, after the 1968 student revolt, there were some young people who wished they could wash away the original sin of not having been born workers and contribute to the emancipation of labour:[3]

> In Western democracies, at least, social movement organizers, authorities, and police had negotiated routines that greatly minimized the violence of social movement claim making. Organizers had also begun creating international alliances even more actively than their nineteenth-century predecessors had managed.[4]

Diminished and on the defensive because of economic restructuring and the end of the welfare state, factory workers lost their centrality in the rebirth of the crowd that was observed in the twenty-first century – which, among other consequences, loosened the bonds that tied the radicalized segments to the popular movement. This crowd, say Hardt and Negri, 'is an internally different, multiple social subject whose constitution and action is based not on identity or unity (or, much less, indifference) but on what it has in common'.[5]

Although there are often violent nuclei within the crowd, they are usually in the minority. They have become more visible in recent public disturbances, so that, as Sidney Tarrow noted, 'the violence and intolerance that we have seen during the first decade of the new century constitute a frightening trend'. The *black bloc,* deployed in Italy, Greece, Ukraine, Catalonia, Brazil, Chile and Mexico, is a tactic employed in the struggle principally, but not exclusively, by neo-anarchist groups. Anonymity, one of the features of preindustrial protest (for example, Captain Swing or the Luddites), via identifying marks such as black shirts to provide easy recognition and simultaneously state identity, and organization in compact, variably sized blocks known as 'affinity groups' are two of its outstanding features. Located in strategic positions, moving backwards and forwards in concert, each group performs a particular task with the relevant tools (pliers, blowtorches, etc.) during charges on the police. The goal, as a Mexican neo-anarchist states, is 'to protect the protesters, whether anarchists or not', 'so that they form a homogeneous mass, which means "we are all one, we have no leaders and no limits"'.[6]

Because of their origins as a social *autodefensa* group, their mode of deployment and particularly their employment as shock troops, black blocs are sometimes considered to be urban guerrillas. If they are so considered, then it is important to emphasize their basic difference from the urban guerrillas of the second half of the twentieth century: the latter operated at a distance from the masses, but the new guerrillas act *within* and not *outside* the popular arena.[7] The radical social movements of the 1960s and 1970s failed because of 'repression, partly because of exhaustion and a thin social base, and partly because of changes in the ideological tone of struggles in the Third World (end of the Cultural Revolution in China, socialist wars in Indochina, end of "focoism" in Latin America)'.[8]

Social inequality detonates violence in its most visible form ('subjective': Žižek; 'counter-violence': Balibar) distinct from systemic violence (anonymous and objective, naturalized by ideology), a constituent of domination and creator of the emergency conditions of the subjective violence or counterviolence; also, according to Tilly, it undermines democracy when differences between members of the commonality crystallize into ethnic, gender or social categories, deepening when public policies solidify this state of affairs and, as Mike Davis points out, 'construct epistemological walls around *gecekondus*, *favelas*, and *chawls* that disable any honest debate about the daily violence of economic exclusion'.[9]

Unfortunately, these ingredients (social inequality, racism, poverty, exclusion and classism) are all part of reality in Mexico: extreme inequality is not counterbalanced by effective policies that tend towards equity, and systemic violence is shamelessly displayed in different spheres of community life. To make matters worse, the war against organized crime has spread violence, both quantitatively and geographically, throughout the country,[10] with instances of cruelty rising to levels unimaginable even in the hardly peaceful twentieth century.

In addition, being besieged by crime and suffering the continual murder of their leaders, certain segments of civil society adopted forms of action that were also violent:[11] citizens' *autodefensa* groups in rural areas and the black bloc in urban demonstrations.[12] This chapter looks at this method of struggle in recent protests, clarifies its relationship with neo-anarchism, ascertains its forms of action and evaluates its presence within the popular movement.

The Black Bloc

The black bloc emerged in Germany in response to the largest post-war police operation in the country, which evicted an anti-nuclear protest camp in 1980. Each year, local farmers and peace activists still try to block the route of the *Castor* train, which transfers nuclear waste from the La Hague plant in France to Gorleben. As in any conflict, the methods of the adversaries adapt to the actions and reactions of the other side. Faced by the wave of arrests that occurred in various parts of Germany, in addition to the eviction of squatters, some activists wore black clothes as a distinctive uniform at demonstrations and masks in order to avoid being identified by police, and, on *Black Friday*, December 1980, destroyed an expensive shopping area in Berlin. Anarcho-punk music, anti-racist groups and images in the media allowed this strategy to spread to other Western countries.[13]

The black bloc tactic, which was also employed in the Netherlands, made its debut in Washington DC in a protest outside the Pentagon in 1989. Ten years later, at the World Trade Organization (WTO) summit in Seattle, a group of protesters damaged the premises of GAP, Starbucks and Old Navy. In Mexico, the striking students of the National University:

> protested outside the embassy because of the attacks suffered by social organizations in Seattle at the protest against World Trade Organization summit. They burned flags and threw firecrackers at the building. Before and after the attack, the strikers stoned certain businesses in the Zona Rosa, smashing the mirrors and windscreens of over 10 vehicles and even stole a pair of flags from the Café Milano.[14]

Subsequently, there came Davos, Cancún, Prague, Melbourne, Nice and Zurich. In Genoa, during the 2001 G-8 meeting, a large contingent damaged banks and shops, in addition to destroying cars. During the Third Summit of the Americas (Quebec) in the same year, the black bloc took charge of bringing down the protective barrier that stopped demonstrators trying to get into the city centre: the police attacked not only the black bloc, but also the whole protest. A senior police commander who had faced the Genoa riot admitted frankly 'that the government was not trying to maintain order, *but manage disorder*'.[15] As Tarrow has stated:

> although classical anarchism all but disappeared with the Bolshevik revolution, the urge to foster participatory decentralization was reborn in the participatory movements of the 1960s in both Europe and the United States, in the peace movements of the 1980s, and in the global justice movement after the Seattle anti-World Trade Organization (WTO) campaign of 1999.[16]

On 21 December 2003, various Italian neo-anarchist groups signed an 'open letter to the anarchist and anti-authoritarian movement', calling for the internationalization of the libertarian struggle. This led to the birth of the Federación Anarquista Informal (FAI – Informal Anarchist Federation), a label that possibly unites and gives coherence to the activity of different groups. Since that time, a number of violent acts (particularly parcel bombs sent to executives of Italian corporations) have been justified by adherents of the FAI. The letter became the manifesto of libertarian organization.

Exercising their autonomy, each individual or group associated with the FAI commits to it for one specific act only (including the process of development) in order to be free to join different causes in other contexts. In any event, the FAI allows its members (individuals or groups) to use its initials, adding the particular denomination of each organization. The understanding is that anyone who belongs to it must abide by the fundamental pact of mutual support. It is a federation because 'it is diffuse and horizontal', without leaders, what Ernesto Laclau calls one of the most powerful myths of the 'totally reconciled society'; it is anarchist to the extent that it is in favour of the destruction of the state and capital, and is against the exploitation of man by man and of nature by man; it is informal since it lacks any 'notion of being in a vanguard'.[17]

Occupy Oakland, the Arab Spring, the Greek and Italian movements that reject austerity policies, and recent Brazilian protests also had a black bloc present. In July 2011, hooded youths threw objects at various fast food establishments and at an Oakland branch of the Wells Fargo Bank. A demonstration of 25,000 people in February 2012 turned Syntagma Square in Athens into a battlefield between the police and the shock group, which, equipped with gas masks, threw Molotov cocktails at the parliament building where the vote would be taken on the draconian spending cuts imposed by the European Union on an economy mired in the worst recession in the last sixty years. It was as bad as this: the imposition of 'the depoliticized technocratic model wherein bankers and other experts are allowed to squash democracy'.[18]

The Conspiracy of Fire Cells (SPF in Greek) has been active in Greece since 2008 and was incorporated into the FAI three years later. It has a repertoire of struggle that includes painting slogans, smashing the windows of banks and luxury shops, arson attacks and explosive packages, as well as the execution of 'representatives of the system'. The aim of this libertarian group is to put an end to the 'Civilization of Dominion' over people and nature entrenched in our own psyche and to lay the foundations of all human relations 'on passion' (Fourier would have something to say about that). Thus, the true conflict is not that which exists between classes, but that which places the rebel in opposition to the conformist, the individual in opposition to the willing slave. This break with an order that produces and reproduces social and mental slavery requires the permanent and (necessarily violent) insurrection of individuals and communities so 'that every single day may be an act of hostility directed against the modern way of life',[19] the only attitude consistent with the emancipation of power:

With our attacks on the system, we shift fear onto the enemy's side. We make those who have power – the bosses, the rich, journalists, judges ... remain restless and continually looking over their shoulders. Every 'suspicious vehicle', any motorbike that just happens to overtake on his side, someone 'weird' who they might already have seen somewhere or an 'imponderable' gesture could be a message of rage, ready to explode against them with full force. With the force of anarchy against the order they represent and serve.[20]

Wearing masks and balaclavas, in January 2013, young people dressed in black marched in Cairo with national flags and anarchist emblems, shouted slogans against the Muslim Brotherhood and tried to remove the wire barrier guarding the presidential palace, at that time the residence of Mohamed Morsi. The moment of greatest tension occurred in a demonstration in Rome, which was attended by about 70,000 people, when about 200 masked individuals separated from a column, throwing stones and bottles in the environs of the Ministry of Economy, torching several cars and then confronting the police in a pitched battle.[21]

The black bloc was prominent in Rio de Janeiro and São Paulo in June 2013 with the unexpected social protest that revealed the dark side of the 'Brazilian miracle', which, despite spectacular economic growth and the expansion of the middle class, has not overcome the social segregation that lies in its origins as an independent nation. Preceded by the largest number of strikes recorded since 1996, the most numerous popular demonstrations Brazil has ever seen denounced the squandering of public money on the upcoming massive sporting events and the corruption of the political class. In addition, they demanded better public services for the population, salary increases for teachers and the extension of universal rights. Those involved in the June protest were from the extreme left and the extreme right, though most of the demonstrators, and predominantly the younger ones, were participating for the first time. The demonstrations led to bloody clashes between the military police, inherited from the dictatorship and known for their brutality, and young anarchists (many barely in their teens) armed with catapults. Despite the initial hostility that these violent and belligerent allies aroused, they did generate a certain sympathy among the teachers during the October demonstrations when they took up positions as human shields between protesters and the military police. Given the demonstrations planned for the World Cup, the Brazilian government set up a riot police.[22]

The many confusing elements in the protest against the swearing-in of Enrique Peña Nieto included the deployment of the black bloc in Mexico City. It had already hit out at the police in the massive march on 7 July in protest against the presidential election. Following the pattern described above, according to a newspaper article, 'it was a structured and organized campaign of rebellion, it had coordination between factions, intelligence, operational capacity, propaganda and human resources'.[23]

A few weeks before the presidential changeover, between forty and sixty people joined the 'camp' that several groups of students from the movement #YoSoy132 had set up at the Monument to the Revolution in the previous June. At dawn on 1 December, some of those young-sters 'brought supermarket trolleys loaded with bottles, flammable materials (including thermite), wooden crates, baseball bats and back-packs that were also "loaded"'. These materials would be used a few hours later by a contingent of youths who, with their faces covered and some wearing t-shirts with red spots, forced an opening in the impos-ing metal fence that the federal police had erected to block access to San Lázaro, first by knocking down a panel, then crashing a rubbish lorry into the wire barrier.[24] Meanwhile, other groups of hooded youths wrecked street fittings nearby.

At around midday, the operation was repeated in Avenida Juárez, this time targeting the franchises of transnational corporations. The Mexico City Head of Government at the time, Marcelo Ebrard, blamed the damage on 1 December on the 'Bloque Negro' (black bloc), the 'Cruz Negra' (Black Cross) and the 'Coordinadora Estudiantil Anarquista' (Anarchist Student Coordination). The police indiscriminately beat up and captured anyone on the perimeter. One activist was mortally wounded in the police action. The Mexico black bloc, while disavow-ing 'senseless violence', admitted 'that yesterday's "destruction" had been done by the population in a *natural* response to the violence pro-voked by the state for so many years'.[25]

A twenty-one-year-old vegan, who consumes no animal products, who read Bakunin at the age of fifteen and who is currently an activist for the Frente de Liberación Animal (Animal Liberation Front), ex-plains their participation in the marches: 'it is about smashing the win-dows of some establishment or a cash machine, taking money from there and "distributing it to the people"'. Youngsters generally go for establishments that represent 'power' – 'the Oxxos run by Femsa and Bancomer cash-machines because they support bullfighting'.[26]

The second significant deployment of the black bloc tactic occurred during the 2 October demonstration that has, for forty-five years, com-memorated the massacre at the Plaza de las Tres Culturas. At about 4:30 p.m., youths mainly aged fifteen to twenty forced their way into the demonstration in the Eje Central on the corner of Avenida Juárez, destroyed some of the fittings in the Alameda, stole goods from shops and threw firecrackers, Molotov cocktails, chunks of concrete, pipes and sticks at the police.[27] For the third time in less than a year, this street became the arena for confrontation between neo-anarchists and the police, resulting in thirty-two injured officers and 102 arrests; to date, two of these have been sentenced to nearly six years in prison. The police made random arrests of anyone near the scene; while Sub-comandante Marcos gave his blessing to the neo-anarchists, asking 'Was there actually "any other choice"?', mocking, in passing, the peaceful civil resistance of Andrés Manuel López Obrador, his true competitor in the area of nonconformity: 'Is this turning off the lights a trick to avoid seeing anarchists?'[28]

Neo-anarchists

Violence found fertile ground among some of the groups that were radicalized in the 1999 UNAM student strike, which was set off by the rector's disrespectful decision to modify the General Regulation of Pay-ments (one of the causes of the 1987 Consejo Estudiantil Universitario movement). The use of force to achieve the occupation of the faculties and institutes, the widespread anti-intellectualism among young rebels (which isolated them from the rest of the university community) and the shock tactics, revealing some training in street fighting, indicate a change in attitude in the student body and a break with preceding movements. The experience of the Consejo General de Huelga (Gen-eral Strike Council), including being defeated and dispersed, was the reference point from which some of the more rigid and intransigent positions among the UNAM students would emerge, and later spread to other public universities in Mexico City. Neo-anarchists claim some of the acts of that movement as their own: 'alteration of murals, paint-ings, *okupied* [sic] auditoriums and classrooms, clashes with riot po-lice, hired thugs and conservative students'.[29]

Another cardinal reference point for the polarization of social move-ments was the 'Oaxaca commune', which lasted six months. The teachers of Section 22 of the Sindicato Nacional de Trabajadores de la Educa-ción (SNTE – National Union of Education Workers) went on strike on 22 May 2006 and occupied the historic centre of Oaxaca City with the support of a number of social groups. By the middle of June, the teachers had carried out three mass demonstrations and had facilitated the establishment of the Asamblea Popular de los Pueblos de Oaxaca (APPO – Popular Assembly of the Peoples of Oaxaca). Within this broad coalition, some of the young participants identified as anarchists. Each of the six mobilizations was larger than the one before and incorporated virtually every sector of the state. Faced by a situation it was unable to contain, the federal government ordered 4,500 police into Oaxaca City to bring it back under control. In the operation carried out on 29 October, security forces used armoured vehicles, tear gas, water cannon and firearms. Even so, it took ten hours to remove the barricades erected in August and recover the old Antequera historic centre.[30]

The crushing of the 'Oaxaca commune' claimed the lives of twenty-six people and resulted in many wounded, prisoners, destruction, torture and humiliation, terrorizing the civilian population.[31] As other guerrilla organizations had done, the Comando Magonista de Liberación (Magonista Liberation Commando) and the Tendencia Democrática Revolucionaria-Ejército del Pueblo (Revolutionary Democratic Tendency-People's Army) – a splinter group of the Ejército Popular Revolucionario (EPR – Popular Revolutionary Army) – issued a statement that read:

> We unconditionally support the effort made by the Oaxacan people to achieve their goals in a peaceful manner. We call on the media and opinion leaders to desist from concealing knowingly and tendentiously distorting the ferocious repression carried out by the government against the Oaxacan people. And we warn the ruling elite that by withdrawing the legal and peaceful means of struggle in our country, they will be solely responsible for the escalation of the social and political conflict currently in progress, as well as the armed revolutionary response.[32]

The student strike and the Oaxacan movement for self-government, both of which were finally crushed, represented an important experience for later social struggles. Both ended with the intervention of the federal police and strengthened radical tendencies, in the sense that they realised it is always useless to negotiate with the state because the only thing that public power seeks from negotiating is to gain time and then to repress subordinates when the time comes. To this must be added the war against organized crime, which, without an explicit objective, was also designed to contain outbreaks of social rebellion that emerged at the end of the first PAN administration.[33] The hardening of the state's attitude, the incessant murder of social leaders and the indifference shown to popular demands by the government of Felipe Calderón resulted in harsher responses by social movements and a repositioning of the guerrillas, who, as part of their military strategy ('prolonged popular war'), formed mass fronts to provide legal and active presence in these movements.

In the recent protests in Mexico City, there has been talk of participation by the Frente Popular Revolucionario (Popular Revolutionary Front), a remnant of the Oaxacan insurrection; the Frente Oriente

(Eastern Front), based in Mexico City and its metropolitan area, which formed the Asamblea Popular de los Pueblos de Oriente (Popular Assembly of the Towns of the East); as well as other small groups from different university schools (the Colegios de Ciencias y Humanidades (CCH – Colleges of Sciences and Humanities), for example). The Militants of the Frente Oriente identify themselves as 'communists with a proletarian perspective', though they have allowed the 'anarchists' to join their contingent during marches. A section of the hooded group who seized the rector's offices at the UNAM in April 2013 came from the CCH (others were linked with UACM strikers). In the same month, masked youths occupied the rector's offices at the UAM Iztapalapa for a few hours and, in November, others occupied the UAM Xochimilco Dean's offices.[34]

The fact that these groups converge at demonstrations and have enemies in common does not indicate an ideological affinity among all of them: some claim to be communists, others anarchists, others environmentalists and still others have more specific commitments. What does seem to be clearer is the geographical space where they come from: eastern Mexico City and the Mexico State conurbation. Both are historically significant in terms of popular movements. Chalco was the town where Julio López took up arms against Mexico State landowners in 1868. Towards the end of the 1960s, the spearhead of the popular urban movement that changed the relationship between governors and the governed in Mexico City, the Campamento 2 de Octubre, was set up in Iztacalco. In 2006, the Vicente Fox government repressed the people of San Salvador Atenco, Mexico State, who, organized as the Frente de los Pueblos en Defensa de la Tierra (Community Front in Defence of Land), stopped him building an airport on *ejido* lands in Texcoco as an alternative to Mexico City's Benito Juárez Airport. The movement's leaders spent four years in prison.[35]

Of the fifty-five acts claimed by anarchist groups in 2011, such as clashes with police and attacks on iconic companies owned by private capital (bank branches, luxury hotels, transnational cafes, car dealerships, etc.), most are attributed to the Células Autónomas de Revolución Inmediata Práxedis G. Guerrero, (the Práxedis G. Guerrero Autonomous Cells for Immediate Revolution), the CCF/FAI-México, the Frente de Liberación Animal (Animal Liberation Front), the Frente de Liberación de la Tierra (Earth Liberation Front) and las Individualidades Inclinadas hacia lo Salvaje (Individualities Inclined to Savagery) (see Table 7.1).

Two-thirds of the events occurred in Mexico City and the State of Mexico (see Table 7.2). This is explicable as Mexico City is where the

Table 7.1 Anarchist Actions in 2011

Organization	Total	%
Células Autónomas de Revolución Inmediata – Práxedis G. Guerrero	12	22
CCF/FAI-México	9	16
Frente de Liberación de la Tierra/ Frente de Liberación Animal	5	9
Individualidades Inclinadas hacia lo Salvaje	4	7
Célula Insurreccional Mariano Sánchez Añón (Mariano Sánchez Añón Insurrectional Cell)	2	4
FAI	2	4
FAI-Ácrata (FAI-Anarchist)	1	2
Célula Anarquista Revolucionaria Insurreccional (Insurrectional Revolutionary Anarchist Cell)	1	2
Anarquistas Individuales en Solidaridad (Individual Anarchists in Solidarity)	1	2
Anonymous	18	32
	55	100

Source: *Insurrectionary Anarchism in Mexico 2011*, pp. 4–11

Table 7.2 Locations of Anarchist Actions in 2011

State	Total	%
Mexico City	23	42
Mexico State	15	27
Veracruz	5	9
Guanajuato	1	2
Tamaulipas	1	2
Hidalgo	1	2
Oaxaca	1	2
Coahuila	1	2
Chihuahua	1	2
Jalisco	1	2
Not given	5	8
	55	100

Source: *Insurrectionary Anarchism in Mexico 2011*, pp. 4–11

embassies are located (several events were in solidarity with anarchists from other countries), it is the seat of the republic's powers, and there are numerous corporations and banks, while the State of Mexico has very important industrial plant and is home to several higher education institutions. In this regard, it is important to note that the goals of these organizations include besieging the 'techno-industrial system'.[36]

The groups appear to be local because their acts are generally concentrated in relatively closely spaced geographical areas. Nine acts of sabotage carried out by the Células Autónomas de Revolución Inmediata – Práxedis G. Guerrero took place in Mexico City, one in the State of Mexico and two in unspecified locations (possibly Mexico City); their targets were multinationals, embassies and public figures. The Frente de Liberación de la Tierra went for targets in Mexico State (explosives at a luxury car dealership and a police station); the first act being in solidarity with political prisoners belonging to the Greek CCF.[37]

The Individualidades Inclinadas hacia lo Salvaje sent explosive packages to higher education institutions and research centres in Mexico City (two packages) and the State of Mexico (two packages). As the CCF/FAI-Mexico is a federation, its acts covered more locations in the country: three in Mexico City, three in Mexico State, one in Jalisco, one in Chihuahua and another in an unspecified location: it had textile factories and retail chains in their sights. The Frente de Liberación Animal placed bombs in cash machines in the State of Mexico and tried to set fire to an Austrian-owned farm.

Let us pause a moment to look at some of the violent episodes of the Células Autónomas de Revolución Inmediata Práxedis G. Guerrero, the most active libertarian nucleus, published in a compendium with information from various anarchist sites, also attaching photographs of the damage that, in many cases, can be confirmed in the press.

In the last week of February 2011, the Células Autónomas sent explosive packages to the directors of Reclusorio Preventivo Varonil Norte (Men's Prison – North) and Centro Varonil de Readaptación Psicosocial (Men's Psycho-Social Re-adaptation Centre), both in Mexico City. The motive was to protest against the recruitment of prison guards, as prisons destroy human dignity and generate greater problems than those they claim to solve. There were no casualties. Around the same time, it also sent an explosive device to the director of Monsanto Mexico because of the damage Monsanto causes to the environment. Apparently, there were no fatal consequences. On the night of 26 April, a dozen youths set up barricades in Insurgentes in solidarity with one of the prisoners of the 2006 APPO movement, in protest against the murder of a Guerrero ecologist, and demanding the release of several Chilean anarchists. At dawn on 23 May, the Células Autónomas detonated homemade bombs at branches of Bancomer and Santander banks due to their corporate responsibility in the arms race and the pollution of the planet. The city prosecutor at the time, Miguel Ángel Mancera, said that such acts 'have nothing to do with the country nor with the city', so it was possible that they emanated from the 'international arena'.[38]

In September 2001, a Células Autónomas explosive device damaged a police car in Iztapalapa and the group set off a homemade bomb in the Customer Service Centre of the Federal Electricity Commission in Iztacalco, causing no injuries. In one case, this was to draw attention to the police brutality used to subjugate the Atenco movement; in the other, to draw attention to the destruction of nature caused by hydro-electric plants. Before the end of the year, the targets were Norberto Rivera, Miguel Ángel Mancera and the Italian Institute of Culture. Cardinal Rivera was selected as the representative of an oppressive, archaic and intolerant church, as an accomplice of domination and as responsible for the mental control of the population; city prosecutor Mancera was targeted to protest against the policy of law and order applied in the city 'so beloved by Social Democrats', and the Institute was targeted in solidarity with an imprisoned Italian anarchist and against the repressive state.[39]

Another anarchist publication reports various acts of sabotage between August and September 2012, carried out in Mexico City (three), Mexico State (two), Veracruz (one), Nuevo León (one), Puebla (one) and Oaxaca (one). Apart from the groups mentioned above, there also appear in this publication the Iniciativa Anarco-Insurreccionalista de Ofensiva y Solidaridad Julio Chávez López-FAI (Julio Chavez Lopez-FAI Anarcho-Insurrectionalist Initiative of Offence and Solidarity) and the Núcleo Antagonista Anarquista de Ajusticiamiento 25 de Noviembre-FAI (25 November-FAI Antagonist Anarchist Execution Nucleus). Following the pattern of the previous year, the Células Autónomas de Revolución Inmediata Práxedis G. Guerrero continued its crusade against bank branches and the CCF/FAI-México continued theirs against manufacturing industry.[40]

In the closing days of 2013, neo-anarchists recovered the Justo Sierra auditorium (the *Che Guevara*), which had been occupied by various student groups since the 1999 strike, after pushing out those who had 'brutally' closed it, declaring themselves to be 'masters and owners'.[41] Rather than opening it up to the university community, the objective seems to have been to make a forum available for the Simposio Internacional de las Jornadas Informales Anarquistas (International Symposium of Informal Anarchist Days), which was held a week later and was attended by '250 people aged between 25 and 60 years. Some 50 were foreigners from countries such as the United States, Italy and Spain', including Constantino Cavalleri, author of *El anarquismo en la sociedad posindustrial* [*Anarchy in Post-industrial Society*] (1999), and Jean Weir of Elephant Editions. Alfredo Maria Bonanno, the Italian author of *El placer armado* [*Armed Joy*] (1977), was deported by the Mexican immigration authorities from Benito Juárez Airport before he could attend. Greek political prisoners sent a written contribution to the event. Possibly linked to this, at the beginning of 2014, two Canadians and one Mexican were arrested on charges of throwing Molotov cocktails at the building of the Secretaría de Comunicaciones y Transportes (Ministry of Communications and Transport) in Mexico City.[42]

The implications of what historical anarchism called 'direct action' are various. The most immediate is that it denies politics because, in the first place, it considers politics to be inherently spurious; and, second, the most powerful contemporary party formations seek a hypothetical centre, which leads to the dilution of differences, and consequently choosing between party A or B is meaningless. In any case, power belongs not to the people, but to big capital. Moreover, the return of the PRI to the presidency would demonstrate the failure of the democratic path that the left had envisaged and hoped for since it adopted the electoral route following the political reform of 1977. The insistent message in Mexican neo-anarchistic documents is to the effect that the 'social democrats' (i.e. the PRD authorities) are obeying authoritarian orders by imprisoning young rebels, in line with that anti-political direction in which every act of government is seen as being coercive. From this perspective, power is not to be taken, but destroyed.

In public demonstrations, the act itself in principle precludes any negotiation with authority, not only by neo-anarchists, but also with all those involved in the protest. The radical stance, even if it is still clearly a minority position, is affirmed in the act of force and imposes its own logic on the whole social movement. It has no ulterior motives, for, even though its stated enemies are the state and capital ('attacking private property, and their servile guardians, it claims the superiority of life over the dictatorship of objects', as the Coordinadora de las Sombras (Coordination of Shadows) stated shortly after the events of 2 October 2013), it is consummated in the action: each thing that is destroyed or each policeman put out of action is more than just the *means* in a long-term struggle – as classical anarchism would have understood it when imagining a future – as they constitute the very object of the action. For postmodern rebels, they are the ultimate purpose in a present that has no horizon: 'they would not let us dream, now we will not let them sleep', they warn.[43]

Conclusion

The growth and geographical expansion achieved by neo-anarchism during this century so far stands out, developing in Europe (Greece, Italy and Germany), the Arab world (Egypt) and Latin America (Brazil, Chile and Mexico), although its presence can also be seen in public disturbances in multiple locations (Vancouver and Toronto, 2010; London, 2011; Los Angeles, 2012). The streets are now theirs. In spite of the fact that these are small decentralized groups, their demonstrated capacity for action and articulation is not insignificant, and the project promoted by the Greek CCF to form the 'Black International' (International Working People's Association (IWPA)) should be taken into account. Although anarchism never disappeared as a political ideology, easily adapting to a rebel ethos that is not limited to a particular historical period, its expansion in the era of globalization contrasts with the ebb in socialist thought on the left and the increasingly evident inability of liberalism to tackle the current civilizational crisis.

The neo-anarchist position poses head-on questions of the way of being in today's society, the instrumental rationality that provides the foundations for its technological development and the cynical reasoning that governs its public ethics. A present-day scenario characterized by unemployment, exclusion, racism, violence and the destruction of nature feed this disenchanted perspective in which the explosion of a Molotov cocktail represents a liberating act and chaos represents desirable order as, for better or worse, it is the only result that our intentional act can attain – nihilistic insofar as it lacks purpose and presumes the fracturing of historicity:

> The nihilism of contemporary culture is not only the crisis of values and the absence of shared transcendences: it is also the fact that the action of man does not inflame more between the two poles of tradition and revolution ... Neither history nor the future but the timeliness of the present moment is the horizon for the action of the contemporary man.[44]

However, while this may be so, along with Žižek some of us may still regret 'that opposition to the system cannot articulate itself in the guise of a realistic alternative, or at least a meaningful utopian project, but [can] only take the shape of a meaningless outburst', showing 'a grave illustration of our predicament' and 'a spirit of revolt without revolution'.[45]

Notes

1. Rudé, *The Crowd in History*; Thompson, *Customs in Common*, p. 89. I cite the latter.
2. The change in the social movement repertoire in the nineteenth century reduced or put an end to their violence. Tilly and Wood, *Social Movements 1768–2008*.
3. On this topic, see Robert Linhart's formidable novel *L'Établi*. [*The Assembly Line*]
4. Tilly and Wood, *Social Movements 1768–2008*.
5. Hardt and Negri, *Multitude*. As outlined by Laclau, you can see the plebs transformed into 'the people' in his *La razón populista*. In a pessimistic diagnosis, Alain Touraine believes that 'the world of the oppressed has become so diverse and fragmented that it will not be able to produce a historical actor, that is to say, a will to collective action that will have consequences for the orientation of society'. Touraine, *After the Crisis*.
6. Tarrow, *Power in Movement*; cited in '¿Quiénes protestaron el 1 de diciembre and por qué? I' [Who Protested on 1 December and Why?], *Animal Político*, 25 November 2013.
7. The adventurous violence that Pereyra speaks of in *Política y violencia*, p. 38.
8. Arrighi, Hopkins and Wallerstein, *Antisystemic Movements*.
9. Žižek, *Violence*; Balibar, *Violencias, identidades y civilidad*, p. 107; Tilly, *Democracy*; Davis, *Planet of Slums*. Against domination, the violent response of subordinates contains 'a de facto legitimacy'. Balibar, 'La necesidad cívica de la sublevación', p. 294.
10. Escalante Gonzalbo, 'Homicidios 2008–2009', pp. 38 ff.; Hope, 'Violencia 2007–2011', p. 40.
11. Illades and Santiago, *Estado de Guerra*, pp. 131 ff.
12. Violent forms of the repertoire of contention are the easiest to initiate as they require few resources. Tarrow, *Power in Movement*.
13. 'Black blocs sao politizados e expressam revolta contra injustiças sociais, diz pesquisador' [Black Blocs are Politicized and Express Revolt against Social Injustice, Says Researcher], *Rede Brasil Atual*, 28 October 2013.
14. 'Quien resulte responsable' [Whoever is Responsible], *Reforma*, 23 January 2000.
15. Agamben, 'El gobierno de la inseguridad', p. 28, my emphasis.
16. Tarrow, *Power in Movement*.
17. *Europol Te-Sat 2013*. Retrieved 12 October 2016 from https://www.europol.europa.eu/sites/default/files/publications/europol_te-sat2013_lr_0.pdf, pp. 31–33; APA, 'Chronologie de la FAI'. Retrieved 12 October 2016 from http://apa.online.free.fr/article.php3?id_article=236; Laclau, *On Populist Reason*; 'Carta abierta al movimiento anarquista and antiautoritario' [Open

Letter to the Anarchist and Anti-authoritarian Movement], 21 December 2003. I cite the latter.

18. 'Black Bloc and Occupy Oakland', *Corrente*, 11 June 2011; 'Grecia: piazza Syntagma si svuota: arrivano i black bloc' [Syntagma Square is Empty: The Black Bloc Arrives], *Blitz Quotidiano*, 12 February 2012; Žižek, *The Year of Dreaming Dangerously*. I cite the latter.

19. Conspiración de Células del Fuego, 'Red Anarquista Internacional de Acción and Solidaridad' [Fire Cells Conspiracy, 'International Anarchist Network of Action and Solidarity'], 12 January 2011. Retrieved 12 October 2016 from http://liberaciontotal.lahaine.org/?p=311&print=1; Conspiración de Células del Fuego, *La nueva guerrilla urbana anarquista*, pp. 47, 44, 59.

20. Conspiración de Células del Fuego, *La nueva guerrilla urbana anarquista*, p. 29.

21. '"Bloque negro" hace presencia en Egipto' ['Black Bloc' Present in Egypt], *24 Horas*, 26 January 2013; 'Roma si ferma per il corteo in centro Sos infiltrati, espulsi 5 black bloc' [Rome Stops for the Parade in the Centre. Infiltrators SOS, Five Black Bloc Expelled]. http://roma.repubblica.it/cronaca/2013/10/19/news/roma_si_ferma_per_il_corteo_in_centro_sos_inf iltrati_espulsi_5_black_bloc-68911866/

22. Marcelo Badaró, 'Sobre toupeiras e bumerangues: as jornadas de junho e as lutas socias em curso no Brasil' [Moles and Boomerangs: The Days of June and Ongoing Social Struggles in Brazil], *Rubra Colectivo*, 18 October 2013; Singer, 'Rebellion in Brazil', p. 31; Secco, 'As Jornadas de Junho', p. 71; Alberto J. Olvera, 'Movilizaciones masivas en Brasil: de la normalización neoliberal a la esperanza democrática' [Massive Mobilizations in Brazil: From Neoliberal Normalization to Democratic Hope], *Este País*, November 2013, p. 42; 'Brasil crea policía antimotines para el Mundial' [Brazil Creates Riot Police for the World Cup], *El Universal*, 3 January 2013.

23. 'Bloque Negro and EPM-LN' [Black Bloc and EPM-LN], *Reporte Índigo*, 3 December 2012.

24. Cited in Adolfo Gilly, 'La provocación del primer día' [The Provocation of the First Day], *La Jornada*, 17 December 2012.

25. '¿Quiénes protestaron el 1 de diciembre and por qué? I'; 'Muere el activista Kuykendall, herido en el operativo policiaco el 1 December 2012' [Kuykendall, the Activist Wounded in 1 December, 2012 Police Operation, Dies], *La Jornada*, 26 January 2014; 'Indemnizarán a detenidos el 1 December 2012' [Those Arrested on 1 December 2012 to Be Compensated], *La Jornada*, 11 April 2014. 'Comunicado de Bloque Negro México sobre los acontecimientos del 1 de diciembre' [Communiqué from Mexico Black Bloc on the Events of 1 December], *Webguerrillero. Periódico digital de las izquierdas del siglo xxi*, 2 December 2012. Retrieved 12 October 2016 from http://periodicodigitalwebguerrillero.blogspot.mx. Emphasis added. According to a newspaper article, the Cruz Negra Anarquista [Anarchist Black Cross] was formed in 2006 and the Coordinadora Estudiantil Anarquista [Anarchist Student Coordinator] in 2010. 'Grupos anarquistas,

la mano que creo el caos en la Ciudad de México' [Anarchist Groups, the Hand that Created Chaos in Mexico City], *El País*, 2 December 2012.

26. '¿Quiénes protestaron el 1 de diciembre and por qué? I'. (OXXOs are convenience stores. Femsa is the company that produces Coca Cola in Mexico.)

27. 'Scattered attacks' do not require much coordination or large amounts of violence, which allows small (violent) cores of (non-violent) social movements to carry them out. Tilly, *The Politics of Collective Violence*, pp. 171, 173.

28. 'Violencia en marcha del 2 de octubre; encapuchados atacan con bombas molotov' [Violence at 2 October March; Masked Men Attack with Molotov Cocktails], *Imagen Radio*, 2 October 2013; 'EL Bloque negro (¿anarquista?) en los medios mexicanos' [(Anarchist?) Black Bloc in the Mexican Media), *Radio Nederland Internacional*, 2 November 2013; 'Líder del Bloque Negro, uno de los detenidos del 2OctMx'[Leader of Black Bloc, one of Those Detained 20 October], *El Universal*, 3 October 2013; '"Precio" por protestar: 5 años and 9 meses' ['Price' for Protesting: Five Years and Nine Months], *Proceso*, 26 January 2014; 'Lluvia de amparos contra los abusos del gobierno capitalino' [Inundation of Constitutional Relief Countersuits against Mexico City Government Abuses], *Proceso*, 6 April 2014; cited in 'Censura el *Subcomandante Marcos* ataques a anarquistas and las "reformas estructurales"' [Subcomandante Marcos Censures 'Structural Reforms" and Attacks on Anarchists], *La Jornada*, 5 November 2013.

29. *Rabia and Acción*, No. 9, January 2012, On the radicalization of the strikers, see Meneses Reyes, 'Memorias de la huelga estudiantil de la UNAM, 1999–2000', pp. 84 ff.; 'A causa de la alteración del mural de David Alfaro Siqueiros, detuvieron a tres activistas' [Three Activists Detained for Alteration to Siqueiros Mural], *Reforma*, 24 July 1999.

30. 'Cronología del conflicto en Oaxaca' [Chronology of the Conflict in Oaxaca], *El Universal*, 30 October 2006; Sotelo Marbán, *Oaxaca*, p. 147; Estrada Saavedra, 'La anarquía organizada', pp. 915, 910.

31. Osorno, *Oaxaca sitiada*, pp. 289, 282.

32. Centro de Documentación de los Movimientos Armados (CEDEMA – Centre for the Documentation of Armed Movements), Comando Magonista de Liberación and la Tendencia Democrática Revolucionaria-Ejército del Pueblo, 'Comunicado núm. 2' [Magonista Liberation Commando and the Democratic Revolutionary Tendency-People's Army, 'Communique No. 2'], Oaxaca, 27 November 2006.

33. Illades and Santiago, *Estado de Guerra*, p. 68.

34. Arturo Rodríguez García, 'El Estado es el violento' [The State is the Violent One], *Proceso*, 19 May 2013; cited in '¿Quiénes protestaron el 1 de diciembre and por qué? I'; 'Encapuchados toman rectoría de la UNAM' [Hooded Protesters Occupy Rectory of the UNAM], *El Universal*, 20 April 2013; 'Encapuchados toman la rectoría de la UAM Iztapalapa' [Hooded Protesters Occupy Rectory of the UAM Iztapalapa], *Excélsior*, 24 April 2013; 'Toman "encapuchados" rectoría de UAM Xochimilco' ['Hooded' Protesters Occupy Rectory of the UAM Xochimilco], *Milenio*, 6 November 2013.

35. Marván Laborde, 'De la ciudad del presidente al gobierno propio, 1970–2000', pp. 498 ff.; 'Liberan a los doce presos atenquenses' [Twelve Atenco Prisoners Freed], *La Jornada*, 1 July 2010.
36. Marco Appel, 'Alarma por los anarquistas mexicanos' [Alarm over Mexican Anarchists], *Proceso*, 21 April 2013; Marco Appel, 'Anarquistas: lo del 1 de diciembre fue "autodefensa"' [Anarchists: 1 December was 'self-defence'], *Proceso*, 16 December 2012; 'Grupo anarquista se adjudica atentados a Mexibús' [Anarchist Group Claims Responsibility for Mexibus Attacks], *El Universal*, 1 November 2015.
37. Conspiración de Células del Fuego, 'Liberación total ... Contra toda forma de dominación and en defensa de la Tierra' [Total Liberation ... against All Forms of Domination and in Defence of the Earth], liberaciontotal .lahaine.org.
38. Ibid., pp. 12, 15, 17, 19; 'Alertan cárceles del DF por el envío de explosivos' [Mexico City Prisons Warned of Explosives Shipment], *El Universal*, 12 March 2011; 'Explotan bombas caseras en bancos Santander and Bancomer' [Homemade Bombs Explode at Santander and Bancomer Banks], *La Crónica de Hoy*, 23 May 2011. I cite the latter.
39. *Insurrectionary Anarchism in Mexico 2011*, pp. 27, 32–33, 39–41, 43; 'CFE descarta lesionados por explosión de bomba casera en cajeros' [CFE Rules out Injuries from Homemade Bomb Explosion at Cash Machines], *Periódicodigital.mx*, 23 September 2011; 'Envían paquete explosivo al cardenal Rivera' [Explosive Package Sent to Cardinal Rivera], *El Universal*, 26 November 2011; 'Explosivo en la PGR era para Mancera' [Explosive at PGR was for Mancera], *El Universal*, 28 November 2011; 'Estalla artefacto en el Instituto Italiano de Cultura de la Ciudad de México' [Device Explodes at the Italian Institute of Culture in Mexico City], *La Prensa*, 12 December 2011.
40. *Conspiración Ácrata*, No. 8, November 2012; 'Hallan artefacto explosivo en sucursal bancaria de la colonia Obrera' [Explosive Device Found at Bank Branch in the Obrera Borough], *Excélsior*, 18 September 2012.
41. Cited in 'Anarquistas echan del auditorio de Filosofía a grupos que lo tomaron hace cuatro años' [Anarchists Throw out Groups Who Occupied Philosophy Faculty Auditorium Four Years Ago], *La Jornada*, 21 December 2013. Three months later, the displaced student 'collectives' unsuccessfully attempted to reclaim the space. 'Disputan dos grupos ocupación del auditorio *Che* Guevara' [Two Groups Dispute Occupation of the *Che Guevara* Auditorium], *La Jornada*, 4 March 2014; 'Los 15 años del secuestro del *Che Guevara*' [The Fifteen-Year Seizure of the *Che Guevara*], *Milenio*, 25 February 2016.
42. 'Deportan del Aeropuerto Internacional de la Ciudad de México a líder anarquista' [Anarchist Leader Deported from Mexico City International Airport], *El Universal*, 28 December 2013; Conspiración de Células del Fuego, *Seamos peligrosos... por la difusión de la Internacional Negra*, 2013 [Let's be dangerous ... in favour of the spread of the Black International, 2013]; 'Definen hoy situación por detenidos por bombas molotov' [Legal

Situation of Those Detained for Molotov Cocktails to Be Decided Today],
El Universal, 9 January 2014. The three detainees would be released a year
and a half later for lack of evidence. 'Falla PGR al acusar a extranjeras
anarquistas' [PGR Failure in Accusation of Foreign Anarchists], *Reforma*,
1 May 2015.

43. 'Los encapuchados responden ... ¡Con la revuelta no podrán!' [Hooded
Protesters Respond ... They Won't Be Able to Handle the Revolt!], www
.proceso.com. The Greek neo-anarchists say, 'We choose the shadows of
the moon to plan our plots. So, as soon as the darkness of night bids us
welcome, we become the bottle of nitro-glycerine balancing on the head
of a pin.' Conspiración de Células del Fuego, *La nueva guerrilla urbana
anarquista*, p. 63.

44. Volpi, *El nihilismo*, p. 143.

45. Žižek, *Violence*; Žižek, 'Answers without Questions'. In the same sense,
Balibar, Touraine and Arrighi: 'insurrection only makes sense if you join in
a process of transformation of institutions'. Balibar, 'La necesidad cívica
de la sublevación' (The need for civic revolt], p. 298; we have observed 'the
absence of organized reactions among employees and the general public',
so that 'an extreme asymmetry between an economic world overwhelmed
by the financial sphere and the possibilities of social action must be recognized'. Touraine, *After the Crisis*. 'Without strategy, there is no reason what-
soever to believe that there will be an invisible hand that ensures that the
transformation takes place in the desired direction, even if it does finally
cause the collapse of the capitalist world-economy'. Arrighi, Hopkins and
Wallerstein, *Antisystemic Movements*.

Chapter 8

The Autumn of Discontent

The international economic crises of 2008 and 2011 led not only to the impoverishment of millions of people but also damaged the reputation of the political class. And little wonder: the association between corrupt business practices of big capital and the venal politicians who made them possible made it clear that they did not exactly owe a duty to their constituents. Saint-Simon considered politicians to be members of the parasitical classes, and the conviction that the economy has destroyed the autonomy of politics is currently on the rise; we are experiencing a process of 'de-democratization'.[1]

Despite its broad social base, the regime that came to power as a result of the Mexican Revolution did not consolidate the public reputation of the political class; on the contrary, it fuelled the conviction that honesty was not among its civic virtues. One might think that democratic legitimacy would have improved the public opinion of politicians, but judging by the polls on trust in institutions, political parties consistently come last as far as public trust is concerned. Furthermore, in what should have been noted with concern, in the 2009 midterm election – when an obstinate campaign was carried out against the political establishment – a total of nearly two million blank ballots were cast, the highest figure ever registered. By 2013, the first Encuesta Iberoamericana de Juventudes (Ibero-American Youth Survey) showed that it was young Spaniards and Mexicans who had the highest levels of distrust for institutions, including, undoubtedly, the political class.[2]

The disenchantment of youth cannot be explained away by a rebel ethos that is prevalent in that stage of life (Daniel Cohn-Bendit called on the young to distrust anyone over thirty),[3] but is a direct response to young people being members of the age group hardest hit by the very poor growth of the Mexican economy over the past three decades, frequently being the victims of police extortion and currently making up the reserves of the forces of organized crime. It is unsurprising, therefore, that university students took prominent parts in 1986, 1999, 2012 and 2014: in 1986 and 1999 to preserve *quasi*-free public education, in 2012 against private television's alliance with the PRI, and in 2014 supporting the demand for the return alive of the forty-three students who went missing in Iguala on the night of 26 September 2014 alive.

There was also the revival of the teachers' movement caused by educational reform, which far surpassed social reaction against other structural reforms (for example, energy), where greater resistance had been expected, given the powerful reference point of revolutionary nationalism in the collective imagination. However, that was not what happened: a sectorial claim was stronger than one with historical roots – whether or not we conceive of it as myth – and affected a larger proportion of the population.

But social mobilization was not limited to the cities. In certain regions where organized crime had a significant presence, vigilante groups formed to protect the population. Although the phenomenon is not new (for example, armed resistance to the *caciques* and landowners' 'guardias blancas'), what stands out is how fast and how widely the community's *autodefensa* groups spread. Even in places like Tepalcatepec, Michoacán, armed mobilization had overtones of popular insurrection, and this explains the federal government's haste to restore control and promote the fantasy of the rule of law in the state.

Beyond the obviously violent nature of the self-defence groups, straddling the boundary between criminal violence and a negligent state (itself a form of violence, according to scholars), what stands out is that this repertoire is frequently used in collective action. Possibly, the phenomenon is related to the fact that Mexican society has naturalized violence, and violence moreover allows social movements to economize means, producing immediate effects.[4] We might also add that the discrediting of the political class as a whole – because of its proximity to the world of money (legal or illegal) and consequently to corruption – leads to the assumption that there are no substantive differences between the parties and therefore no options for change that do not involve direct action. If this is so, I do not consider that this violent repertoire already dominates social mobilization, but, undoubtedly, affects the collective imaginary, showing itself to be superior to its strength (via television or press images, and the rejection it causes in sectors that are not mobilized) and thus allowing it to overpower the other players involved.

What has happened in recent years to explain the revival and radicalization of social movements? Why are young people again taking to the streets? How has organized civil society reacted to the return of the PRI? Why are violent forms of collective action on the rise? What is the state response to social mobilization? What are the consequences of this for developing Mexican democracy? These are some of the questions that guide this chapter, which, rather than offering answers, attempts to add some elements to the public debate.

'They were Taken Alive: We Want Them Back Alive'

Although with the return of the PRI, the strategy against crime employed by the state has followed the guidelines set by the previous administration, both the emphasis on structural reforms and the emergence of social movements have put human rights problems and the penetration of organized crime into various areas of the state's spheres of activity on the back burner in public debate. Nonetheless, the extrajudicial execution of twenty-one alleged criminals by the army in San Pedro Limón (Tlatlaya, State of Mexico) on 30 June 2014 and the murder of six people in Iguala on 26 September 2014, plus the aforementioned forced disappearance of forty-three student teachers from the Escuela Normal Rural Isidro Burgos, Ayotzinapa, has made these pending issues pressing once again, exacerbated by government inaction. The news of Tlatlaya, and especially Ayotzinapa, flew around the world, shocking international public opinion. In Mexico, it provoked expressions of solidarity and outrage unseen since 1968 or 1985.

Several factors established the Iguala massacre as an event – 'the effect that seems to exceed its causes', as characterized by Žižek[5] – within national consciousness: first, the evidence that public force is obedient to crime and acts against society; second, because it dealt with poor youths in one of the most neglected states in the country; third, due to the incapacity of the state to protect the population, or even of carry out a decent investigation into the dreadful facts. Furthermore, as noted above, the federal government's deliberate intention of silencing the media with respect to the violence – the events at Iguala took public opinion by surprise when it was 'bombarded' by daily accounts of government success ('Move Mexico!') and the celebrated harmony of the main political parties (Pact for Mexico) – also fed into this process. Finally, it was thanks to the Ayotzinapa students' substantial group cohesion and ability to mobilize, a relative advantage compared with other victims of mass crimes (e.g. San Fernando).

The mobilization for Ayotzinapa has united all those involved in collective action in recent years – the Movimiento por la Paz con Justicia y Dignidad (MPJD – Movement for Peace with Justice and Dignity), students, teachers and *autodefensa* groups – with their peaceful and violent components. Thus, the strength of the current protest not only lies in the chanting of the slogan 'They were taken alive: we want them back alive' – the slogan of Rosario Ibarra de Piedra's Eureka Committee – but the cumulative effect of the other mobilizations. This slogan, I think, supplies the content that Ernesto Laclau called the 'empty signifier', a space within which the specific demands in the popular field are unified: it is simultaneously one and all.[6]

In contrast, the dimensions of the event shrank the already diminished political class, which, from their respective positions, party initials, tendency or tribe could only come up with the tactic of distancing themselves from the 'barbarity'. A tragedy occurred: in principle, no one was responsible – there were only victims. While this showed the wisdom of burying one's head in the sand, social mobilization began in Chilpancingo, with the governor and the municipality of Iguala as its targets. From then on, the Coordinadora Estatal de Trabajadores de la Educación de Guerrero (CETEG – State Coordinator of Education Workers of Guerrero) would take the lead in Chilpancingo, the state capital, acting as the organized base supporting the other social forces, including the militant students and parents from Ayotzinapa. And, with their violent repertoire, dissident teachers coloured the whole movement in the city. On 29 September, some three thousand people marched up to the local Congress 'to demand the impeachments of Governor Angel Aguirre Rivero and the mayor of Iguala, Jose Luis Abarca Velazquez'. Once the meeting was over, youths from the Federación de Estudiantes Campesinos y Socialistas de México (FECSM – Mexican Federation of Socialist and Peasant Students) 'smashed the windows of the entrance to the library'. There was simultaneously a small demonstration in Acapulco. In the evening, about a thousand people marched in Chilpancingo again, holding candles 'to demand of federal and state governments that justice be done for the murdered students ... as well as for the footballer David Josue García Evangelista, who died on the same day, and for the other two victims of armed aggression in Iguala'.[7]

The demonstration that took place on 2 October in Chilpancingo was much larger; the contingent occupied a stretch of the Autopista del Sol (the major highway from Mexico City to Acapulco) over three kilometres long. This was attended by students from the FECSM, teachers from the CETEG, teachers and students of the Autonomous University of Guerrero and the Colegio de Bachilleres, peasants, housewives, students and parents from Ayotzinapa. The protest demanded that the forty-three students missing in Iguala be presented alive and reiterated the demands for the suspension of Aguirre Rivero and the criminal prosecution of both Abarca Velazquez and Felipe Flores Velazquez, head of the city police and the mayor's cousin. Only a few slogans were painted on public buildings, while in Morelia, about five thousand people commemorating the massacre at the Plaza de las Tres Culturas offered support to the student teachers of Guerrero. A day earlier, students of the Instituto Politécnico Nacional (IPN – National Polytechnic Institute) had marched to the Interior Ministry demanding the repeal of internal regulations, the cancellation of the new curricula and the resignation of the Institute's director.[8] By this time, Abarca Velazquez and his security chief had already escaped (there being no arrest warrant against them), the governor was silent and the federal government continued without making any response or initiating any investigation.

The FECSM temporarily occupied the premises of Guerrero's Attorney General on 7 October, pasting photographs of the missing onto the walls. The ministry police officers who were responsible for guarding the building fled at the approach of about five hundred students willing to take it by force. Later, accompanied by the parents of the missing, they moved to the Autopista del Sol, where they took over the toll booths and allowed motorists free passage. That afternoon, three hundred members of the UPOEG, the Guerrero *autodefensa* group, started the Caravana por el Desarrollo y la Paz (Caravan for Peace and Development) moving towards Iguala, later joining the search for the missing begun by the state government. That same day, the national President of the PRD, Carlos Navarrete, offered a 'heartfelt' apology to the parents of the missing students. By then, the federal government had made its first arrests, starting with twenty-two city policemen, and the EPR was already talking about 'a crime of the state'.[9]

On 8 October, the movement received a response from outside Guerrero – demonstrations in approximately 25 states chanting the slogan: 'They were taken alive: we want them back alive.' According to the press, 'the demonstrations took place in small municipalities, with gatherings of 300 people, to large cities like Guadalajara, where about 7,000 people came together'. In San Cristobal de las Casas, about 20,000 Zapatistas held a silent march by way of mourning. In Guanajuato and Leon, places where this type of action goes against the grain, more than two thousand students and citizens, who were also outraged by the murder of a student at the hands of the police, came together, carrying candles and banners. For a second consecutive day, a crowd in Chilpancingo took to the streets, repeating their demands. In Tlapa de Comonfort, some fifty youths attacked the city hall. In Mexico City, thousands of people demanded the return of the missing students and the suspension of Aguirre Rivero. Left-leaning intellectuals and leaders (including Cuauhtémoc Cárdenas, who was jeered and attacked by a small group that called him a coward, a traitor and a murderer) joined the protest. Yet, it was only when the demands spread beyond the borders of Guerrero that President Peña Nieto alluded to the problem, noting 'signs of institutional weakness in parts of the country'.[10]

The CETEG began a strike on 9 October and, the following day, a rally in Chilpancingo, which included the Consejo de Ejidos y Comunidades Opositoras a La Parota (Council of Ejidos and Communities Opposed to La Parota). The local branch of the Cámara Nacional de Comercio (CANACO – National Chamber of Commerce) insisted on the suspension of Aguirre Rivero, calling for a 'popular assembly' on 15 October. For its part, the local Congress initiated the parliamentary process to deprive Abarca Velazquez of his constitutional immunity (*fuero*). On 12 and 13 October, there were demonstrations in Chilpancingo and other parts of Guerrero. On 13 October, 'students, teachers and parents set offices ablaze and smashed windows at the state's government palace and the town hall'. In Ayotzinapa two days later, the Asamblea Nacional Popular (ANP – National People's Congress) was formed, with the participation of the CETEG and other social organizations. In addition to demanding the return of the missing students, the dismissal of Aguirre Rivero and the suspension of the branches of government in the state, the ANP also aimed at the establishment of 'a constituent assembly of the people of Guerrero, creating the best possible conditions for political, social and economic, cultural proposals, where democracy derives from the sovereignty of the people, working with the appointment of an honourable government' – in short, to refound the state. That same day, but this time in Ciudad Universitaria, Mexico City, a demonstration of students from a wide range of backgrounds chanted the slogans 'Justice!', 'We want them back alive!' and 'Peña Out!' in the context of the first forty-eight-hour general strike at the university.[11]

On 17 October, a remarkable demonstration took place along the Miguel Aleman coast road in Acapulco, with the crowd chanting: 'Assassins and police are the same filth!' and 'Terror comes from the state!' There were also demonstrations in seven other states. Five days later, a march in Iguala, featuring the participation of the CETEG and the FECSM, retraced the route of the missing students, insisting on Aguirre Rivero's resignation, Abarca Velazquez's punishment and the suspension of the branches of government in the state, a demand which, as noted above, had been proposed by the ANP. Teachers set fire to the town hall and vandalized Plaza Tamarindos, a shopping centre in Iguala. In other parts of the state, there were more mobilizations. On 22 October, the second general strike began at the university. The following day, Aguirre Rivero finally announced that he would ask Congress to grant him a leave of absence. Before the end of the month, the ANP began to occupy town halls throughout the state and set up municipal councils.[12]

Illustrations 8.1–8.14 Romuald de Richemont, 'Mexico: 43 Students Still Missing. November 20, Mexican Revolution Day Protest, 2014'

Illustration 8.2

Illustration 8.3

Illustration 8.4

Illustration 8.5

Illustration 8.6

Illustration 8.7

Illustration 8.8

Illustration 8.9

Illustration 8.10

Illustration 8.11

Illustration 8.12

Illustration 8.13

Illustration 8.14

'It was the State'

But neither depriving Abarca Velazquez of immunity nor Aguirre Rivero's leave of absence slowed down the mobilization. On 5 November,
students in the Zócalo in Mexico City were shouting 'They were taken
alive; we want them back alive!', along with a chorus of 'Peña Out!' and
adding 'It was the state!' against the background of the third university
general strike, this time lasting seventy-two hours; there was also a
proposal for an indefinite national strike starting on 20 November. Acts
of protest for Ayotzinapa were held in twenty-two states. One day later,
alleged neo-anarchists torched a Metrobus and Ciudad Universitaria
station, while a contingent of teachers and various social organizations occupied the State Palace of Justice in Chilpancingo.[13]

The presentation of the results of the investigation by the Attorney
General of the Republic on 7 November sparked further social anger.
According to the official theory, the missing students had been executed by the Guerreros Unidos and it would not even be possible to
recover their cremated bodies, as the ashes had been dumped in the
Cocula River. As evidence, the prosecutor presented to the media nothing more than statements made by three suspects and few charred
human remains.[14] At night, young people from different backgrounds
assembled at the Ángel de la Independencia, carrying candles and banners reading 'It wasn't drug traffickers, it was the State', 'Peña Out',
'They were taken alive: we want them back alive' and the MPJD slogan
'We've had it up to here!' reappearing.[15]

The violence got worse in Mexico City and in Chilpancingo on 8
November as a result of the frustration many felt, given the adverse
results. In Mexico City, a small group, presumed to be a small group of
neo-anarchists, attempted to set fire to the main gate of the National
Palace.[16] The slogan 'Ayotzinapa lives! The state is dead!' appeared. And
in Chilpancingo, about six hundred students from the FECSM torched
trucks near the Government Palace, which was extensively damaged.
Even though Aguirre Rivero had fallen and an interim governor was in
office, the Movimiento Popular Guerrerense (MPG), believed to be part
of the ANP, 'agreed to compel the disappearance of the three branches
of government and proposed the creation of municipal citizen committees and popular councils to govern from the districts, neighbour-
hoods and communities of the state's 81 municipalities'.[17]

Community police appeared in Chilpancingo on 9 November, the
date when the '43 for 43' march arrived in Mexico City, walking from
Iguala. The following day, hooded student teachers blocked access to
Acapulco International Airport for four hours. On 12 November, the

CETEG mobilization included torching PRI headquarters, which had already been attacked on multiple occasions, and the state Congress building, as well as some cars. In solidarity on the following day, Michoacán student teachers destroyed the PRI building in Morelia and closed the airport. Those in Oaxaca blocked in employees of the Ciudad Judicial for a time. Hours later, Acapulco's shopkeepers and hoteliers requested federal intervention to stop the social mobilization doing further damage to their businesses by driving away tourism. On 15 November, a CNTE contingent marched to the Zócalo in Mexico City. The previous day, the FECSM and the CETEG had also marched in Chilpancingo.[18]

A month and a half after the events of Iguala, the Mexican Supreme Court, with one of its judges acting as spokesperson, made a reference to the slaughter and urged the new judges to 'make it known to citizens that, in every sentence, in every agreement, in every decision we make, that we are listening to their demands for justice'. The legislature was not far behind and, in the budget proposal for 2015, allocated an additional 400 million pesos to rural teacher training colleges, channelling 50 million pesos to Ayotzinapa 'so that students would not have to make street collections to support their curricular activities'.[19] After a tour of China and Australia and in the midst of the most severe crisis of his administration (though he was really trying to get away from it while his cabinet tried to sort out the situation), Peña Nieto returned, emboldened: instead of accounting for himself,[20] he required others to account for themselves. Turning the volume up, a little later he denounced an 'orchestrated effort to destabilize the country' and 'attack the plan that his government is promoting'.[21]

Some days earlier, the EPR had claimed responsibility for the bombing of the Soriana store in Valle de Aragon (Ecatepec) in protest against the disappearance of the forty-three students and calling for the establishment of a truth commission 'to investigate the disappearance of the students, to be constituted by family representatives, the rural teacher training college, town representatives and independent organizations'. Meanwhile, the parents of the missing students formed three caravans to travel the country and demand that their children be returned alive. At daybreak on 20 November, two explosive devices exploded at Banamex and Scotiabank cash machines in Naucalpan and, at night, three demonstrations came together at the Zócalo in Mexico City, again demanding that the students be returned alive. At the meeting, the parents of the missing affirmed their determination to change 'this country once and for all; we are ready to send these institutions to hell because they are no use anymore'. When the majority of participants had withdrawn, there was apparently a confrontation between the police and a group of suspected infiltrators, but, according to the testimony of those detained (who were released ten days later for lack of evidence), what really happened was that the Mexico City police had attacked passers-by.[22]

After 20 November, the demonstrations reduced in their intensity in Mexico City, but in the State of Guerrero, they continued with the same force. IPN students had very successful negotiations to end the strike at the institution and restart classes on 15 December at certain schools and on 7 January in the remainder. With their violent repertoire, members of the CETEG (occupying the city centre of Chilpancingo) attacked the offices of the Guerrero State Attorney General (1 December), burned the busts of former state governors (3 December), occupied the offices of the Instituto Nacional Electoral (INE – National Electoral Institute) on 8 December and publicly humiliated local leaders of the PRD and Movimiento Ciudadano (MC), forcing them to march along the side road of the Autopista del Sol with banners saying 'We are PRD crooks' and 'Peña Nieto Out!' (9 December). As had been agreed during the establishment of the ANP, the parents of the missing students demanded the suspension of the branches of government in Guerrero, while the student teachers demanded the cancellation of the 2015 elections, not because of the state was apparently ungovernable, but because 'elections do not solve the problems of the people'. The 14 December confrontation between federal police and CETEG teachers and Ayotzinapa students resulted in twenty-five wounded. On 26 December, the parents of the missing students called for nonparticipation in the 2015 election at the Monument to the Revolution in Mexico City, which would represent 'the beginning of the revolution', while in Iguala, protesters demanded that the student teachers kidnapped on 26 September, in their view being illegally held by the army, be presented alive.[23]

In the new year, the CETEG spoke out in favour of cancelling the elections, establishing municipal councils elected via popular assemblies and the suspension of the branches of government in the state. After a violent clash between military police and student teachers, teachers and 'support groups' (all hooded), who attempted to gain access to the headquarters of the 27th Infantry Battalion in Iguala, the National Ministry of Defence agreed to allow the parents of the Ayotzinapa students and the Comisión Nacional de Derechos Humanos (CNDH – National Human Rights Commission) to visit the military headquarters to verify that the missing students were not there.[24]

On 26 January, in Mexico City, a massive demonstration, led by the parents of the missing students and seconded by CNTE teachers from various states, restated the demand that the forty-three student teachers be returned alive, accusing the army of holding them illegally. On Army Day (19 February), hooded students threw stones and explosive devices at the headquarters of the 35th Military Zone in Chilpancingo. On 27 February, the 9th Global Action for Ayotzinapa was held with much lower attendance. In Guerrero, Michoacán and Oaxaca, it was basically the CNTE that mobilized. In Mexico City, approximately three thousand people marched and, in addition to the teachers and trade unionists, there were a number of neo-anarchists, who vandalized public monuments on their way along Paseo de la Reforma.[25]

At the rally that concluded the ceremony, Felipe de la Cruz, the spokesman for the parents of the missing students, called for nationwide sabotage of the electoral process with a cryptic argument:

> No to the elections! Polling officials are members of the people and the people are tired. And if the polling officials are Mexican and have dignity and courage in their hearts, they will reject the elections with all their stationery, and boxes and all the rest. We will make sure they do not install the polling booths. We will not boycott the vote, because if there are no polling booths, there will be nowhere to vote.[26]

Meanwhile, indifferent to the social crisis, the political parties in Guerrero selected their candidates.

Six months after the forced disappearance of the student teachers, only a small group of students at public universities in Mexico City took to the streets, evidencing the fact that by then, the movement had lost momentum. Earlier, at the INE, a committee of parents of the kidnapped 43 students met with advisers to request the suspension of the June elections in Guerrero. It was dissident teachers who mobilized, in Guerrero as well as Oaxaca and Michoacán, more to block educational reform in their respective states than in pursuit of the ever more unlikely presentation of the Ayotzinapa student teachers alive. However, by then, even that had weakened, this being demonstrated by the fact that by mid-April, a significant number of teachers had abandoned the occupation of the Zócalo in Chilpancingo. With meagre attendance, at the end of the month, student teachers, CETEG teachers and parents held a march in the state capital, during which five cars were set on fire, leading to a clash with the police. The only demonstration outside Guerrero was a small one in Guadalajara. Moreover, the acting governor made an agreement with the MPG 41, including positions for teachers and student teachers, in addition to a building and an amnesty for social leaders.[27]

The election campaigns were overshadowed by the Iguala tragedy, by the inability of the candidates to make proposals that gave citizens any expectation of justice and by the conviction of many that, in fact, the true elector in Guerrero was crime. With the PRD having no intention of disassociating itself from the deposed governor Aguirre Rivero, one of those responsible for the fateful night of 26 September – by default at the very least – the path was clear for the return of the PRI to the state executive. Furthermore, the teachers' failed antipolitical strategy, in addition to challenging the federal government on a non-negotiable issue, also cleared the way for the PRI steamroller, the most experienced actor in conflicts like these. Victory in the election for governor would go to the PRI candidate Héctor Astudillo Flores with 40.94 per cent of the vote, six percentage points ahead of the PRD candidate. In Tlapa, on election day itself, the federal police killed Antonio Vivar Díaz, the leader of the MPG in the city, who had attempted to prevent the holding of elections.[28]

On 15 July, relatives of the Ayotzinapa student teachers tried to gain access to the headquarters of the 27th Infantry Battalion in Iguala, but were repelled by military police using tear gas. At the end of the month, parents of students formed two caravans to travel the country and insist on the search for the missing students. The Grupo Interdisciplinario de Expertos Independientes (GIEI – Interdisciplinary Group of Independent Experts), sent by the CIDH at the request of the Mexican government, presented its report on 7 September. It highlighted the muddle of the official investigation. Although this re-ignited public debate, it did not lead to the first anniversary being marked by a revival of social mobilization. As part of the protests, on 22 September, student teachers clashed with state police in Iguala. On 26 September, there were demonstrations of students and teachers in about twelve states, in addition to the demonstration in Mexico City, where parents of the victims gave speeches. Vidulfo Rosales, their lawyer, called for 'the formation of a broad front that will contribute to the radical transformation of this country'. During the march, a group of masked men caused a certain amount of destruction in the Paseo de la Reforma. During the investiture of Governor Astudillo Flores, students and parents threw stones and Molotov cocktails at the local congress building. In addition, disappointed by the lack of student support, the parents of the missing students occupied the facilities of the teacher training college on 3 February 2016, complaining: 'It is not fair that we the parents have to go to steal the buses and they do not want to do it. It is not fair that we should take part in caravans when they do not. So, what kind of school of conscience is this?'[29]

Conclusion

Mexican democracy may have advanced in electoral matters, but what is highly disturbing is that the relationship between governors and governed has certainly not altered substantially, especially if we take into account the national emergency resulting from the costly war on organized crime, the crisis in security policy and the failure of the state's efforts on human rights. Similarly, the moral crisis of the political class is no cause for celebration; rather, it should make us look to the future with doubt, because as long as the rules of the political game do not change and the symbiosis between politics (both micro and macro) and big business does not yield,[30] it is highly unlikely that things will improve. However, this not only assumes an institutional change that does away with what remains of the authoritarian state, but transcends the neoliberal historical bloc that emerged in the 1980s from the alliance (and now fusion) of capital, a (growing) segment of the political class and crime.[31]

Social mobilization can contribute to both the democratization of the regime and to making explicit the unacceptable deficit in justice suffered by broad swathes of the population. Extreme inequality and injustice light the bonfire of social violence, as we have seen repeatedly in the contemporary history of the State of Guerrero. Noting the virulence achieved by the conflict – triggered by the inescapable demand for the presentation of the students missing in Iguala alive – the unalloyed authoritarianism of *caciques* and rulers, the brazen presence of organized crime across the whole of the state and the guerrilla activity of the last half a century, the conditions for a new cycle of violence exist and we must not ignore the warning signs we see before us. The torching of the headquarters of the three branches of government and offices of the main political forces, while, at the same time, the ANP states its intention of founding the state anew from the bottom up show the radical nature of the movement and, to judge from what we have seen, there is no credible negotiating partner in either the state government or, even less so, in a political class that has become discredited by the complicities that led to the events in Iguala.[32]

Although intermingled and identified with the same cause, the logic of the student movement in Mexico City, and perhaps other parts of the country, is different (though not divorced) from the protest in Guerrero. The student movement, which is generally peaceful, is primarily focused on the authoritarian matrix that the Mexican regime retains, on discrediting the political class and on increasing respect for human rights. Organization into local assemblies, coordination in an inter-university assembly and the demand that power be transparent link the new student activism with the #YoSoy132 movement. However, the basic difference between the current protest and the preceding one is that it rejects the entire political class, while #YoSoy132 was focused on the return of the PRI.

Today, as before, the risk is that the student movement will fall apart due to a lack of foundations that give it coherence and continuity when the inevitable backlash comes. This would also require the presence of clear leadership, which the dominant antipolitical discourse does not encourage, or, alternatively, that better integrated and more deter-mined but smaller groups (neo-anarchists) impose their violent reper-toire on the movement as a whole, as happened in the mobilization of 1 December 2012, with the attack in November 2014 on the gates of the National Palace and the outrages that took place during the demon-stration on 2 October 2015.

In the Guerrero and Mexico City mobilizations, there emerged an antipolitical discourse that we cannot ignore. The Guerrero mobili-zation, which is anchored in the tradition of rural rebellion and the communalist perspective, assumes that social organization of itself generates the structures of government, providing order from the bot-tom up, and is equipped with its own institutions for policing and im-parting justice. One of the demands of the ANP is therefore for the validation of 'community policing as the *only* form of popular security and justice in the state of Guerrero'. When the time comes, the state would be integrated by the group of sovereign peoples gathered in the nation.[33] Seen in this way, politics would be unnecessary.

Whether this perspective is correct or not, the truth is that it is lim-ited, given that the form of government for which the ANP is fight-ing would, in the best of cases, only work for homogeneous societies, as perhaps certain indigenous towns are, but would be inoperable in diversified societies and densely populated urban centres with greater social stratification and where coexisting conflicting interests coex-ist. If we add in the sectoral primacy of the CETEG's demands, the Guerrero-based movement risks remaining isolated in the absence of a national perspective, even indeed if it should be successful in some of its demands. It can be noted that activism outside the state de-clined and it perhaps only attracts 'neo-anarchists' who also share the CETEG's violent repertoire.

The antipoliticism of young people, except for the neo-anarchists, who are trying do away with all politics, is more accurately a rejection of party politics, following the line that party interests cause social movements to fragment and survive parasitically at their expense, the clearly weak supposition being that what is social is good in itself and that politics (understood as its party-political form) is the opposite. Furthermore, anything that moves towards decreasing the organization's horizontality, or any attempt to make representatives permanent, is presumably harmful. Unfortunately, the illusion of ending politics reduces the movement's reach and allows others to fill this space (on this topic, the Arab Spring has taught us some important lessons). What is even worse in the present circumstances is that it deprives society of the opportunity to remove the corrupt political class and build the necessary politics on new foundations.

Notes

1. Touraine, *After the Crisis*; Jameson, *Representing Capital*; Agamben, 'El gobierno de la inseguridad', p. 33; Žižek, *The Year of Dreaming Dangerously*; Castells, *Redes de indignación y esperanza*, p. 21; Iglesias, *Disputar la democracia*, p. 155; Balibar, 'El comunismo como compromiso, imaginación y política', p. 39.
2. 'Jóvenes mexicanos, los que menos confían en las instituciones' [Young Mexicans Have Least Confidence in Institutions], *Milenio*, 22 August 2013.
3. Bartra calls it a 'shrivelled myth' in 'La abeja, la araña y las moscas', p. 106.
4. Tarrow, *Power in Movement*.
5. Žižek, *Event*, my emphasis.
6. Laclau, *La razón populista*, pp. 124–25.
7. 'Miles demandan en Chilpancingo juicio político al gobernador Aguirre Rivero' [Thousands in Chilpancingo Demand Impeachment of Governor Aguirre Rivero], *La Jornada*, 30 September 2014. The FECSM was formed in 1935 to coordinate students from each of the schools and support their demands. It currently calls itself an 'underground organization', working with five areas of action: education, culture, sports, production and politics. Civera Cerecedo, 'Normales rurales', pp. 16, 19.
8. 'Megamarcha en Chilpancingo en demanda de hallar normalistas' [Megamarch in Chilpancingo Demanding that Students Be Found], *La Jornada*, 3 October 2014; 'Huélum en completo orden; se organizan para evitar infiltraciones de porros' [IPN March in Order; Organized to Prevent Infiltration by Thugs], *Excélsior*, 1 October 2014.
9. 'Toman normalistas la Procuraduría General de Justicia de Guerrero; exigen presentar vivos a los desaparecidos' [Student Teachers Occupy the Guerrero State Prosecutor's Office; Demand that the Disappeared Be Presented Alive], *La Jornada*, 8 October 2014; 'Vuelve a Iguala el "usted disculpe"' ['I Beg Your Pardon' Returns to Iguala], *La Jornada*, 8 Octo-

ber 2014; '"Liberen a policías detenidos o aténganse a las consecuencias", amenaza cártel en Iguala' [Iguala Poster Threatens 'Free Arrested Police or Face the Consequences'], *La Jornada*, 7 October 2014; 'EPR: 'fue un crimen de Estado' [EPR: It was a State Crime]', *La Jornada*, 6 October 2014.

10. 'Marcha en 25 estados para pedir justicia por Ayotzinapa' [Marches in 25 States Seeking Justice for Ayotzinapa], *La Jornada*, 9 October 2014; 'Miles exigen la aparición de los normalistas y la salida de Aguirre' [Thousands Demand the Appearance of the Student Teachers and the Resignation of Aguirre], *La Jornada*, 9 October 2014; 'Agresión a Cuauhtémoc Cárdenas' [Cuauhtémoc Cárdenas Assaulted], *La Jornada*, 9 October 2014; 'Hay señales de debilidad institucional en el país' [Signs of Institutional Weakness in the Country], *La Jornada*, 9 October 2014.

11. 'Maestros, ejidatarios e la iniciativa privada piden la salida de Aguirre' [Teachers, *Ejidatarios* and Private Enterprises Call for Aguirre to Go], *La Jornada*, 11 October 2014; '"En Guerrero no hay gobierno", dicen empresarios y estudiantes' [There is No Government in Guerrero, Say Businessmen and Students], *La Jornada*, 13 October 2014; 'El gobierno ve a la guerrilla detrás de las movilizaciones en Guerrero' [Government Thinks Guerrillas behind Demonstrations in Guerrero], *Proceso*, 19 October 2014; 'Destrozos en el Palacio de Gobierno de Chilpancingo' [Destruction at Government Palace in Chilpancingo], *La Jornada*, 14 October 2014; *Plan de acción de la Escuela Rural de Ayotzinapa y organizaciones sociales estatales en la Asamblea Popular #Ayotzinapa, 2014* [*Action Plan of Ayotzinapa Rural School and State Social Organizations in the People's Assembly #Ayotzinapa, 2014*]; 'Miles de universitarios manifestaron rabia e indignación por el caso Iguala' [Thousands of University Students Expressed Anger and Outrage over Iguala Case], *La Jornada*, 16 October 2014. I cite the last three.

12. 'Más indignación por los 43 desaparecidos de Ayotzinapa' [More Outrage over the Missing Ayotzinapa 43], *La Jornada*, 18 October 2014; 'Marcha de 20 mil personas exige en Iguala justicia para los normalistas' [20,000 March in Iguala Demanding Justice for Student Teachers], *La Jornada*, 23 October 2014; 'La defenestración de Aguirre, paso a paso' [Defenestration of Aguirre, Step by Step], *Proceso*, 26 October 2014; 'Tomadas, 28 alcaldías por el caso Ayotzinapa' [Occupied, 28 Town Halls over Ayotzinapa Case], *La Jornada*, 29 December 2014.

13. '"¡Fuera Peña!", exigen miles en el Zócalo' ['Peña Out!' Demand Thousands in the Zocalo], *La Jornada*, 6 November 2014; 'En 22 estados, solidaridad con Ayotzinapa' [Solidarity with Ayotzinapa in 22 States], *La Jornada*, 6 November 2014; 'Incendian camión y estación del Metrobús CU: 2 detenidos' [Bus and CU Metrobus Station Torched: Two Held], *El Universal*, 6 November 2014; 'Toman organizaciones magisteriales y sociales oficinas federales y locales' [Teachers' and Social Organizations Occupy Federal and Local Offices], *La Jornada*, 7 November 2014.

14. After one more confession, that of a hitman nicknamed *El Cepillo*, the prosecutor presented the final version of the events at Iguala on 27 January 2015. Guilty of not merely verbal but conceptual excess, he said they had come to 'the historical truth of the facts'. Unless we think of ourselves

as a theocracy, truth is not a matter for the state (unlike justice, which is). 'La PGR va ahora por los integrantes de los Rojos' [PGR Now Going for the Members of the Reds], *Milenio*, 29 January 2015. For a critique of the official attempt to close the case, see Jesús Silva-Herzog Márquez, 'Pasar la página' [Turn the Page], *Reforma*, 2 February 2015. So far, the remains of only one of the students (Alexander Mora Venancio) have been identified, but, as stated in the report of the Argentine experts who have been assisting with the case, 'there is not sufficient scientific certainty nor physical evidence that the remains recovered from the San Juan River by experts from the PGR and partly by the EAAF correspond to those removed from the dump at Cocula, as stated by those indicted by the PGR. Charred and burnt human remains were recovered from both the San Juan River and the dump at Cocula. For the time being, evidence linking the two sites is essentially testimony'. EAAF, 'Identificación de uno de los 43 normalistas desaparecidos de Ayotzinapa' [Identification of One of the 43 Missing Ayotzinapa Student Teachers], 7 December 2014.

15. 'PGR: los 43 habrían sido ejecutados y calcinados' [PGR: All 43 were Executed and Burned], *La Jornada*, 8 November 2014; 'Nace en el Ángel propuesta de un paro nacional' [Proposal for a National Strike Put Forward at el Ángel], *La Jornada*, 8 November 2014.

16. A few days later, UNAM students unmasked one of those who participated in the torching and discovered him to be an infiltrator. 'Descubren estudiantes rostro de "infiltrado"' [Students Unmask 'Infiltrator'], *El Universal*, 17 November 2014.

17. 'Vandalizan anarquistas contra Palacio Nacional' [Anarchists Vandalize National Palace], *El Universal*, 9 November 2014; 'Esto apenas empieza, advierten normalistas' [This is Just the Beginning, Student Teachers Warn], *La Jornada*, 9 November 2014.

18. 'Marcha la CRAC-PC para exigir la presentación con vida de 43 normalistas' [CRAC-PC Marched to Demand the Live Presentation of 43 Student Teachers], *La Jornada*, 10 November 2014; 'La justicia, otra desaparecida: integrantes de la marcha 43 por 43' [Justice: Another Disappearance, Say the 43 for 43 Marchers], *La Jornada*, 10 November 2014; 'Manifestantes bloquearon cuatro horas las actividades en el aeropuerto de Acapulco' [Protesters Blocked Activities at Acapulco Airport for Four Hours], *La Jornada*, 11 November 2014; 'CETEG quema sede del PRI en Chilpancingo' [CETEG Torches PRI Headquarters in Chilpancingo], *El Universal*, 12 November 2014; 'Maestros incendian pleno del Congreso de Guerrero y autos' [Teachers Torch Guerrero Congress as Well as Cars], *El Universal*, 12 November 2014; 'Se expande protesta normalista en Morelia' [Student Teacher Protest Expands in Morelia], *El Universal*, 12 November 2014; 'Normalistas destrozan sede del PRI en Morelia y cierran aeropuerto' [Student Teachers Destroy PRI Headquarters in Morelia and Shut Down Airport], *La Jornada*, 13 November 2014; 'Piden en Acapulco intervenga el ejército; 'no generaremos más violencia', responde' [Army Asked to Intervene in Acapulco; Reply: 'We Will Not Cause More Violence'], *La Jornada*, 14 November 2014; 'Marcha la CNTE del Monumento a la Revolución al

Zócalo' [CNTE Marches from Monument to the Revolution to Zócalo], *El Universal*, 15 November 2014; 'Marchan 8 mil personas en Chilpancingo para exigir que se presente con vida a normalistas' [8,000 March in Chilpancingo Demanding Presentation of Student Teachers Alive], *La Jornada*, 15 November 2014.

19. 'Cimbra a México la violencia desmedida, afirma la Corte' [Excessive Violence is Battering Mexico, Court Affirms], *El Universal*, 14 November 2014; 'Asignan a normales rurales $400 millones adicionales' [Additional $400 Million Allocated to Rural Teacher Training Colleges], *La Jornada*, 14 November 2014.

20. The recent newspaper discovery of an extravagantly costly residence for the President's family, allegedly the property of one of his government contractors, has reduced the current federal administration's credibility to zero. 'From the "Mexican Moment" to the "'Mexican Mess" reports *The Financial Times*', *Sin Embargo*, 14 November 2014.

21. 'El Estado, facultado a usar la fuerza para restablecer el orden' [The State is Empowered to Use Force to Restore Order], *La Jornada*, 16 November 2014; cited in 'Peña Nieto denuncia "afán orquestado para desestabilizar al país"' [Peña Nieto Denounces 'Orchestrated Effort to Destabilize the Country'], *Animal Político*, 19 November 2014. The head of the President's Office told the foreign press: 'We are not going to replace reforms with high impact theatrical acts, we are not interested in successful 72-hour media cycles. We will be patient in this new cycle of reforms. We will not give way even if the public demands blood, nor satisfy the cravings of journalists. It will be the institutions that get us out of the crisis, not displays of bravado.' Cited in *El País*, 7 December 2014.

22. 'Se adjudica el EPR explosión en Soriana de Ecatepec' [EPR Claims Responsibility for Explosion in Soriana Ecatepec], *El Universal*, 14 November 2014; 'Salió de Tixtla la primera caravana de padres de alumnos desaparecidos' [First Caravan of Parents of Missing Students Has Left Tixtla], *La Jornada*, 14 November 2014; 'Arrojan explosivos en dos bancos de Naucalpan' [Explosives Thrown into Two Naucalpan Banks], *El Universal*, 20 November 2014; cited in 'El gobierno sabe dónde están los 43 normalistas' [The Government Knows Where the 43 Student Teachers are], *La Jornada*, 21 November 2014; 'Enfrentamiento frente a Palacio Nacional' [Clash outside National Palace], *La Jornada*, 21 November 2014; 'Salen de prisión los 11 detenidos el 20 de noviembre' [The Eleven Arrested on 20 November Leave Prison], *Animal Político*, 30 November 2014.

23. 'Establecen fechas para reiniciar clases en el IPN' [Dates Agreed for Restarting Classes at IPN], *El Universal*, 11 December 2014; Vandalizan instalaciones de la procuraduría de Guerrero' [Guerrero Attorney General's Offices Vandalized], *El Universal*, 1 December 2014; 'Integrantes de la CETEG queman bustos de ex gobernadores de Guerrero y tiran reja' [Members of CETEG Burn Busts of Former Guerrero Governors and Demolish Barrier], *La Jornada*, 4 December 2014; 'CETEG "clausura" instalaciones del INE en Guerrero' [CETEG 'Closure' of INE Facilities in Guerrero], *El Universal*, 8 December 2014; 'La CETEG retiene a miembros

del Sol Azteca y los obliga a expresar "somos ratas del PRD'" [CETEG Holds PRD Members, Forces Them to State 'We are PRD Crooks'], *La Jornada*, 10 December 2014; 'Exigen padres de los normalistas desaparecer poderes en Guerrero' [Parents of Missing Student Teachers Demand Disappearance of Powers in Guerrero], *La Jornada*, 10 December 2014; 'Aumenta la presión popular para impedir los comicios en Guerrero' [Popular Pressure to Thwart Elections in Guerrero Increases], *La Jornada*, 11 December 2014; 'Choca la policía federal con maestros y normalistas, hay 25 heridos' [Federal Police Clash with Teachers and Student Teachers. 25 Wounded], *El Universal*, 15 December 2014; 'Padres de normalistas llaman a no votar' [Parents of Student Teachers Call for Nonparticipation in Voting], *La Crónica de Hoy*, 26 December 2014; 'Derriban una puerta de instalaciones del 41 Batallón de Infantería de Iguala' [Door at 41st Infantry Battalion Headquarters in Iguala Demolished], *La Jornada*, 27 December 2014; Rosalía Vergara, 'Investigar a la policía federal y al ejército, clamor de los familiares' [Families Cry out for Investigation of Federal Police and Army], *Proceso*, 28 December 2014.

24. 'Apuestan en Guerrero a consejos populares' [Betting on Popular Advice in Guerrero], *Reforma*, 3 January 2015; 'Reactivan búsqueda de los normalistas' [Search for Student Teachers Restarted], *Reforma*, 15 January 2015. According to the acting governor, 'Mexico City anarchists' were responsible for the vandalism in Guerrero. '"Anarcos" del DF cometen vandalismo en Guerrero: Ortega' [Mexico City 'Anarchists' Commit Vandalism in Guerrero. Ortega], *El Universal*, 20 January 2015.

25. 'Agreden cuartel en Chilpancingo' [Headquarters in Chilpancingo Attacked], *Reforma*, 20 February 2015; 'Reclaman justicia' [They Demand Justice], *Reforma*, 27 February 2015; 'Reaparecen anarquistas y vandalizan' [Anarchists Reappear and Commit Vandalism], *El Universal*, 27 February 2015.

26. Cited in 'Reaparecen anarquistas y vandalizan'.

27. 'Medio año de dolor y de desesperación' [Half a Year of Pain and Despair], *Reforma*, 27 March 2015; 'Fracción de CETEG abandona plantón en Chilpancingo' [Section of CETEG Abandons Chilpancingo Occupation], *Milenio*, 15 April 2015; 'Prenden protesta en Chilpancingo' [Protest Started in Chilpancingo], *Reforma*, 27 April 2015; 'La CETEG secuestra y quema cinco vehículos' [CETEG Seizes and Burns Five Vehicles], *Milenio*, 27 April 2015; 'Guerrero premia a movimiento social y la CETEG' [Guerrero Rewards Social Movement and CETEG], *El Universal*, 19 May 2015.

28. 'Guerrero: entre el terror y el desencanto de votar' [Guerrero: Between Terror and the Disillusionment of Voting], *Proceso*, 17 May 2015; 'En Guerrero impusieron a sangre y fuego los comicios' [Elections in Guerrero Imposed by Blood and Fire], *La Jornada*, 10 June 2015; 'Las mafias del PRI guerrerense se frotan las manos' [The PRI's Guerrero Mafias are Rubbing Their Hands Together], *Proceso*, 14 June 2015.

29. 'Padres de los 43 intentan entrar a cuartel en Iguala' [Parents of the 43 Attempt to Enter Iguala Headquarters], *Milenio*, 15 July 2015; 'Enfrentamientos entre un grupo de normalistas y la policía estatal' [Clashes be-

tween Group of Student Teachers and State Police], *El País,* 23 September 2015; 'Se movilizan en varios estados al cumplirse un año de la tragedia' [Several States Mobilize on First Anniversary of Tragedy], *La Jornada,* 27 September 2015; 'Anuncian padres de los 43 frente amplio radical' [Parents of the 43 Announce Radical Broad Front], *Milenio,* 27 September 2015; '"No habrá olvido", claman miles a un año de la tragedia en Iguala' ['There Will Be No Forgetting', Cry Thousands One Year after Iguala Tragedy], *La Jornada,* 27 September 2015; 'Choque entre normalistas y antimotines dejó dos policías con quemaduras' [Clash between Student Teachers and Riot Police Leaves Two Policemen with Burns], *El Universal,* 29 October 2015; 'Surge el primer desacuerdo entre los padres de los 43 y la base estudiantil de Ayotzinapa' [First Disagreement Arises between Parents of the 43 and Ayotzinapa Student Base], *Interacción,* 3 February 2016.

30. The process at local level is nicely analysed in Ugalde, '¿Por qué más democracia significa más corrupción?', p. 14.
31. González Rodríguez, *Campo de guerra,* p. 22.
32. Raymundo Rivapalacio, 'Guerrero: empezó la insurrección iv' [Guerrero Began the Fourth Insurrection], *El Sur,* 14 November 2014. See Chapter 5 above.
33. *Plan de acción de la Escuela Rural de Ayotzinapa y organizaciones sociales estatales en la Asamblea Popular #Ayotzinapa,* 2014 [*Action Plan of Ayotzinapa Rural School and State Social Organizations in the People's Assembly #Ayotzinapa,* 2014], my emphasis. An excellent analysis of this perspective can be found in Adolfo Sánchez Rebolledo, 'Guerrero, la tragedia sin fin' [Guerrero, Endless Tragedy], *La Jornada,* 22 January 2015.

Sources and Bibliography

Archives

Archivo General de la Nación (AGN – General Archive of the Nation).
Archivo Gregorio y Marta Selser, Universidad Autónoma de la Ciudad de México (AGMS-UACM – Gregorio and Marta Selser Archives, Autonomous University of Mexico City).
Archivo Histórico de la Casa de la Cultura Jurídica en el Estado de Querétaro (AHCCJEQ – Historical Archives of the House of Legal Culture in the State of Querétaro).
Archivo Histórico de la Embajada de España en México (AHEEM – Historical Archives of the Spanish Embassy in Mexico), Comisión Mixta Hispano Mexicana de Reclamaciones (CMHMR – Joint Hispano-Mexican Claims Commission), Biblioteca Daniel Cosío Villegas, El Colegio de México (Daniel Cosío Villegas Library, Colegio de México).
Archivo Histórico del Estado de Querétaro (AHEQ – Historical Archives of the State of Querétaro).
Archivo Histórico Genaro Estrada de la Secretaría de Relaciones Exteriores, México (AREM – Genaro Estrada Historical Archives of the Ministry of Foreign Affairs, Mexico).
Colección Porfirio Díaz, Universidad Iberoamericana (CPD-UIA – Porfirio Díaz Collection, Universidad Iberoamericana).
Embajada de España en México, *Relaciones diplomáticas hispano-mexicanas (1826–1917)*, selección de Javier Malagón Barceló (Mexico, El Colegio de México, 1949), micropelícula (51 rollos) [Spanish Embassy in Mexico, *Spanish-Mexican diplomatic relations (1826–1917)* Javier Malagón Barceló selection (Mexico, El Colegio de México, 1949), microfilm (fifty-one rolls)].
Instituto Internacional de Historia Social, Ámsterdam (IISG – International Institute of Social History, Amsterdam).

Documents

Asamblea Nacional Popular, *Plan de acción de la Escuela Rural de Ayotzinapa y organizaciones sociales estatales en la Asamblea Nacional Popular #Ayotzinapa*, 15 October 2014 [*Action Plan of Ayotzinapa Rural School and State*

Social Organizations in the People's Assembly #Ayotzinapa, 15 October 2014].

'Asociaciones registradas en el Departamento de Trabajo hasta mayo del año de 1913' [Associations Registered with the Department of Work up to May 1913], *Boletín del Departamento de Trabajo*, año 1, no. 1, July 1913, n.p.

'Carta abierta al movimiento anarquista y antiautoritario' [Open Letter to the Anarchist and Anti-authoritarian Movement], 21 December 2003, *Conspiración. Publicación anarquista intermitente*, no. 1, 2004, p. 26.

Comando Magonista de Liberación y la Tendencia Democrática Revolucionaria-Ejército del Pueblo, 'Comunicado no. 2' [Magonista Liberation Commando and the Democratic Revolutionary Tendency-People's Army, 'Communique No. 2'], Oaxaca, 27 November 2006.

Comando Popular Revolucionario 'La Patria es Primero' (CPR-LPEP), 'Comunicado guerrillero no. 3' [Guerrilla Press Release No. 3], 2 October 2005.

Comité Clandestino Revolucionario Indígena-Comandancia General del EZLN, Quinta Declaración de la Selva Lacandona [Fifth Declaration of the Lacandon Jungle] (1998).

Conspiración de Células del Fuego [Fire Cells Conspiracy], *La nueva guerrilla urbana anarquista* [The New Anarchist Urban Guerrilla] (Atenas, Internacional Negra, 2013).

———, *Seamos peligrosos … por la difusión de la Internacional Negra* [*Let's Be Dangerous … in favour of the Spread of the Black International*] (n.p., Internacional Negra Ediciones, 2013).

Coordinadora Regional de Autoridades Comunitarias-Policía Comunitaria (CRAC-PC), 'Comunicado de las comunidades fundadoras de la Coordinadora Regional de Autoridades Comunitarias-Policía Comunitaria' [Press Release from the Founding Communities of the Regional Coordination of Community Authorities – Community Police], Territorio comunitario, 2 June 2013.

Defensa del derecho territorial patrio elevada por el pueblo mexicano al Congreso General de la Nación, pidiendo la reconquista de la propiedad territorial para que nuevamente sea distribuida entre todos los ciudadanos habitantes de la República por medio de leyes agrarias y la organización general del trabajo, por la serie de leyes protectoras con los fondos que se han de crear de un Banco Nacional de Avíos [*Defence of national land law raised by the Mexican people to the General National Congress, calling for the re-conquest of property in land so that it shall once again be distributed among all citizen-inhabitants of the Republic through agrarian laws and the general organization of work, by the series of protective laws having funds to create a National Bank of Loans*] (Mexico, Tipografía de José Reyes Velasco, 1877).

'Directorio de asociaciones en la República' [Directory of Associations in the Republic], *Boletín del Trabajo. Órgano del Departamento del Trabajo*, volume 1, no. 1, January 1918, pp. 52–56.

Equipo Argentino de Antropología Forense (EAAF), 'Identificación de uno de los 43 normalistas desaparecidos de Ayotzinapa' [Identification of One of the Forty-Three Missing Trainee Teachers from Ayotzinapa], 7 December 2014.

Ejército Revolucionario del Pueblo Insurgente (ERPI), 'Poder popular, partido y ejército de masas' [Popular Power, Party and Army of the Masses], 1999.
Europol Terrorism Situation and Trend Report 2013 (Van Deventer, The Netherlands, European Police Office, 2013).
Human Rights Watch, 'Mexico: Crisis of Enforced Disappearances'. Retrieved 12 October 2016 from https://www.hrw.org/news/2013/02/20/mexico-cris is-enforced-disappearances.
Insurrectionary Anarchism in Mexico 2011. (no imprint)
International Crisis Group, 'Justice at the Barrel of a Gun: Vigilante Militias in Mexico', 28 May 2013.
La Convención Radical. Antología [*The Radical Convention. An Anthology*], introduction by Arturo Obregón, review and classification of subjects by Liborio Villalobos Calderón (Mexico, CEHSMO, 1978).
Liga Mexicana de Defensa de los Derechos Humanos (LIMEDDH), 'Informe sobre la matanza de El Charco' [Report on the El Charco Massacre], 1999.
Movimiento Revolucionario Lucio Cabañas Barrientos (MRLCB), 'Comunicado no. 5' [Press Release No. 5], 28 June 2005.
Parametría, *El desafuero de López Obrador* [Removal of López Obrador's Political Immunity from Prosecution], 2004.
'Plan Socialista' [Socialist Plan], in García Cantú, 1969, pp. 67–71.
'Relación de los gremios, artes y oficios que hay en la nobilísima Ciudad de México (1788)' [Report of the Guilds, Arts and Trades Existing in the Most Noble City of México (1788)], Biblioteca Nacional, ms. 1388 (451), in Kicza, 1986, pp. 228–29.
UNODC (United Nations Office on Drugs and Crime) *World Drug Report 2015. Executive Summary* (Vienna, 2015).
UPOEG (Unión de Pueblos y Organizaciones del Estado de Guerrero), '¿Quiénes somos?' [Who are We?], 2014, 5 pp.

Bibliography

Agamben, Giorgio, 'El gobierno de la inseguridad' [The Government of Insecurity], in Laval et al., 2012, pp. 25–35.
Aguayo Quesada, Sergio, *La Charola. Una historia de los servicios de inteligencia en México* [*The Badge. A History of the Intelligence Services in Mexico*] (Mexico, Grijalbo, 2001).
Aguilar Camín, Héctor, 'La captura criminal del Estado' [The Criminal Capture of the State], *Nexos*, January 2015, pp. 19–31.
Aguilar Valenzuela, Rubén and Jorge G. Castañeda, *El narco: La guerra fallida* [*Drugs: The Failed War*] (Mexico, Punto de Lectura, 2009).
Anderson, Benedict, *Under Three Flags: Anarchism and the Anti-Colonial Imagination* (New York and London, Verso, 2005).
Anderson, Perry, *Components of the National Culture*, in 'The Repressive Culture' (New Left Review, 1968).

Anderson, Rodney D. 'Race and Social Stratification: A Comparison of Working-Class Spaniards, Indians, and Castas in Guadalajara, Mexico in 1821'. *Hispanic American Historical Review*, vol. 68, no. 2, 1988, pp. 209–43.

Arrighi, Giovanni, Terence K. Hopkins and Immanuel Wallerstein, *Antisystemic Movements* (New York and London, Verso, 1989).

Arrom, Silvia Marina, *Popular Politics in Mexico City: The Parian Riot, 1828* (Arrom and Ortoll, 1996), pp. 71–95.

Arrom, Silvia Marina, and Servando Ortoll (eds), *Riots in the Cities: Popular Politics and the Urban Poor in Latin America, 1765–1910* (Wilmington, DE, Scholarly Resources Inc., 1996).

Ávila Coronel, Francisco, 'Problemas para el estudio de la guerrilla del Partido de los Pobres (PDLP), Atoyac, Guerrero (1972–2012)' [Problems Involved in Studying the Guerrilla of the Partido de los Pobres (PdlP) Atoyac, Guerrero (1972–2012)], UNAM, Facultad de Filosofía y Letras, Thesis for Master's degree in History, 2013.

Balibar, Étienne, *Violencias, identidades y civilidad* [*Violence, Identities and Civility*] (Barcelona, Gedisa, 2005).

———, 'El comunismo como compromiso, imaginación y política' [Communism as Commitment, Imagination and Politics], in Žižek (ed.), 2011, pp. 21–48.

———, 'La necesidad cívica de la sublevación' [The Civic Need for Revolt], in Laval et al., 2012, pp. 281–99.

Barbosa Cano, Fabio, *La CROM, de Luis N. Morones a Antonio J. Hernández* [*The CROM, from Luis N. Morones to Antonio J. Hernández*] (Puebla, UAP, 1980).

Bartra, Armando, *Guerrero bronco. Campesinos, ciudadanos y guerrilleros en la Costa Grande* [*Rough Guerrero. Peasants, Citizens and Guerrillas on the Costa Grande*], 1996 (Mexico, Era, 2000).

Bartra, Roger, 'La abeja, la araña y las moscas' [The Bee, the Spider and the Flies], *Fractal*, no. 63, 2011, pp. 101–8.

Bellingeri, Marco, *Del agrarismo armado a la Guerra de los pobres 1940–1974* [*From Armed Agrarianism to the War of the Poor 1940–1974*] (Mexico, Juan Pablos/Secretaría de Cultura de la Ciudad de México, 2003).

Bezucha, Robert J., *Modern European Social History* (Lexington, MA, D.C. Heath, 1972).

Bojórquez, Juan de Dios, *La inmigración española en México* [*Spanish Immigration into Mexico*] (Mexico, Crisol Special Edition, 1932).

Bosteels, Bruno, 'Detrás de Ayotzinapa' [Behind Ayotzinapa], *Memoria*, no. 256, 2015, pp. 14–17.

Bustamante Álvarez, Tomás, 'Periodo 1934–1940' [The 1934–1940 Period], in Salazar Adame et al., 1987, pp. 335–54.

Braudel, Fernand, *History and the Social Sciences: The Longue Durée*, Translated by Immanuel Wallerstein, *Review* vol. 32, no. 2, 2009, pp. 25–55.

Casanova, Julián, *La historia social y los historiadores ¿Cenicienta o princesa?* [*Social History and Historians. Cinderella or Princess?*], 2nd edn (Barcelona, Crítica, 2003).

Castañeda, Carmen (ed.), 'Élite, clases sociales y rebelión en Guadalajara y Jalisco, siglos xviii y xx' [*Elites, Social Classes and Rebellion in Guadalajara and Jalisco in the Nineteenth and Twentieth Centuries*] (Guadalajara, El Colegio de Jalisco/Gobierno de Jalisco, 1988).

Castellanos, Laura, *México armado 1943–1981* [*Armed Mexico 1943–1981*] (Mexico, Era, 2007).

Castells, Manuel, *Redes de indignación y esperanza* [*Networks of Outrage and Hope*] (Madrid, Alianza, 2012).

Cerutti, Mario, and Óscar Flores, *Españoles en el norte de México. Propietarios, empresarios y diplomacia, 1850–1920* [*Spaniards in the North of Mexico. Proprietors, Entrepreneurs and Diplomacy, 1850–1920*] (Monterrey, UANL/ Universidad de Monterrey, 1997).

Chávez Orozco, Luis, *Datos para la prehistoria del socialismo en México* [*Data for the Prehistory of Socialism in Mexico*] (Mexico, Secretaría de la Economía Nacional, 1935).

Civera Cerecedo, Alicia, 'Normales rurales. Historia mínima del olvido' [Rural Teacher Training Colleges. A Minimal History of Forgetting], *Nexos*, March 2015, pp. 16–19.

Coatsworth, John H., *Los orígenes del atraso. Nueve ensayos de historia económica de México en los siglos xviii y xix* (The Origins of Backwardness. Nine Essays on the Economic History of Mexico in the Nineteenth and Twentieth Centuries)(Mexico, Alianza, 1990).

Combes, Hélène, Sergio Tamayo and Michael Voegtli (eds), *Pensar y mirar la protesta* [*To Think and Watch Protest*] (Mexico, UAM, 2015).

Considérant, Victor, *México. Cuatro cartas al mariscal Bazaine* [*Mexico. Four Letters to Marshal Bazaine*], edited, preliminary study and notes by Carlos Illades, translation by Hilda Domínguez Márquez (Mexico, Instituto Mora/ UAM, 2008).

Cumberland, Charles Curtis, *Mexican Revolution, The Constitutionalist Years*, (Austin and London, University of Texas Press, 2010).

D'Eramo, Marco, 'Populism and the New Oligarchy', *New Left Review*, no. 82, 2013, pp. 7–40.

Davies, Keith A., 'Tendencias demográficas y urbanas durante el siglo xix en México' [Demographic and Urban Trends in Mexico in the Nineteenth Century], *Historia Mexicana*, no. 120, 1972, pp. 481–524.

Davis, Mike, *Planet of Slums* (New York and London, Verso, 2006).

De Mauleón, Héctor, 'De la red a las calles' [From the Internet to the Streets], *Nexos*, September 2012, pp. 35–42.

_____, "Guerreros Unidos" [The Guerreros Unidos Gang], *Nexos*, February 2016, pp. 20–27.

Delgado Larios, Almudena, *La Revolución mexicana vista desde España 1910– 1931* [*The Mexican Revolution as Seen from Spain*] (Mexico, Publicaciones Cruz, 2010).

Escalante Gonzalbo, Fernando, 'Homicidios 2008–2009: la muerte tiene permiso' [Homicides 2008–2009: Death Has Permission], *Nexos*, January 2011, pp. 36–49.

Espinosa, Valeria, and Donald B. Rubin, 'Did the Military Interventions in the Mexican Drug War Increase Violence?', *The American Statistician*, vol. 69, no. 1, 2015, pp. 17–27.

Estrada Saavedra, Marco, 'La anarquía organizada: las barricadas como el subsistema de seguridad de la Asamblea Popular de los Pueblos de Oaxaca' [Organized Anarchy: Barricades Used as a Security Subsystem by the Asamblea Popular de los Pueblos de Oaxaca], *Estudios Sociológicos*, vol. XXVIII, no. 84, 2010, pp. 903–39.

———, 'Sistema de protesta: política, medios y el #Yo soy 132' [System of Protest: Politics, Media and the #YoSoy132 Movement], *Sociológica*, vol. XXIX, no. 82, 2014, pp. 83–123.

Fillieule, Olivier, and Danielle Tartakowsky, *La manifestation* (Paris, Les Presses de Sciences Po, 2008).

Flores, Francisco A., *Historia de la medicina en México desde la época de los indios hasta el presente* [*History of Medicine in Mexico from the Time of the Indians to the Present Day*], foreword by Porfirio Parra, 4 vols (Mexico, Oficina de la Secretaría de Fomento, 1886).

Flores Torres, Óscar, *Revolución mexicana y diplomacia española. Contrarrevolución y oligarquía hispana en México, 1909–1920* [*Mexican Revolution and Spanish Diplomacy. Counterrevolution and the Spanish Oligarchy in Mexico 1909–1920*] (Mexico, INEHRM, 1995).

———, 'Revolución mexicana y diplomacia española. La burguesía de Monterrey y los *gachupines* en el Nuevo León radical de 1914' [Mexican Revolution and Spanish Diplomacy. The Monterrey Bourgeoisie and the *Gachupines* in the Radical Nuevo Leon of 1914], in Cerutti and Flores Torres, 1997, pp. 201–3.

Frost, Elsa Cecilia, Michael C. Meyer and Josefina Zoraida Vázquez (eds), *El trabajo y los trabajadores en la historia de México* [*Work and Workers in Mexican History*] (Mexico/Tucson, El Colegio de México/University of Arizona Press, 1979).

Fuentes Mares, José, *Historia de dos orgullos* [*A History of Two Prides*] (Mexico, Océano, 1984).

Gamboa Ojeda, Leticia, *Los empresarios de ayer* [*Yesterday's Businessmen*] (Puebla, UAP, 1985).

Garavito, Rosa Albina, *Sueños a prueba de balas. Mi paso por la guerrilla* [*Bulletproof Dreams. My Time with the Guerillas*] (Mexico, Cal y Arena, 2014).

García Cantú, Gastón, *El socialismo en México. Siglo xix* [*Socialism in Mexico. Nineteenth Century*] (Mexico, Era, 1969).

Gasparello, Giovanna, 'Policía Comunitaria de Guerrero, investigación y autonomía' [Community Police in Guerrero, Investigation and Autonomy], *Política y Cultura*, no. 32, 2009, pp. 61–78.

Gibler, John, 'Afán de impunidad' [The Rule of Impunity], in Osorno, 2011, pp. 139–65.

Giddens, Anthony, *Out of the Orrery: E.P. Thompson on Consciousness and History*, in *Social Theory and Modern Sociology* (Cambridge, Polity Press, 1987).

Gill, Mario, 'Los Escudero de Acapulco' [The Escuderos of Acapulco], *Historia Mexicana*, no. 10, 1953, pp. 291–308.

Gomezjara, Francisco A. *María de la O y Benita Galeana, precursoras del feminismo socialista en Guerrero* [*María de la O and Benita Galeana, Forerunners of Socialist Feminism in Guerrero*] (Chilpancingo, UAG, 1982).

González Casanova, Pablo, *La democracia en México*, [*Democracy in Mexico*], 7th edn (Mexico, Era, 1975).

_____, *En el primer gobierno constitucional, 1917–1920* [*In the First Constitutional Government*] (Mexico, Siglo Veintiuno, 1980).

González Loscertales, Vicente, 'La colonia española de México durante la revolución maderista, 1911–1913' [The Spanish Colony in Mexico during the Madero Revolution, 1911–1913], *Revista de la Universidad Complutense*, no. 107, 1977, pp. 341–65.

_____, 'Bases para el análisis socioeconómico de la colonia española de México en 1910' [Bases for the Socio-economic Analysis of the Spanish Colony in Mexico in 1910], *Revista de Indias*, nos. 155–58, 1979, pp. 267–95.

_____, 'Los españoles en la vida social y económica de Méjico, 1910–1930' [The Spanish in the Social and Economic Life of Mexico, 1910–1930], Universidad Complutense, Doctorate Thesis in Communication Sciences, 2015.

_____, *El empresario español en Puebla, 1880–1916* [*The Spanish Businessman in Puebla, 1880–1916*]. (n.p., n.d.)

González Navarro, Moisés, *Población y sociedad en México (1900–1970)* [*Population and Society in Mexico (1900–1970)*], 2 vols (Mexico, UNAM, 1974).

González Navarro, Moisés et al., *El poblamiento de México. México en el siglo xix* [*The Peopling of Mexico. Mexico in the Nineteenth Century*] (Mexico, CONAPO, 1993).

González Rodríguez, Sergio, *Campo de guerra* [*Battlefield*] (Barcelona, Anagrama, 2014).

_____, *Los 43 de Iguala* [*The Iguala 43*] (Barcelona, Anagrama, 2015).

Grillo, Ioan, *El narco. En el corazón de la insurgencia criminal mexicana* [*The Narco. At the Heart of the Mexican Criminal Insurgency*] (Mexico, Tendencias, 2012).

Guerrero Gutiérrez, Eduardo, 'La estrategia fallida' [The Failed Strategy], *Nexos*, December 2012, pp. 25–36.

_____, 'La dictadura criminal' [The Criminal Dictatorship], *Nexos*, April 2014, pp. 44–52.

_____, 'El estallido de Iguala' [The Explosion of Iguala], *Nexos*, November 2014, pp. 44–49.

_____, '¿Bajó la violencia?' [Did Violence Decrease?], *Nexos*, February 2015, pp. 20–28.

_____, 'La inseguridad 2013–2015' [Insecurity 2013–2015], *Nexos*, January 2016, pp. 40–52.

Gutiérrez, Florencia, *El mundo del trabajo y el poder político. Integración, consenso y resistencia en la Ciudad de México a fines del siglo xix* [*The World of Work and Political Power. Integration, Consensus and Resistance in Mexico City in the Late Nineteenth Century*] (Mexico, El Colegio de México, 2011).

Hart, John Mason, *Anarchism and the Mexican Working Class, 1860–1931* (Austin, University of Texas Press 1978).

Hardt, Michael, and Antonio Negri, *Multitude: War and Democracy in the Age of Empire* (New York, Penguin, 2004).

Hayek, Friedrich A., 'Historia y política', in Hayek et al., 1973, pp. 9–33.

Hayek, Friedrich A. et al., *El capitalismo y los historiadores* [*Capitalism and the Historians*] (Madrid, Unión Editorial, 1973).

Hermosa, Jesús, *Manual de geografía y estadística de la República Mexicana* [*Manual of Geography and Statistics of Mexico*] (Paris, Rosa & Bouret, 1857).

Hernández Chávez, Alicia y Manuel Miño Grijalva, eds., (1991), *Cincuenta años de historia en México* [*Fifty Years of History in Mexico*], 2 vols., México, El Colegio de México.

Hill, Christopher, *The World Turned Upside Down: Radical Ideas during the English Revolution* (London, Penguin, 1972).

Hobsbawm, Eric J., *Primitive Rebels: Studies in Archaic Forms of Social Movement in the 19th and 20th Centuries*. Manchester University Press, 1953, 1963, 1971.

_____, *Worlds of Labour: Further Studies in the History of Labour* (London, Weidenfeld & Nicolson, 1984).

_____, *Age of Extremes: The Short Twentieth Century 1914–1991* (London, Michael Joseph Ltd., 1994).

_____, *Interesting Times: A Twentieth-Century Life* (London, Allen Lane, 2002).

Hobsbawm, Eric J., and George Rudé, *Captain Swing: A Social History of the Great English Agricultural Uprising of 1830* (London, Lawrence & Wishart, 1969).

Hope, Alejandro, 'Violencia 2007–2011. La tormenta perfecta' [Violence 2007–2011. The Perfect Storm], *Nexos*, November 2013, pp. 36–41.

Huitrón, Jacinto, *Orígenes e historia del movimiento obrero en México* [*Origins and History of the Labour Movement in Mexico*], 3rd edn' (Mexico, Editores Mexicanos Unidos, 1984).

Iglesias, Pablo, *Disputar la democracia. Política para tiempos de crisis* [*Politics in a Time of Crisis*] (Madrid, Akal, 2014).

Illades, Carlos, edited and with an introduction by Carlos Illades, *México y España durante la Revolución mexicana* [*Mexico and Spain during the Mexican Revolution*] (Mexico, SRE, 1985).

_____, *Presencia española en la Revolución mexicana, 1910–1915* [*The Spanish Presence during the Mexican Revolution, 1910–1915*] (Mexico, UNAM/ Instituto Mora, 1991).

_____, 'Reclamaciones españolas: índice de expedientes fallados' [Spanish Claims: Index of Settled Cases], *Secuencia*, no. 24, 1992, pp. 179–216.

_____, 'Poblamiento y colonización: las políticas públicas, 1854–1910' [Population and Colonization: Public Policies 1854–1910], in González Navarro et al., 1993, pp. 134–47.

_____, 'Los propietarios españoles y la Revolución mexicana' [Spanish Proprietors and the Mexican Revolution], in Lida (ed.), 1994, pp. 170–89.

_____, *Hacia la república del trabajo. La organización artesanal en la Ciudad de México, 1853–1876* [*Towards the Republic of Work. Artisan Organization in Mexico City, 1853–1876*] (Mexico, El Colegio de México/UAM, 1996).

_____, 'Los trabajadores y la república: El Gran Círculo de Obreros de México en las fiestas cívicas' [The Workers and the Republic: The Great Circle of Workers of Mexico in Civic Festivities], *Journal of Iberian and Latin American Studies*, vol. 5, no. 1, 1999, pp. 1–14.

_____, *Estudios sobre el artesanado urbano del siglo xix* [*Studies of Urban Artisans in the Nineteenth Century*], 2nd edn (Mexico, Miguel Ángel Porrúa/UAM, 2001).

_____, *Rhodakanaty y la formación del pensamiento socialista en México* [*Rhodakanaty and the Formation of Socialist Thought in Mexico*] (Barcelona, Anthropos/UAM, 2002)

_____, *Las otras ideas. Estudio sobre el primer socialismo en México, 1850–1935* [*The Other Ideas. Study of the First Socialism in Mexico 1850–1935*] (Mexico, Era/UAM, 2008).

_____, *Guerrero. Historia breve* [*Guerrero: A Short History*] (Mexico, FCE/El Colegio de México/Fideicomiso para Historia de las Américas, 2010).

_____, *De la Social a Morena. Breve historia de la izquierda en México* [*From the Social to Morena. A Brief History of the Left in Mexico*] (Mexico, Jus, 2014).

Illades, Carlos, and Teresa Santiago, *Estado de guerra. De la guerra sucia a la narcoguerra* [*State of War. From the Dirty War to the Narco War*] (Mexico, Era, 2014).

Illades, Carlos, and Mario Barbosa (eds), *Los trabajadores de la Ciudad de México 1860–1950. Textos en homenaje a Clara E. Lida* [*Workers in Mexico City from 1860 to 1950. Texts in Tribute to Clara E. Lida*] (Mexico, El Colegio de México/UAM, 2013).

Illades, Carlos, and Andrey Schelchkov (eds), *Mundos posibles. El primer socialismo en Europa y América Latina* [*Possible Worlds. The First Socialism in Europe and Latin America*], prologue by Enrique Semo (Mexico, El Colegio de México/UAM, 2014).

Illades, Esteban, *La noche más triste. La desaparición de los 43 estudiantes de Ayotzinapa* [*The Saddest Night. The Disappearance of the 43 Ayotzinapa Students*] (Mexico, Grijalbo, 2015).

Illades, Esteban, Juan Pablo García Moreno and Kathya Millares, 'México se mueve: crónica de una marcha' [Mexico Moves: Chronicle of a March], *Nexos*, 21 November 2014.

Jameson, Fredric, *Representing Capital: A Reading of Volume One* (New York and London, Verso, 2011).

Jarquín, María Teresa, 'La población española en la Ciudad de México según el Padrón General de 1882' [The Spanish Population in Mexico City According to the General Census of 1882], in Lida, 1981. pp. 197–98.

Judt, Tony, *Ill Fares the Land* (New York, Penguin, 2010).

Katz, Friedrich, *La guerra secreta en México* [*The Secret War in Mexico*], 2 vols (Mexico, Era, 1983).

_____, 'Introducción: las revueltas rurales en México' [Introduction: Rural Revolts in Mexico], in Katz (ed.), 1990, I, pp. 9–24.

_____ (ed.), *Revuelta, rebelión y revolución. La lucha rural en México del siglo xvi al siglo xx* [*Revolt, Rebellion and Revolution. Rural Struggle in Mexico from the Sixteenth Century to the Twentieth Century*], 2 vols (Mexico, Era, 1990).

Katz, Friedrich et al., *La servidumbre agraria en la época porfiriana* [*Agrarian Serfdom during the Porfiriato*] (Mexico, SEP, 1976).

Kenny, Michael (ed.), *Inmigrantes y refugiados españoles en México (siglo xx)* [*Spanish Immigrants and Refugees in Mexico, Twentieth Century*] (Mexico, Ediciones de la Casa Chata, 1979).

Kicza, John E., *Colonial Entrepreneurs: Families and Business in Bourbon Mexico City* (Albuquerque, University of New Mexico Press, 1983).

Kriedte, Peter, Hans Medick and Jürgen Schlumbohm (with Herbert Kisch and Franklin F. Mendels), *Industrialization before Industrialization: Rural Industry in the Genesis of Capitalism* (New York, Cambridge University Press, 1981).

Kuschick, Murilo, 'Investigación político-electoral. Elección presidencial en México, 2006' [Political-Electoral Research. Presidential Election in Mexico, 2006], *Sociológica*, no. 65, 2007, pp. 189–216.

Laclau, Ernesto, *La razón populista* [*On Populist Reason*] (New York and London, Verso, 2005).

Laval, Christian et al., *Pensar desde la izquierda. Mapa del pensamiento crítico para un tiempo de crisis* [*Thinking from the Left. Map of Critical Thinking for a Time of Crisis*] (Madrid, Errata Naturae, 2012).

Leal, Juan Felipe, *Del mutualismo al sindicalismo en México* [*From Mutualism to Unionism in Mexico*] (Mexico, El Caballito, 1991).

Lear, John, *Workers, Neighbors, and Citizens. The Revolution in Mexico City* (Lincoln, NE, University of Nebraska Press, 2001).

———, 'El trabajador cualificado de la Ciudad de México en los años de la Revolución' [The Skilled Worker in Mexico City in the Years of the Revolution], in Sanz Rosalén, Piqueras and Arenas (eds), 2005, pp. 331–42.

Le Bon, Gustave, *The Crowd: A Study of the Popular Mind* (Radford, VA, Wilder Publications, 2008).

'Ley del Pueblo', in García Cantú, 1969, pp. 369–74.

Lida, Clara E., 'México y el internacionalismo clandestino del ochocientos' [Mexico and the Clandestine Internationalism of the 1800s], in Frost, Meyer and Vázquez (eds), 1979, pp. 879–83.

———, 'Los españoles en México. Del porfiriato a la postrevolución' [The Spanish in Mexico. From the Porfiriato to the Post-revolution], in Sánchez-Albornoz (ed.), 1988, pp. 322–42.

———, 'La inmigración española en México: un modelo cualitativo' [Spanish Immigration into Mexico: A Qualitative Model], in Hernández Chávez and Miño Grijalva, 1991, pp. 201–15.

——— (ed.), *Tres aspectos de la presencia española en México durante el porfiriato* [*Three Aspects of the Spanish Presence in Mexico during the Porfiriato*] (Mexico, El Colegio de México, 1981).

——— (ed.), *Una inmigración privilegiada. Comerciantes, empresarios y profesionales españoles en México en los siglos xix y xx* [*Privileged Immigration. Spanish Businessmen, Entrepreneurs and Professionals in Mexico in the Nineteenth and Twentieth Centuries*] (Madrid, Alianza, 1994).

Lida, Clara E., and Carlos Illades, 'El anarquismo europeo y sus primeras influencias en México después de la Comuna de París: 1871–1881' [European Anarchism and its Early Influences on Mexico after the Paris Commune: 1871–1881], *Historia Mexicana*, no. 201, 2001, pp. 103–49.

Linhart, Robert, *L'Établi*. [*The Assembly Line*], translated by Margaret Crosland (Amherst, MA, University of Massachusetts Press, 1981). Consulted as *De cadenas y de hombres*.

Lofredo, Jorge, 'La otra guerrilla mexicana. Aproximaciones al estudio del Ejército Popular Revolucionario' [The Other Mexican Guerrilla. Approaches to the Study of the Popular Revolutionary Army], *Desacatos*, no. 24, 2007, pp. 229–46.

Luquín Romo, Eduardo, *La política internacional de la Revolución constitucionalista* [*The International Policy of the Constitutionalist Revolution*] (Mexico, INEHRM, 1957).

Mac Gregor, Josefina, 'España entre dos caminos: Villa y Carranza' [Spain between Two Paths: Villa and Carranza], *Eslabones*, no. 2, 1991, pp. 44–54.

———, 'Agentes confidenciales en México: España y su primer contacto oficial ante la Revolución constitucionalista' [Confidential Agents in Mexico: Spain and its First Official Contact with the Constitutionalist Revolution], *Secuencia*, no. 24, 1992, pp. 75–106.

———, *México y España del porfiriato a la Revolución* [*Mexico and Spain from the Porfiriato to the Revolution*] (Mexico, INEHRM, 1992).

———, *Revolución y diplomacia: México y España 1913–1917* [*Revolution and Diplomacy: Mexico and Spain 1916–1917*] (Mexico, INEHRM, 2002).

———, 'Villa y los españoles: una relación difícil en tiempos difíciles' [Villa and the Spanish: A Difficult Relationship in Difficult Times], in Sánchez Andrés, Pérez Vejo and Landavazo (eds), 2007, pp. 401–24.

Macías Cervantes, César Federico, *Genaro Vázquez, Lucio Cabañas y las guerrillas en México entre 1960 y 1974* [*Genaro Vázquez, Lucio Cabañas and Guerrilla Movements in Mexico between 1960 and 1974*] (Puebla, BUAP/ Universidad de Guanajuato, 2008).

Madrazo, Alejandro y Ángela Guerrero, 'Más caro el caldo que las albóndigas' [The Broth Cost More than the Meatballs], *Nexos*, December 2012, pp. 45–53.

Martí Soler, Miquel, *L'Orfeó Català de Mèxic, 1906–1986* [*The Orfeó Català in Mexico 1906–1986*] (Barcelona, Curial Edicions Catalanes, 1989).

Martínez, Christopher, 'Transnational Criminal Organizations. Mexico's Commercial Insurgency', *Military Review*, 2012, pp. 58–62.

Marván Laborde, Ignacio, 'De la ciudad del presidente al gobierno propio, 1970–2000' [From the President's City to Self-Government, 1970–2000], in Rodríguez Kuri (ed.), 2012, pp. 483–563.

Meneses Reyes, Marcela, 'Memorias de la huelga estudiantil de la UNAM, 1999–2000' [Memoirs of the UNAM Student Strike, 1999–2000], UNAM, Facultad de Ciencias Políticas y Sociales, Doctorate in Political and Social Sciences Thesis, 2012.

Merino, José, Jessica Zarkin and Eduardo Fierro, 'Desaparecidos' [Missing], *Nexos*, January 2015, pp. 11–17.

Meyer Cosío, Lorenzo, *El cactus y el olivo. Las relaciones de México y España en el siglo xx* [*The Cactus and the Olive: Relations between Mexico and Spain in the Twentieth Century*] (Mexico, Océano, 2001).

Montemayor, Carlos, *Guerra en el Paraíso* [*War in Paradise*]. Collected Works vol. 1. (Mexico, FCE, 2006 [1991]).

_____, *La violencia de Estado en México. Antes y después de 1968* [*State Violence in Mexico. Before and after 1968*] (Mexico, Random House, 2010).

Montgomery, David, *Citizen Worker: The Experience of Workers in the United States with Democracy and the Free Market during the Nineteenth Century* (New York, Cambridge University Press, 1993).

Moore, Jr., Barrington, *Injustice: The Social Bases of Obedience and Revolt* (London, Macmillan, 1978).

Moreno Lázaro, Javier, 'La otra España. Empresas y empresarios españoles en la Ciudad de México durante la Revolución' [The Other Spain. Spanish Companies and Entrepreneurs in Mexico City during the Revolution], *América Latina en la Historia Económica*, no. 27, 2007, pp. 111–56.

Nettlau, Max, *Actividad anarquista en México* [*Anarchist Activity in Mexico*], edited and with an introduction by Jacinto Barrera Bassols, translated by Diana Stoyanova Tasseva and Lucrecia Gutiérrez Maupomé (Mexico, INAH, 2008).

Oikión Solano, Verónica, and Marta Eugenia García Ugarte (eds), *Movimientos armados en México, siglo xx* [*Armed Movements in Mexico, Twentieth Century*], 3 vols (Mexico, El Colegio de Michoacán/CIESAS, 2008).

Olveda, Jaime, 'Proyectos de colonización en la primera mitad del siglo xix' [Colonization Projects in the First Half of the Nineteenth Century], *Relaciones*, no. 42, 1990, pp. 23–47.

Osorno, Diego Enrique, *Oaxaca sitiada. La primera insurrección del siglo xxi* [*Oaxaca under Siege. The First Insurrection in the Twenty-First Century*], prologue by Lorenzo Meyer (Mexico, Grijalbo, 2007).

_____, *País de muertos. Crónicas contra la impunidad* [*Country of the Dead. Chronicles against Impunity*], introduction by Diego Enrique Osorno (Mexico, Debate, 2011).

Paoli Bolio, Francisco José, and Enrique Montalvo Ortega, *El socialismo olvidado de Yucatán: elementos para una reinterpretación de la Revolución mexicana* [*The Forgotten Socialism of the Yucatan: Elements for a Reinterpretation of the Mexican Revolution*] (Mexico, Siglo Veintiuno, 1977).

Pereyra, Carlos, *Política y violencia* [*Politics and Violence*] (Mexico, FCE, 1974).

Pérez Acevedo, Martín y Lisette Griselda Rivera Reynaldos, 'Propietarias españolas en México ante los efectos de la Revolución: pérdidas patrimoniales y búsqueda de indemnizaciones, 1910 a 1938' [Spanish Proprietresses in Mexico and the Effects of the Mexican Revolution: Capital Losses of Property and the Pursuit of Compensation, 1910 to 1938'], *Revista de Indias*, vol. LXXII, no. 256, 2012, pp. 771–98.

Pérez Herrero, Pedro, 'Algunas hipótesis de trabajo sobre la inmigración española a México: los comerciantes' [Some Working Hypotheses on Spanish Immigration into Mexico: Shopkeepers], in Lida (ed.), 1981, pp. 103–77.

Pérez Toledo, Sonia, *Trabajadores, espacio urbano y sociabilidad en la Ciudad de México 1790–1867* [Population and Social Structure in Mexico City 1790–1842] (Mexico, Miguel Ángel Porrúa/UAM, 2011).

———, in collaboration with Herbert S. Klein, *Población y estructura social de la Ciudad de México 1790–1842* [*The Population and Social Structure of Mexico City 1790–1842*] (Mexico, Miguel Ángel Porrúa/UAM/CONACYT, 2004).

Piccato, Pablo, *City of Suspects. Crime in Mexico City, 1900–1931* (Durham, NC, Duke University Press, 2001).

Pla Brugat, Dolores, 'Españoles en México (1895–1980). Un recuento' [The Spanish in Mexico (1895–1980). An Account], *Secuencia*, no. 24, 1992, pp. 107–20.

Posada Noriega, Juan, *México ante el derecho internacional. Las reclamaciones españolas* [*Mexico and International Law. Spanish Claims*] (Mexico, Imprenta Manuel León Sánchez, 1930).

Priestland, David, *The Red Flag: Communism and the Making of the Modern World* (London, Allen Lane, 2009).

Quintero Romero, Dulce María and América Libertad Rodríguez Herrera, 'Organizaciones sociales: nuevos actores políticos en Guerrero' [Social Organizations: New Political Actors in Guerrero], *Política y Cultura*, no. 30, 2008, pp. 39–66.

Rangel Lozano, Claudia E.G. and Evangelina Sánchez Serrano, 'La guerra sucia en los setenta y las guerrillas de Genaro Vázquez y Lucio Cabañas en Guerrero' [The Dirty War in the 1970s and Guerrilla Movements of Genaro Vázquez and Lucio Cabañas in Guerrero], in Oikón Solano and García Ugarte (eds), 2008, II, pp. 495–525.

Reina, Leticia, *Las rebeliones campesinas en México, 1819–1906* [*Peasant Revolts in Mexico 1819–1906*] (Mexico, Siglo Veintiuno, 1980).

Reyes Heroles, *El liberalismo mexicano*, III [Mexican Liberalism]. (Mexico, Fondo de Cultura Económica, 1982).

Rhodakanaty, Plotino C., *Obras* [*Works*]. Edited, foreword and notes by Carlos Illades, compiled by María Esther Reyes Duarte (Mexico, UNAM, 1998).

Rhodakanaty, Plotino C., and Juan de Mata Rivera, *Pensamiento socialista del siglo xix* [*Socialist Thought in the Nineteenth Century*]. Edited, foreword and notes by Carlos Illades, compiled by María Esther Reyes Duarte (Mexico, UNAM, 2001).

Ribera Carbó, Anna, *La Casa del Obrero Mundial. Anarcosindicalismo y revolución en México* [*The Casa del Obrero Mundial. Anarcho-Syndicalism and Revolution in Mexico*] (Mexico, INAH,2010).

Richmond, Douglas, 'Confrontation and Reconciliation: Mexicans and Spaniards during the Mexican Revolution, 1910–1920', *The Americas*, vol. XLI, 1984, pp. 215–28.

Rivera Velázquez, Jaime, 'El abismo michoacano' [The Michoacán Abyss], *Nexos*, September 2013, pp. 44–51.

Rosales Suasti, José, 'Los socialistas libertarios: rebeldes incomprendidos del Distrito de Querétaro, 1879–1884' [Socialist Libertarians: The Misunderstood Rebels of the District of Querétaro, 1879–1884], *Gaceta del Archivo Histórico Municipal de Querétaro*, 2006, pp. 3–5.

_____, 'La rebelión campesina socialista queretana 1879–1884 y el congreso anarquista de Londres de 1881' [The Querétaro Campesino Socialist Rebellion 1879–1884 and the 1881 London Anarchist Congress], *El Retorno de los Bárbaros*, no. 0, 2011, pp. 1–14.

Rodríguez Kuri, Ariel (ed.), *Desabasto, hambre y respuesta política [Shortages, Hunger and Political Response, 1915]*, (México, D.F.: Ediciones ¡Uníos!, Colección Sábado Distrito Federal 2000).

_____, *Historia política de la Ciudad de México desde su fundación hasta el año 2000 [Political History of Mexico City from its Founding until 2000]* (Mexico, El Colegio de México, 2012).

Rudé, George F.E., *The Crowd in History: A Study of Popular Disturbances in France and England, 1730–1848* (New York, John Wiley & Sons, 1964).

_____, *The Crowd in the French Revolution* (Oxford, Oxford University Press, 1967).

_____, 'Ideology and Class Consciousness' *(*Part I of *Ideology and Popular Protest)* (London, Lawrence & Wishart, 1980).

Salazar Adame, Jaime et al., *Historia de la cuestión agraria mexicana. Estado de Guerrero [The History of the Mexican Agrarian Question. State of Guerrero]* (Mexico, CEHAM/UAG/Gobierno del Estado de Guerrero, 1987).

Sánchez-Albornoz, Nicolás (ed.), *Españoles hacia América la emigración en masa, 1880–1930 [Spanish Mass Emigration to America, 1880–1930]* (Madrid, Alianza, 1988).

Sánchez Andrés, Agustín, Tomás Pérez Vejo and Marco Antonio Landavazo (eds), *Imágenes e imaginarios sobre España en México siglos xix y xx [Images and Imaginaries of Spain in Mexico in the Nineteenth and Twentieth Centuries]* (Mexico, Porrúa/Universidad Michoacana de San Nicolás de Hidalgo/CONACYT, 2007).

Sanz Rosalén, Vicent and José Antonio Piqueras Arenas (eds), *En el nombre del oficio. El trabajador especializado: corporativismo, adaptación y protesta [In the Name of the Trade. The Skilled Worker: Corporatism, Adaptation and Protest]* (Madrid, Biblioteca Nueva, 2005).

Secco, Lincoln, 'As Jornadas de Junho' [The Days of June], in Vainer et al., 2013, pp. 71–78.

Semo, Enrique, *México: del antiguo régimen a la modernidad* [Mexico: From the Old Regime to Modern Times], (México. UNAM-UACJ, 2012).

Sewell, Jr., William H., *Work and Revolution in France: The Language of Labour from the Old Regime to 1848* (New York, Cambridge University Press, 1980).

Sicilia, Javier, *Estamos hasta la madre [We've Had it up to Here!]* (Mexico, Planeta, 2011).

Sierra, Justo, *México su evolución social [Mexico: Its Social Evolution]*, 3 vols (Barcelona, Santiago Ballescá, 1900–1902).

Singer, André, 'Rebellion in Brazil. Social and Political Complexion of the June Events', *New Left Review*, vol. 85, 2014, pp. 19–37.

Soboul, Albert, *The French Revolution, 1787–1799: From the Storming of the Bastille to Napoleon* (New York, Random House, 1975).

———, *A Short History of the French Revolution, 1789–1799* (Berkeley, University of California Press, 1977).

Sotelo Marbán, José, *Oaxaca. Insurgencia civil y terrorismo de Estado* [*Oaxaca. Civil Insurgency and State Terrorism*] (Mexico, Era, 2008).

Spencer, Herbert, *The Man versus the State, with Six Essays on Government, Society, and Freedom* (Indianapolis, Liberty Classics, 1981 [1884]).

Stedman Jones, Gareth, *Languages of Class: Studies in English Working Class History, 1832–1982* (Cambridge, Cambridge University Press, 1983).

Taibo II, Paco Ignacio and Rogelio Vizcaíno, *Las dos muertes de Juan R. Escudero. La comuna de Acapulco 1918–1923* [*The Two Deaths of Juan R. Escudero. The Acapulco Commune 1918–1923*] (Mexico, Joaquín Mortiz, 1990).

Tamayo, Sergio, 'Dinámica de la movilización. Movimiento poselectoral y por la democracia' [Dynamics of Mobilization. Post-election and Pro-democracy Movement], *Desacatos*, no. 24, 2007, pp. 249–74.

Tanck de Estrada, Dorothy, 'La abolición de los gremios' [The Abolition of Guilds], in Frost, Meyer and Vázquez (eds), 1979, pp. 311–31.

Tarrow, Sidney G. *Power in Movement: Social Movements and Contentious Politics* (Cambridge, Cambridge University Press, 2011).

Teitelbaum, Vanesa, 'Asociación y protesta de los artesanos al despuntar la década de 1860' [Craftsmen's Association and Protest at the Beginning of the 1860s], in Illades and Barbosa (eds), 2013, pp. 51–80.

Thompson, Edward Palmer, 'The Peculiarities of the English', *The Socialist Register*, 1965, pp. 311–62.

———, *The Making of the English Working Class* (London, Victor Gollancz Ltd., 1980).

———, *Customs in Common* (New York, The New Press, 1991).

Thomson, Guy P.C., and David G. LaFrance, *Patriotism, Politics, and Popular Liberalism in Nineteenth Century Mexico. Juan Francisco Lucas and the Puebla Sierra* (Wilmington, DE, Scholarly Resources Inc., 1999).

Tilly, Charles, *European Revolutions, 1492–1992* (Oxford, Blackwell, 1993).

———, *Contention and the Urban Poor in Eighteenth- and Nineteenth-Century Latin America*, in Arrom and Ortoll (eds), 1996, pp. 225–42.

———, *The Politics of Collective Violence* (New York, Cambridge University Press, 2003).

———, *Democracy* (New York, Cambridge University Press, 2007).

Tilly, Charles, and Lesley J. Wood, *Social Movements, 1768–2008*, 2nd edn (Boulder, Paradigm, 2009).

Torre, Wilbert, *Narcoleaks. La alianza México-Estados Unidos en la guerra contra el crimen organizado* [*Narcoleaks. The Mexico–US Alliance in the War against Organized Crime*], prologue by Yuri Herrera (Mexico, Grijalbo, 2013).

Touraine, Alain, *After the Crisis* (Hoboken, NJ, Wiley, 2014).

Turner, John Kenneth, *Barbarous Mexico* (Chicago, Kerr & Company, 1911).

Tutino, John, *From Insurrection to Revolution in Mexico: Social Bases of Agrarian Violence 1750–1940* (Princeton, Princeton University Press, 1987).

Ugalde, Luis Carlos, 'Por qué más democracia significa más corrupción' [Why More Democracy Means More Corruption], *Nexos*, February 2015, pp. 8–15.

Urbina Villagómez, Mirtha Leonela, 'Reconstrucción de una memoria negada: la lucha agraria de las comunidades indígenas en el Bajío y la Sierra Gorda (1876–1884)' [Reconstruction of a Suppressed Memory: The Agrarian Struggle of the Indigenous Communities of the Bajío and the Sierra Gorda (1876–1884)], in Wright Carr et al., 2012, pp. 148–71.

Vainer, Carlos et al., *Cidades rebeldes. Passe libre as manifestações que tomaam as ruas do Brasil* [*Rebel Cities. Free Pass for the Demonstrations that Took to the Streets of Brazil*] (São Paulo, Boitempo, 2013).

Valadés, José Cayetano, *El socialismo libertario mexicano, siglo XIX* [Mexican Libertarian Socialism, Nineteenth Century] (Culiacán, UAS, 1984).

Villaseñor, José, 'El Gran Círculo de Obreros de México' [The Great Circle of Mexican Workers], *Historia Obrera*, no. 4, 1975, pp. 25–32.

Voegtli, Michael, '¿Cómo manifestar la diversidad? Las marchas del 'movimiento LGBTTTI' en la Ciudad de México (1878–2011)' [How Should Diversity Demonstrate? LGBT Marches in Mexico City (1878–2011)], in Combes, Tamayo and Voegtli (eds), 2015, pp. 451–99.

Volpi, Franco, *El nihilismo* [*Nihilism*], 2nd edn (Argentina, Biblos, 2011).

Walker, David W., 'Porfirian Labor Politics: Working Class Organizations in Mexico City and Porfirio Diaz, 1876–1902', *The Americas*, vol. XXXVII, no. 3, 1981, pp. 257–89.

Wright Carr, David Charles et al. (eds), *La memoria histórica de los pueblos subordinados* [*The Historic Memory of Subordinated Peoples*] (Guanajuato, Universidad de Guanajuato, 2012).

Womack, Jr., John, *Zapata and the Mexican Revolution* (New York, Alfred A. Knopf, 1968).

Yankelevich, Pablo, 'Denuncias e investigaciones contra españoles. Orígenes y desenvolvimiento de una conducta social y práctica política en el México revolucionario' [Complaints and Investigations against Spaniards. Origins and Development of Social Behaviour and Political Practice in Revolutionary Mexico], in Sánchez Andrés, Pérez Vejo and Landavazo (eds), 2007, pp. 425–64.

Zamora Lomelí, Karla Beatriz, 'Conflicto y violencia entre el Estado y los actores colectivos. Un estudio de caso: el Frente de Pueblos en Defensa de la Tierra en San Salvador Atenco, Estado de México, 2001–2009' [Conflict and Violence between the State and Collective Actors. A Case Study: The Community Front in Defence of Land in San Salvador Atenco, State of Mexico, 2001–2009], El Colegio de México, Doctorate in Social Sciences Thesis, 2010.

Žižek, Slavoj, *Violence: Six Sideways Reflections* (London, Profile Books, 2009).

———, 'Answers without Questions' in Žižek (ed.), 2013.

———, *The Year of Dreaming Dangerously* (New York and London, Verso, 2012).

———, *Event (Philosophy in Transit)* (New York, Penguin, 2014).

———, (ed.), *The Idea of Communism, 2. The New York Conference* (2011) (New York and London, Verso, 2013).

Zuloaga Rada, Mariana, 'La diplomacia española en la época de Carranza:

iberoamericanismo e hispanoamericanismo, 1916–1920' [Spanish Diplomacy in the Carranza Period: Ibero-Americanism and Hispano-Americanism 1916–1920], *Historia Mexicana*, no. 180, 1996, pp. 807–42.

Media

24 Horas, Mexico City
Animal Político, Mexico City
Ariete, Mexico City
El Cantábrico, Santander
El Correo de Asturias, Oviedo
El Diario, Mexico City
El Economista, Mexico City
El Financiero, Mexico City
El Hijo del Trabajo, Mexico City
El Imparcial, Mexico City
El Monitor Republicano, Mexico City
El País, Madrid
El Socialista, Mexico City
El Sur, Acapulco, Gro.
El Universal, Mexico City
Excélsior, Mexico City
Interviú, Madrid
La Crónica de Hoy, Mexico City
La Firmeza, Mexico City
La Internacional, Mexico City
La Jornada, Mexico City
La Jornada Guerrero, Acapulco, Gro.
La Libertad, Mexico City
La Nación, Buenos Aires
La Prensa, Mexico City
La Revolución Social, Puebla, Pue.
La Sombra de Arteaga, Querétaro, Qro.
La Verdad. Hoja política e independiente, Querétaro, Qro.
La Voz de México, Mexico City
¡Luz!, Mexico City
Milenio, Mexico City
The New York Times, New York
Proceso, Mexico City
Reforma, Mexico City
Reporte Índigo, Mexico City
Sin Embargo, Mexico City
Tribuna Roja, Mexico City
Periódico Oficial del Gobierno Constitucional del Estado de Coahuila de Zaragoza, Saltillo, Coah.

Webpages

Blitz Quotidiano
Conspiración Ácrata. Publicación de la Tendencia Anarquista Insurreccional
Corrente
Interacción
Margen.org
Periódicodigital.mx
Rabia y Acción
Rede Brasil Atual
Reporte Índigo
Rubra Colectivo
Webguerrillero. Periódico digital de las izquierdas del siglo xxi

Agencies

Agencia de Prensa Asociativa (APA)
Proceso.com
Radio Netherlands Worldwide
Reuters

Index

www.ingramcontent.com/pod-product-compliance
Lightning Source LLC
Chambersburg PA
CBHW070928030426
42336CB00014BA/2583